Ethnic Politics in Israel

This book offers an analysis of contemporary Israeli democracy, examining in particular society and politics from the perspectives of the different ethnic groups outside of the Ashkenazi mainstream.

The author explores the political expressions of the secondary groups in Israel (Mizrahim, Religious, Russians and Palestinian-Arab) and how these groups were treated by the Ashkenazim as a threat to its hegemony over the state. Looking at the instability created by the struggle of these marginal groups against the state, and the discrimination policy practiced by the Ashkenazi "hegemonic ethnic state" regime against the other, non-Ashkenazi, groups, the book illustrates how this has contributed to the failure to establish an "Israeli people."

Ethnic Politics in Israel will be of great interest to students and researchers in the fields of Middle East, Palestinian, Arab, Jewish and Israeli studies, political science, sociology and psychology.

As'ad Ghanem is senior lecturer at the school of political science, University of Haifa. His theoretical work has explored the legal, institutional and political conditions in ethnic states, covering issues such as Palestinian political orientations, the establishment and political structure of the Palestinian Authority, and majority–minority politics in a comparative perspective.

Routledge Studies in Middle Eastern Politics

1. **Algeria in Transition**
Reforms and development prospects
Ahmed Aghrout with Redha M. Bougherira

2. **Palestinian Refugee Repatriation**
Global perspectives
Edited by Michael Dumper

3. **The International Politics of the Persian Gulf**
A cultural genealogy
Arshin Adib-Moghaddam

4. **Israeli Politics and the First Palestinian Intifada**
Political opportunities, framing processes and contentious politics
Eitan Y. Alimi

5. **Democratization in Morocco**
The political elite and struggles for power in the post-independence state
Lise Storm

6. **Secular and Islamic Politics in Turkey**
The making of the justice and development party
Ümit Cizre

7. **The United States and Iran**
Sanctions, wars and the policy of dual containment
Sasan Fayazmanesh

8. **Civil Society in Algeria**
The political functions of associational life
Andrea Liverani

9. **Jordanian–Israeli Relations**
The peacebuilding experience
Mutayyam al O'ran

10. **Kemalism in Turkish Politics**
The Republican People's Party, secularism and nationalism
Sinan Ciddi

11. **Islamism, Democracy and Liberalism in Turkey**
The case of the AKP
William Hale and Ergun Özbudun

12. **Politics and Violence in Israel/Palestine**
Democracy versus military rule
Lev Luis Grinberg

13. **Intra-Jewish Conflict in Israel**
White Jews, black Jews
Sami Shalom Chetrit

14. **Holy Places in the Israeli–Palestinian Conflict**
Confrontation and co-existence
Edited by Marshall J. Breger, Yitzhak Reiter and Leonard Hammer

15. **Plurality and Citizenship in Israel**
Moving beyond the Jewish/Palestinian civil divide
Edited by Dan Avnon and Yotam Benziman

16. **Ethnic Politics in Israel**
The margins and the Ashkenazi center
As'ad Ghanem

Ethnic Politics in Israel

The margins and the Ashkenazi center

As'ad Ghanem

LONDON AND NEW YORK

First published 2010
by Routledge
2 Park Square, Milton Park, Abingdon, Oxon OX14 4RN

Simultaneously published in the USA and Canada
by Routledge
711 Third Ave, New York, NY 10017

Routledge is an imprint of the Taylor & Francis Group, an informa business

© 2010 As'ad Ghanem

Typeset in Times New Roman by
Book Now Ltd, London
First issued in paperback 2013

All rights reserved. No part of this book may be reprinted or reproduced or utilised in any form or by any electronic, mechanical, or other means, now known or hereafter invented, including photocopying and recording, or in any information storage or retrieval system, without permission in writing from the publishers.

British Library Cataloguing in Publication Data
A catalogue record for this book is available from the British Library

Library of Congress Cataloging in Publication Data
Ganim, As'ad.
Ethnic politics in Israel : the margins and the Ashkenazi centre / As'ad Ghanem.
   p. cm. — (Routledge studies in Middle Eastern politics ; 16)
Includes bibliographical references and index.
1. Israel—Ethnic relations—Political aspects. 2. Ethnicity—Political aspects—Israel. 3. Minorities—Israel—Political activity. 4. Group identity—Israel. I. Title.

DS113.2.G36 2009
305.80095694—dc22
                                                        2009022258

ISBN13: 978-0-415-54735-2 (hbk)
ISBN13: 978-0-415-84748-3 (pbk)

To my wife, Ahlam

Contents

List of illustrations — x
Preface — xi

1. Israel as a hegemonic ethnic state and the politics of group identity — 1

2. The Palestinian minority in Israel: resisting the "ethnocratic" system — 22

3. Mizrahi (Oriental) Jews and the Ashkenazi system: incorporation versus separation politics — 60

4. Jewish religious groups and the politics of identity in the "secular-Jewish" state — 79

5. Russian immigrants: imposing multi-culturalism in the public sphere in Israel — 132

6. Group divisions, the external conflict and political instability in Israel since Oslo — 164

7. Conclusion: the future of group politics in Israel — 190

Notes — 195
References — 199
Index — 212

Illustrations

Figure

1.1 Groups in Israel: their position in the "hegemonic ethnic state" system — 17

Tables

2.1 National-emotional affiliation of Palestinian citizens of Israel — 28
2.2 Perception of the disparity between Jews and Palestinians in Israel in key areas of life (2001 survey) — 29
2.3 Opinions regarding desired degree of equality (2001 survey) — 30
2.4 Distribution of the Palestinian vote in Knesset elections, 1949–2006 — 53

Preface

This book is about the political expressions of the secondary groups in Israel (Mizrahim, religious, Russians and Palestinian-Arab), those groups treated by the founding group (the Ashkenazim) as a threat to its hegemony over the state. Political mechanisms of control and hegemony to the territorial, cultural and political margins of the state were used by the Ashkenazi elite against the secondary groups and their elites. The political struggle of the marginal groups against the Ashkenazi domination created a state of instability, in accordance with the group divisions within Israeli society, where group identity and interests define political behavior trends.

The Ashkenazi "hegemonic ethnic state" regime practiced a discrimination policy against the other, non-Ashkenazi, groups (veterans and immigrants alike), and created an authority and social apparatus that legislates ethnic-group affiliation, and even prefered it to civil affiliation. By adopting this policy, the Ashkenazi "hegemonic ethnic regime" paved the way for the development of group struggles indicating the failure of establishing the "Israeli people." Practically, one could define four axes for these struggles that will always obstruct stability of the Israeli political apparatus, while there will be a need for substantial reforms to face these fissures for the apparatus to develop in stability: the secular–religious fissure, the Oriental–Ashkenazi fissure, the Russian–Israeli/Jewish fissure and the Israeli/Jewish–Palestinian fissure within Israel.

In the first chapter I will present the theoretical background for the study, where I maintain that Israel should be classified as a "hegemonic ethnic state" like Turkey, Latvia, Lithuania and Estonia. All these states are described by some scholars' literature as "liberal democracies," but actually should have been classified as ethnic states (for more details about this discussion, see: Ghanem, 1998, 2001a; Rouhana, 1997; Yiftachel, 1997, 1998, 1999; Peleg, 2007). In these states minority group members are offered different limited rights and are integrated to a different limited extent in the states' politics, society, economy and media, although by no means on a par with the majority. The latter, moreover, conducts a long-term policy of control and supervision that guarantees the preservation of majority dominance and the marginalization of the minority groups.

In chapters 2–5 of the book, I will analyze the political conduct among the main secondary groups that struggle against the Ashkenazi domination: religious groups, Orientals, Russian immigrants and Palestinians. Each chapter will start with examining the state policies towards the group, where I claim that as part of the Israeli ethnic state, sophisticated and stratified arrangements were introduced by the state towards different groups. Different policy guidelines were carried out towards the different main secondary groups and a multi-faceted regime was created. As part of this regime different and distinctive sub-regimes are functioning at the same time, with different procedures, regulations and internal logic that is suitable to the intended group. These sub-regimes are implemented along the following lines: *ethnocratic arrangements towards the Palestinian citizens*; *"ethnic democracy" arrangements towards the Orientals and the religious groups*; and *a "multi-cultural" system towards the Russian immigrants*.

Examining the state policies will be followed by analyzing the main political requirements, political organization and political action that were taken by each group in order to try and change the control and exclusion policies conduct by the state and its political, social and cultural elite, the Ashkenazim. In the sixth chapter I will present the complexities of group relations in Israel in the shadow of the Israeli–Palestinian conflict, and in the final chapter I'm proposing to consider basic transformation of the Israeli regime, from a quasi-liberal system to a power-sharing one, where groups will be defined formally as part of the state structure, and as a basic principal on organizing the state and public sphere in Israel.

Part of the information presented in this book was collected while I was a fellow researcher at Madar: the Palestinian center for Israeli Studies in Ramallah, and I want to thank Madar for their support. Over the last few years research assistants helped me to gather my data and classify it. I would like to thank all of them, especially Dr Erez Tzefadia, Riad Bokae, Mohanad Mostafa, Asaf Turjoman and Maor Parsai, and to thank the many people who gave part of their precious time and allowed me to interview them. I would also like to thank Dan Leon and Dr Rosalie Boone, both of whom edited my draft and gave me very useful recommendations for the improvement of the text.

As'ad Ghanem, June 2009

1 Israel as a hegemonic ethnic state and the politics of group identity

Introduction

The Israeli experience of ethnicity, politics and conflict of identities is rooted in the pre-state period, when immigrants in the mandatory Palestine "Jewish Yishov" were forced to deal with conflicts and clashes among the contradictory aspirations and interests of various groups within the Jewish community. During this pre-state period, European Jews dominated Jewish life in the Yishov. At the same time, a small community of immigrants from the Arab states and the Middle East emerged as a distinct "Oriental" group. Following the establishment of the State of Israel in 1948, group identities were empowered by the immigration of Jews from all over the world, especially from the Arab states. In addition, a new Palestinian minority was added to Israel's diversity. This group included those Palestinians who remained under Israeli control following the expulsion operations by the Jewish military forces in 1948.

Israel's experience with the politics of identity reflects experiences occurring worldwide. For example, following the collapse of the Communist Bloc, the process of community crystallization changed dramatically, strengthened by modernization, increasing levels of education, the development of mass media and a considerable rise in expectations regarding individual and community rights. Community members came to see the *collective* as a significant privilege and as essential to the maintenance of their individual and community status.

Developments during the post Cold War era indicate that countries are opening up to each other. Although the state still plays an important role in world affairs, its impact has begun to wane, leading to aroused appetites and demands among minority groups and prompting traditionally dominant groups to prepare their lists of demands as well. This inevitably has led to inter-communal conflicts wherever minority groups exist. Examination of the international context following termination of the Cold War reveals that the most violent conflicts in the world today are those based on inter-communal disputes, such as those taking place in Southern Sudan, Kurdistan, Iraq, Lebanon, Chechnya, Palestine/Israel and so on. All of these groups have applied to the West and to the United States, in particular, for aid in their battles against the state or other oppressors.

The communications revolution of the twenty-first century has intensified ethnic conflicts in two ways. First, communications media transmit information, values, inventions, norms and so on, among the various regions and populations of the world, thereby contributing to specific group identities. It appears that the more similar population groups become with regard to external characteristics such as norms, values, standards of living, and political and social behavior, the greater the obsessive search for attributes that distinguish them from one another. The media tend to sharpen or highlight these differences.

Second, communications media also intensify the determination among groups who have faced discrimination to fulfill their needs just as dominant populations have done. Media enhance group adhesion and elevate the level of group demands; media provide convenient instruments with which to express the views and desires of the group members and leaders, bringing them directly to the tables of governments, international organizations, conferences and universities. Thus communications media have become an important and powerful force in shaping the conflicts which surround intercommunal cooperation.

As ruling or dominant populations seek to perpetuate their rule and superiority, ultimately they stimulate greater awareness among non dominant populations of the gap between themselves and dominant society members, and fuel the desire of non-dominant populations to achieve equality. The dominant groups claim that less dominant groups encounter limited political and economic opposition to their struggles for equality. In actuality, however, competition is rife between the groups as each seeks for its own members: political power, status in the ruling hierarchy, domination over the military, and economic power through control over production, natural resources, high-income positions and employment at all levels in the society. The dominant groups formulate strategies and methods intended to preserve their superiority and domination over resources; traditionally deprived populations seek methods and strategies with which to eliminate the dominance of other groups and race to obtain the same rewards enjoyed by dominant society members.

In these struggles and competitions, cooperation across states or groups often occurs as groups seek maximum control over rewards. Bosnia, South Africa and Northern Iraq provide current examples in which minority groups are prepared to accept the aid of foreign forces in their struggle. In other instances, diverse populations cooperate with each other against those whom they perceive as oppressors (e.g. the Moslems and the Croats against the Serbs in Bosnia; the Singhalese and Moslems against the Tamils in Sri Lanka; and the Turks and a group of Kurds in Turkey who are aligned in cooperation against another faction of the Kurdish society).

All of these developments have created greater awareness of fundamental rights, equality and freedom. Minority groups have developed leaders and spokesmen who have demanded rights for their members as individuals and as groups. This phenomenon has become so widespread that it seems that all ethnic groups – particularly minorities – throughout the world, have voiced their demands. These demands have become the focus of debates, competitions and conflicts. Many observers suggest that the disintegration of the Eastern bloc and the termination of the Cold War were harbingers of these ripening processes that undoubtedly will continue to grow stronger during the post-Cold War era.

This book presents an analytical framework for understanding the level and type of political demands raised by minorities and the political strategies that have been developed by these minorities in order to fulfill their demands. It describes active minorities in Israel: Arabs, Orientals, religious and Russians. These minorities differ along two main parameters: (a) the type of minority and (b) the minority status they hold within the state and the ruling majority context.

Minority claims and strategies for change in deeply divided states

States play major roles in the regulation of politics among the diverse identities that exist within them. As they attempt to find fitting answers to the divisions and conflicts that exist among their populations, these states and their institutions are compelled to invest a great deal of material and ideological effort, both official and unofficial. Virtually every country has populations that consist of different ethnic groups; with rare exceptions (e.g. the Republic of Ireland, North Korea and South Korea), there are no uni-ethnic countries in the world. Consequently, virtually all other countries live with the perpetual need to cope with national, religious, racial and other divisions (Gurr, 1993; Gurr and Harff, 1994; Horowitz, 1985). In the Middle East, for example, all countries are involved in some sort of political identity crisis. Turkey and Iraq must cope with the demands of Kurds. Iran, Saudi Arabia, the Gulf States and Tunisia face problems emanating from ethnic, national, cultural and religious conflicts between fanatical religious groups and secular groups striving to adopt a modern Western orientation. Demands are rising among the Berbers in North Africa, the Southerners in Sudan and a large number of religious minorities around the Arab world (e.g. the Copts in Egypt and the religious sects in Syria and Lebanon). Israel, also, faces similar problems with the Palestinian minority and with Jewish religious, Oriental and Russian groups.

The change strategies used by minority groups and the nature of their political participation at the elite level and in the general public, reflect factors at two levels: (a) the group level and (b) the state or regime level. Group level factors are internal in that they exist within the minority group.

State/regime level factors are external to the group; they characterize the state/regime with which the minority group must contend.

Group level factors

A number of group level factors shape the demands and political expression among minority groups. These factors are critical to promoting a successful struggle for equality with the majority. Four factors, in particular, have critical implications for the alteration of power relations and the allocation of resources between minority and majority groups.

Indigenous vs immigrant status

One factor with important implications for the demands and political expression of minority groups is their status as an indigenous or immigrant minority. The term indigenous describe any ethnic group of people who inhabit a geographic region to which they have the earliest historical connection, although they may live alongside migrants who have populated the region and are usually greater in number. Minorities who are considered indigenous groups, usually have a sense of belonging and self confidence that helps them raise demands related to their collective status, such as demands for self determination and cultural autonomy. On the other hand, minorities who immigrate to a new country searching for economic opportunities usually intend to become integrated into the new society; consequently, their collective demands are absent or limited.

Demographic weight and geographic concentration

The demographic weight and geographic concentration of a minority group vis-à-vis the majority group also have a decisive impact on power relations and resource allocation. The greater the demographic weight of the minority group, the greater its ability to exert pressure on the political system. Size is especially important in an open ethnocracy, in which the minority has an opportunity to participate in the political process and potentially influence the course of events. In such systems, the minority group will find it difficult to change a situation if its membership accounts for only a small percentage of the entire population. However, if it represents a larger percentage of the population (e.g. at least two figures), its voice begins to be heard and it can exert an influence on its situation.

Likewise, geographic concentration influences what the minority group is able to achieve. Dispersion of the group into various parts of the country can weaken its voice and its ability to mobilize or organize effective political action. A minority group's geographic concentration can have decisive impact on the majority and its sense of power. The Canadian case, for example, provides a classic example of how demographic and geographic correspondence proved invaluable in enabling the Francophone minority in Quebec to achieve its goals or make significant progress toward those goals.

Internal solidarity

The ability of a minority group to function as a consolidated ethnic or national group, despite internal differences in approaches and views, is a third group level factor that shapes the demands and political expression of the group. Consolidated minority groups have a single main program for achieving balance or equality with the majority; groups with little or no internal solidarity do not. Minorities in hegemonic ethnic systems are generally subject to a regime of control via which the state endeavors to divide them in order to weaken their action and bargaining power (Lustick, 1980). The success of such a divide-and-conquer policy depends on structural factors within the minority group – differences in ideology, geography or confessional affiliations and the like – that make it impossible for the group to consolidate a uniform position and orient its struggle toward a clear goal. The case of the Arabs in Israel provides a classic example in which group fractionalization and limited internal solidarity have impeded the group's ability to make significant advances in its struggle against the majority (Rouhana and Ghanem, 1998).

Group leadership

The most important factor that shapes the demands and political expression of a minority group, once fundamental demographic, geographic and other characteristics have been accounted for, is the human factor, that is how the group's leadership behaves. The role of minority group leadership is to develop and implement a strategy for the group. The essence of the group's demands, the way in which demands are presented and the timing of their presentation to the majority group all depend chiefly on the leadership of the group. Without a supreme leadership body – manifested in a single person or a unified leadership group – capable of providing effective guidance, the minority group will achieve few, if any, of its goals.

State level factors

State or regime factors critical to a discussion of minority group change strategies and political participation, are those characteristics that address ethnic problems and emphasize the relationship between ethnicity and the state. This connection between ethnicity and state has been the subject of much debate among scholars in various disciplines. The ethnic-related components of a state provide an important standard for measuring the character and depth of its democratic commitment. In this book, I argue that many states that are considered democracies are not, in fact, democracies when one takes an indepth look into their regime's basic components (see also Huntington, 1991). Some of these states should be considered as "ethnic states" with "ethnocratic regimes"; in all domains of life, including the level of formal citizenship, they give preference to one ethnic group over other groups that comprise the total population of the state (Maynes, 1993).

Two principal models can be used to describe how states and regimes deal with ethnic problems and the interaction that occurs between ethnicity and state. These models reflect two archetypes, each of which in turn subsumes two forms. The first archetype is the *civic state* model which, structurally and essentially, prefers democratic and egalitarian components over ethnic-hegemonic ones in interactions with citizens. The civic state model eliminates the dominance of a particular group and the identification of the state with that group. Instead, the model grants full equality to all populations and makes the state neutral in the competition among them. In other words, in this model the state identifies with all groups on an equal basis. The model emphasizes a genuine and sincere attempt to deal with ethnic divisions in ways that guarantee equality among ethnic groups and their members. To this end, the model operates at two levels – an individual level and a group level – and can thus be further sub-divided to reflect a liberal form and a consociational form.

In civic states, competition among citizens as *individuals* is equal before the law. The literature refers to this approach as "liberal democracy." A liberal democracy totally abrogates the dominance of one group and the identification of the state and political system with any particular group. That is, a liberal-democratic system relates to individuals as citizens and not as affiliates of a particular group among those who comprise the population. Officially, a liberal democratic system ignores group composition of the population in its distribution of power centers, choice of symbols and allocation of economic, social and cultural resources. One of the freedoms in such a system is the right of each group to organize on its own, without government assistance or state involvement (Lijphart, 1977; Smooha and Hanf, 1992).

A prerequisite to liberal democracy is a territorial nationalism that recognizes an individual's primordial right to be a member of the citizen nation, a member of the demos. The most prominent examples of states that have adopted a liberal democratic system are France, the United States and Great Britain (Smith, 1991).

At the group level, operation of the civic state model occurs where all citizens are equal, and where ethnic affiliation is strong and the criterion for national affiliation is primarily ethnic. In this situation, the elites of various populations add a group component to the system's liberal elements as a mechanism for dealing with ethnic divisions in the state. Group level democratic arrangements or *consociational democracies* are characterized by the establishment of a federation or confederation wherein representatives of constituent populations agree to divide the power centers, symbols, resources, and economic, cultural and social rewards on the basis of a group key, proportional to each population's size and power. This mechanism eliminates the dominance of any one group and creates sufficiently strong balances that preserve the egalitarian civic system.

A necessary condition for consociational democracy, and the reason this form of government is considered a democracy, rather than merely a coalition of ethnic and national groups, is the existence of all of the fundamental conditions of a civic state (e.g. formal equality between citizens, the trappings of democratic government, changes in government, the rule of law, and competition among political parties and interest groups). In other words, consociational designs are based on the liberal arrangements of a civic state and by no means replace them. Belgium and Switzerland provide current examples of this system (Lijphart, 1977).

The liberal or consociational arrangements of civic states are the only arrangements that can satisfy diverse ethnic and national groups. Because these arrangements recognize basic human needs, they improve group relations and facilitate the peaceful settlement of national, ethnic and civil problems. At the same time, they develop civic values that are shared by all citizens, whatever their ethnic affiliation (Lijphart, 1977; Lustick, 1997).

In civic states, minorities are regarded as legitimate competitors and players; they have an opportunity to contribute to the public good of their people and to the entire citizenry of the state. These opportunities offered by the civic state affect the aims, strategies and political participation of minorities. Consequently, under normal circumstances in civic states, minorities tend to cooperate with the state and the majority in order to contribute to the public sphere. Typically, they demand the right to be integrated or they demand a change of procedures or regulations in order to ease their integration or limited autonomy. They do not, however, tend to raise demands for irredentism, separation or a change in the state regime.

The second archetype that describes how states and regimes deal with ethnic issues is the *ethnic state*. The ethnic state is a reflection of the "hegemonic ethnic project" of the majority; it gives primacy to ethnic affiliation over citizenship in dealing with citizens and their rights; it displays favoritism for one group and its members over other groups that make up the state population (see: Peleg, 2007; Rouhana, 1997; Smooha, 1997; Yiftachel, 2006). Ethnic states are categorized into two sub-types. In the first sub-type, the ethnic dominance is unequivocal and immune to challenge through democratic means. These harsh ethnic states are defined in the literature as *Herrenvolk* democracy or apartheid states, such as the South African partite. In such states, minorities enjoy virtually no basic democratic rights, such as suffrage or the ability to challenge the ethnic hegemony in local courts.

The second ethnic state sub-type includes "lenient" ethnic states in which the ethnic dominance is clear and entrenched, but minorities are still able to participate in the political process. They can vote and challenge decisions made by the majority, but have a limited, and usually ineffectual, ability to exert an equal influence over the political process (Rouhana, 1997).

The hegemonic ethnic group in an ethnic state appropriates the state apparatus and shapes the political system, public institutions, geography, economy and culture, so as to expand and deepen its control over the state and its territory. Political boundaries are vague, often offering privileges, not to minority citizens, but to co-ethnic segments of the dominant population, such as in the diasporas where there is no clearly identified "demos." Ethnic-based politics in these states involve power distribution that polarizes the political body and party system. Rigid forms of ethnic segregation and socio-economic stratification are maintained for minority groups, as expansion of the majority group necessitates the preservation of geographical, political, social and economic separation. A central point is that in ethnic states, the notion of the 'demos' is crucially ruptured. The community of equal resident-citizens (the demos) does not feature highly in the country's policies, agenda, imagination, symbols or distribution of resources. (For more discussion, see: Yiftachel, 2006.)

As a reflection of the diverse policy towards different types of minorities, the state develops a multi-faceted regime or sub-regime components and mechanisms in order to deal differently with a variety of minority types, in accordance with their level of inclusion and exclusion in comparison to the dominant population. On the other hand, minorities develop different strategies and a different orientation towards the state and the dominant population. Two scales can be used in order to identify the "type" of the regime that controls each minority group. The first is related to the level of integration versus the level of separation, and the second is related to the level of equality versus the level of discrimination (see Figure 1.1 concerning the position of the different groups as part of the Israeli ethnic state system).

A hallmark of the ethnic state system is its ability to maintain the dominance of the leading ethno-national group while excluding or marginalizing or, in some cases, assimilating indigenous and/or "external" minorities. Not all minority groups are viewed in the same way. Some are defined as *internal*, whereas others are defined as *external*. The definition ascribed to the group denotes a perceived critical difference between those minorities who are considered part of the 'historical' or 'genetic' nation, and those whose presence is considered mere historical coincidence or a 'danger' to the security and integrity of the dominant ethnos. The ways minority groups are defined and perceived exerts a circular influence on their treatment and on their response to their minority status. For example, the state's treatment of indigenous minorities is generally more openly oppressive than its treatment of immigrant minorities. These minorities are represented and treated, at best, as external to the ethno-national project – at worst, as a subversive threat. Immigrant minorities, on the other hand, are treated better by the state, particularly if they adopt a strategy of *belonging*, that distances them from indigenous or other external minorities.

Hegemonic ethnic states tend to have constant tension between minority and majority groups. Because they structurally privilege one ethnic population over other resident minorities, both within the state and among its diasporas, ethnic states often create or exacerbate ethnic tensions and conflicts. As seen in the cases of Sri Lanka, Estonia and Israel, the dominant group then uses the state apparatus, and international legitimacy according to state sovereignty, to expand its power, resources and prestige, often at the expense of minorities.

Political instability in ethnic states is strongly related to regime illegitimacy among minorities. This results in social disorder and a breakdown of regime functions. As minority groups become disgruntled, their dissatisfaction leads to increased forms of political polarization and intensified waves of anti-governmental protest and violence. The effectiveness of minority mobilization is generally limited, however, as efforts to create integration and equality encounter insurmountable cultural, political, economic and geographical obstacles. Minorities then have numerous response options, including: (a) assimilation, (b) the intensification of their protests, that is escalating levels of violence, or (c) the establishment of competing frameworks of governance and resource allocation, accompanied by disengagement from the state.

The minority group's particular demands in response to the obstacles that thwart their goals reflect the interaction between group variables and those of the state/regime. These interactions lead most frequently to the group's selection of one of the following demand options.

Irredenta and separation

In this option, a national or ethnic group demands self determination. The group develops irredentist movements (wishing to detach itself from one state and join another) or separatist movements (wishing to establish a new state). Demands are usually accompanied by violence and sometimes lead to civil war between the minority group and the majority-controlled central government.

Autonomy

This option calls for minority self determination or self rule within the structure of the current state. Minority groups might demand autonomy in certain spheres of life or might demand extensive autonomy, which, depending on the number of the national groups within the state, might actually result in a bi-national or multi-national state. The most frequent case is of limited autonomy that enables a specific group to lead its own life in certain defined and limited spheres, with the consent of the majority in that state.

Integration

In this option, minority groups demand integration into the life of the state of which they are citizens. The level or degree of integration is a function of the attitude of the government toward the minority group and the degree of pressure under which the group is suffering. Extreme integration refers to total assimilation of the minority into the majority group and elimination of the differences between the groups.

The minority group options presented above are not clear-cut. Not only might these options take other forms (e.g. demand of partition or secession, power-sharing, cantonization, federalism, etc.) (Horowitz, 1985; Peleg, 2007), additionally, two other observations can be made. First, the various options exist on a continuum, with separation and the establishment of a separate independent state at one end, and group assimilation or absorption at the other. Second, in many cases two or more options may coexist. For example, liberal arrangements and equal citizenship can coexist with cultural autonomy for specific minority group members. A variety of these theoretical possibilities exists for the status of minority groups in Israel.

Israel: the politics of identities in theoretical context

Most Israeli social scientists project Israel as a civic state with a liberal democratic system that embraces a policy of absorbing minorities – both indigenous and immigrant – similar to the policies adopted in the open systems of Europe, the USA and Canada (for more details see: Shafir and Peled, 2002; Ram, 1995). Israeli social scientists have proposed, as part of this civic state paradigm, several approaches to understanding the politics of identity in Israel. Shafir and Peled (2002), have noted that until the late 1980s analyses of Israeli society and relations among its various groups were based on three theoretical frameworks: (a) the functionalist approach (Eisenstadt, 1968; 1985; Horowitz and Lisk, 1978, 1989); (b) the elite; and (c) the plurality and struggle approach (Smooha, 1978). Palestinian researchers such as Elia Zureik (1979), Khalil Nakhleh (1977, 1979) and Ghazi Falah (1990), on the other hand, have published research describing Israel as an example of classic colonialism, with an internal structure of contradictions.

In the last two decades, a new wave of critical approaches that attempt to describe the situation of the Israeli state and society has appeared in the social sciences. Recent critics base their research on a number of assumptions missing in previous works, such as: recognizing the need for integrated research, inclusive of all citizens of Israel (both Jewish and Palestinian); assuming that only interests, not social criteria and values, define the course of history; and agreeing that facts on the ground define the nature of the analysis, rather than the intentions or the desires (whether written, or not) which occupy the minds of politicians. A number of theoretical models have been proposed that address these previously missing assumptions. The most important of these models, as they relate to Israeli society, are described in the following sections.

The "cultural diversity" model

Social and political conditions that prevailed in Israel during the 1980s and 1990s resulted in the emergence of a political movement representing Oriental Jews (SHAS, the ultra-orthodox Sephardi party) as well as a growing Arab interest in voting for Arab parties or in support of Arab political movements. Also during this period, Russians emerged as an important political constituency. As a result, a number of researchers began to characterize Israel as a state and society with a multi-cultural system. They maintained that Israel's environment could the be described as one of "cultural diversity," much like that which developed in Western societies such as Canada, Switzerland and even the USA. Therefore, they felt that these societies could be used as suitable models for describing the Israeli society.

The cultural diversity model maintains that all citizens, in addition to their citizenship, are born within a social-cultural group that plays an important role in establishing the values that govern their lives and are vital in their personal and public preferences. The model suggests that society is best understood, not merely by sanctifying individualism, which looks upon a person primarily as a citizen, but also by considering the collective affiliations that influence the person.

In Israel a number of factors stimulate the perception of the state as an example of cultural diversity. First and foremost, the Israeli society contains a number of ethnic, cultural and social blocs (Kildron, 2000; Mawtner, Sagi and Shamir, 1998). Additionally, the following three factors also feed this perception:

1) A clear and distinct set of values, principles and specific ideas exists for each of the populations composing Israeli society. These values promote the formation of a separate identity for each group in the society.
2) Every group has developed claims and concepts to promote its own identity and to intimidate other groups. These relations between the groups result not only in a positive defining of self identity, but also in the superiority of one over the other.
3) A clear political representation for each ethnic-cultural population has been created that includes its own elites, leadership, political parties and movements.

This competition between groups emerged in conjunction with the sharp decline in "nation building," a concept that stemmed from the Zionist movement led by Ben-Gurion and began to develop when the Jewish state was first established in Palestine during the first half of the twentieth century. Decline in the notion of nation building may have resulted from a feeling that the state had achieved its historical mission and that consequently, there was opportunity for individual groups to focus on their own interests, rather than on those of the collective project. Researchers who support this supposition believe that liberalization and the adoption of democratic principles resulted in groups preferring their own interests to those of the general Israeli society. The point of view of some Oriental Jewish, Arab and Jewish religious activists lends further support for this hypothesis. Certainly, the supposition might explain what happened in Israel in 1977 when political power was handed over from the leftist Labor to the rightist Likud, under the leadership of Menahem Begin.

Those who support the "cultural diversity" model as most descriptive of Israel, claim that Israel's choices were limited to confrontation or mutual respect; they maintain that Israeli society chose the latter in harmony with its own cultural diversity. These views were represented by the Israeli academic-cultural establishment and expressed in a 1998 book written by Menachem Mawtner, Avi Sagim and Ronen Shamir and dedicated to the memory of the late Israeli legal expert Professor Ariel Rozon-Tsvi. Despite claims by critics in recent years that the cultural diversity model suitably describes the Israeli state, the state has actually been governed by the Western-Jewish (Ashkenazi) population. Israel is, therefore, closer to a "limited" or "conditional cultural diversity." Some critics are urging a freeing of secondary populations such as Arabs, Russians and religious Jews, from Western hegemony, in the conviction that only then will Israel move toward the status of cultural diversity found in Western democracies (Youna and Shinhav, 2000).

While the cultural diversity model provides a good description of social and cultural conditions as well as a critical approach to understanding these conditions, it fails to provide a satisfactory explanation of other components of Israeli state structure. It leaves unanswered, the basic question, "What are the political/structural ramifications of cultural diversity in the political system?"

The "instinct-civil" model

The "instinct-civil" model, presented by Kimmerling (1999), classifies the Israelis into two groups according to the basic values they adopt. Leftist supporters are described as adopting a democratic-secular-civil approach, expressing their readiness for a liberal approach, and striving for a historic settlement with the Palestinians. Right wing supporters are described as holding an "instinct" identity consisting of a mixture of nationalist and religious inclinations (Kimmerling, 1999).

Projection of an Israeli political map that reflects this political logic reveals a bi-polar political system divided based on two issues: war and peace on one hand and national and religious identity on the other. Opposing poles on the map represent two political camps, one "liberal-civil" and the other "nationalist-conservative." According to relevant scientific literature, this situation suggests that the creation of an "Israeli people" (melting pot) has succeeded, and that the Israeli public behavior mirrors that of voters in Western democratic countries, who can be divided according their degree of liberalism or of conservatism and nationalism.

The "diversified citizenship" model

The "diversified citizenship" model proposed by Shafir and Peled (2002), purportedly presents a comprehensive explanation of the Israeli phenomenon. Analysis of the structural hierarchy of Israeli society, according to this model, indicates three parallel categories of citizenship: liberal, ethnic-nationalist and republican. These three domains have enabled Israeli society to create the present interrelated system. The liberal domain places the Jews, Palestinian citizens and others into one inclusive "status"; the ethnic domain includes only Jews in the classification of social "welfare," and excludes the Palestinian citizens; and the republican domain includes within social "welfare" only the Ashkenazi group, excluding the others (mainly the Mizrahi and religious Jews).

Peled and Shafir (2005) believe that parallel use of these categories provides for the relative success of the Israeli "diversification system" which strives for balance between the exclusion motive of the settlement state and the motive of maintaining Israeli democracy. However, the categories facilitate the continuation of hierarchal classification among Ashkenazim, Orientals and Palestinian citizens. Peled and Shafir (2005) maintain that the Israeli system classifies complete sectors under the umbrella of minimum citizenship, thus excluding these groups – primarily the Orientals and Palestinians in Israel – from real citizenship. Hierarchal approaches, they suggest, are exacerbated during periods of globalization and economic liberalism.

The model presented by Shafir and Peled shows a distorted image of citizenship and of the ruling regime in Israel. Citizenship is typically represented by equal legal relations between the individual and the state. Their presentation of three different types of citizenship is a de facto violation of the concept of citizenship as a system of inclusion. Furthermore, the notion of citizens as a legal entity who own the state is also violated in the Israeli situation, given that the state is identified as a Jewish one that is owned by Jewish people only, rather than by *all* of its citizens. In Israel only Zionist, Western and Ashkenazi Jews enjoy totally the "public wealth and resources" of the state; others have fewer rights. Palestinian citizens are excluded from the formal equality that should be guaranteed through formal citizenship, as are many other groups, such as Oriental Jews, religious Jews and women. Citizenship in Israel, consequently, cannot be considered as "republican" in an authentic, comprehensive liberal sense, as for example in France.

Israel as an "ethnic democracy"

In the early 1990s, the Israeli sociologist Sammy Smooha developed a critical view of the Israeli political system that he described as an "ethnic democracy." Smooha's model addresses contradictions between the character of Israel as a Jewish and a democratic state (Smooha, 1990, 1997).

Smooha argues that Israel cannot claim to possess a harmonious liberal democratic system because the state has not been, nor will it ever be, neutral in dealing with its Jewish citizens as compared to others, particularly Arabs. (Smooha refers to Israel proper within the 1967 Green Line borders, since the occupation was seen as a temporary situation that would quickly be resolved with the establishment of a Palestinian state alongside Israel.) He stresses that the Jewish state does not and cannot ensure the provision of full civil equality to its Arab citizens, nor does it even acknowledge the collective rights of the Arabs. Consequently, Smooha suggests "ethnic state" as the best descriptor of the Israeli system. He emphasizes that the apparent contradiction doesn't disqualify Israel as a democratic state, claiming that Israel continues to enjoy basic features that qualify it as democratic. For example, Israel: (a) ensures for Arabs and all its citizens the right to vote and participate in elections; (b) has adopted a pluralistic party system (including Arab parties), enabling the democratic transfer of power; (c) has an independent judicial system; (d) has independent professional media; (e) has a political apparatus that exerts control over the military establishment and the IDF; and (f) enjoys the unified support of a strong elite and is backed by wide public support.

On the other hand, Smooha ennumerates many deficiencies inherent in the system:

- the exploitation of emergency regulations allowing the authorities to withhold basic rights;
- a lack of any legal framework that defends the rights of minorities or ensures equality for individuals from these minorities;
- existence of a prevalent non-democratic political culture among its citizens; and
- the problematical definition of Israel as a "Jewish state"; and its consequent structure and executive policy.

Smooha acknowledges that Judaism, as the state religion, is not primarily a symbolic issue, or one founded by the Jewish majority of citizens; rather, it is based on political, structural and legal considerations related to the preference for Jews over non-Jews.

The roots of this system go back to the nature of early Jewish settlement in Palestine. Jewish forms of daily life, (e.g. "Hebrew labor"), were emphasized, denying the existence of Palestinian people in the country. Organizations were established to support Jews exclusively well before

1948. Consequently, the Jewish character of the State of Israel and its political system is long-standing.

Current expression of the state's Jewish character occurs in several areas of life and in numerous laws. One example is the "Law of Return" for Jews and their families, even if they are not Jews, but qualify by virtue of their ethnic or religious relationship to Judaism. These laws also define the legal status of international Jewish organizations in Israel such as the World Zionist Organization and the Jewish National Fund (an organization working to take over Arab land and transfer the property to the Jewish people). Innumerable legal and organizational instruments express the intent to sustain Jewish superiority over the other groups in Israel. Political arrangements made by the state ensure an inferior status for Arab political parties and minimize their influence on Israeli policy. The state also continues to reject recognition of any representative country-wide Arab bodies and denies collective rights for Arabs. In summation, the Israeli system not only ensures Jewish superiority, but also seeks to enforce the inferiority of non-Jews in the state.

The "ethnic democracy" model has been subject to much criticism. While many agree with Smooha that Israel cannot be seen as a country with a democratic liberal system, they disagree with his coupling democracy and ethnicity. For example, in my article jointly published with Rouhana and Yiftachel (*Israel Studies*, 2000), we objected to the Smooha model. We stressed that the Israeli system does not take into consideration the basics of democracy, as indicated in Israel's refusal to provide equality to all before the law, its continued efforts at Judaization, and its opposition to adopting a policy of non-discrimination toward non-Jews.

Israel as an "ethnocratic system"

Since the mid-nineties of the twentieth century, the researcher Oren Yiftachel has invested significant effort in explaining the nature of the Israeli entity, especially in its Palestinian–Jewish context, and later in the context of the internal ethnic structure of the Jews within Israel (Yiftachel, 2000, 2006). Yiftachel maintains that Israel represents a model that is well known and widespread in the world: the hegemony of one ethnic group over the geographic space in the state. *Ethnocracy* – the rule of an ethnic group rather than of the demos or citizens – constructs a system that seeks to enforce the hegemony of a nationalist-ethnic group over the state's power systems. The present system in Israel, according to Yiftachel, does not reflect a democratic-Jewish state, but rather constitutes an authoritative Judaizing apparatus controlling a disputed bi-national and multi-ethnic space.

Despite incorporating many features of a national democratic state, the ethnocratic Israeli system creates many and varied obstacles to the development of a civil society capable of forming affiliations beyond ethnic or religious boundaries. The ethnocratic system not only serves as a tool of the reigning group, it also enforces ethnicity as a legitimate classification for denying equality in politics, culture and society. Thus, ethnicity is an institutionalized phenomenon and a springboard for all those conspiring against the establishment of a civil society in Israel.

Yiftachel and Ghanem (2004a, 2004b) subjected the ethnocracy model to theoretical comparative experimental treatment in a co-authored article. In this article, we explained the basic concepts of an ethnocratic system, its components and its effects on interactions between the various groups in Israel. We believe an ethnocratic system is one that can be diagnosed but has scarcely been addressed by specialists in geography, politics and sociology. This system allows for active ethnic expansion and rule. In it, an ethno-nationalist group monopolizes power over geographic spaces or disputed power sources. The system is able to influence distribution and resources in a given area and reflects the public's political identity, ideological goals, governing logic and practical priorities. The state is the basic governance tool that provides institutions, laws and resources and allows for "legislated" forms of violence in order to realize the goals of the system. In actuality, however, the state is much broader and deeper than its apparatuses; it builds the historical narrative, the collective memory and culture, the notions of future organizations, and many other facets, within the ethnocratic society.

Israel as an hegemonic ethnic state and minorities' strategies for change

Although described by some scholars as *liberal democracies*, Israel, with Turkey, Latvia, Lithuania and Estonia, actually should also be classified as ethnic states (see Ghanem, 1998, 2001a; Rouhana, 1997; Yiftachel, 1997, 1998, 1999). In these states, minority group members are by no means on par with the majority group, but are offered different limited rights and are integrated to a limited extent in the states' politics, society, economy and media. These states implement a long-term policy of control and supervision that guarantees the preservation of majority dominance and the marginalization of minority groups.

In Israel *liberal democracy* is declared as the official regime type. However, Israel in fact, exemplifies an *ethnic state* where self preservation of the state and the regime is but a soft cover for hegemony by one ethnic group, to the extent that Israel cannot be numbered among democratic regimes (Ghanem, Rouhana and Yiftachel, 1999; Yiftachel and Ghanem, 2004a, 2004b). State structure and political operation is controlled by one ethnic group, Ashkenazi Jews; the state recognizes this group and its needs as superior in comparison to other groups (see Figure 1.1).

The Ashkenazi sought from the very beginning to establish an "hegemonic ethnic state" with unique ethnic regime structure and considerations based on a clear preference for their interests, rather than a democratic

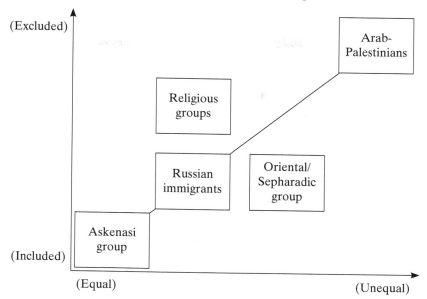

Figure 1.1 Groups in Israel: their position in the "hegemonic ethnic state" system

system with civil interests as its priority (Peleg, 2007; Yiftachel, 1996; Tzefadia and Yiftachel, 2001, 2004). The hegemonic ethnic state regime practiced a policy of discrimination against non-Ashkenazi groups (veterans and immigrants alike). Rather, the state introduced a sophisticated and stratified arrangement towards different groups with different policy guidelines applied towards these groups. By adopting these policies, the ruling Ashkenazi regime failed to establish one "Israeli people," but instead created a multi-faceted regime.

Four main groups struggle against the Ashkenazi hegemony: Palestinians, Orientals, religious and Russian immigrants. The aims and the strategies of each group are a reflection of two levels of factors. The first factor is the type of minority each group represents (e.g. whether the group views itself as an immigrant or an indigenous group) and with whom the group shares common values (i.e. awareness among the group of belonging to a particular national, cultural or religious group). The second factor is the position of the group within the state system where the struggle between groups is an outcome of the discriminatory policy adopted by the founders of the state.

Interaction of these two factors – group type and group position in the state – has produced different and distinctive sub-regulations. Political mobilization methods and semi-political regimes operate according to different procedures, regulations and internal logic deemed suitable to the particular group. Following is a summary of the distinctive interactions that affect Arab, Oriental, religious and Russian minority groups in Israel.

Ethnocratic arrangements affecting Palestinian Citizens and the politics of resistance

The following principles undergird Israeli ethnocratic system political behavior (for details, see Yiftachel, 2006):

- A dominant Jewish ethnic group controls the apparatus of the state.
- Jewish ethnic belonging and religion, rather than citizenship, are the keys to the allocation of resources and power.
- Jewish ethnic domination controls politics, which is organized around status.

Ethnocratic logic provides the analytical frame of reference for understanding the Israeli regime's behavior towards its Palestinian minority and for elucidating relations between various groups. For example, the regime gives broad preference to the Jewish group at the expense of its Palestinian citizens (Kretzmer, 1990; Rouhana, 1997). Specifically:

- immigration policy – in this case, the *law of return* – applies to Jews only;
- a number of land policies (e.g. redemption of the land, Judaization of the Galilee, etc.) apply only to Jews;
- a central role is conferred on religion within the state that symbolizes the boundaries of the privileged ethnicity;
- the flow of capital and development is directed nearly exclusively toward Jewish communities; and
- Hebrew culture is dominant in all public spheres (the Knesset, the courts, the media).

Israel maintains the inferior status of Arabs as compared to Jews through selective discrimination in various spheres and on various levels, so as to maintain the status quo and prevent Arabs from achieving equality (Ghanem, 1998; Ghanem, Rouhana and Yiftachel, 1999). In addition, the Jewish majority is in favor of the ethnic state and supports these policies toward the Palestinian minority (Ghanem, 2003); its support serves as a guarantee that this ethnocracy can continue to function, treating Jews as superior and Arabs as inferior. Chapter 2 will describe the political activity undertaken by the Palestinians in Israel to express their needs and their demand that the ethnocratic regime in Israel be abolished and a democratic, egalitarian regime be created.

The assimilation strategy affecting Orientals and the politics of protest

The State of Israel was established by Jews who immigrated from Europe and America (both Ashkenazi and secular). The majority of Jews who immigrated to Palestine during the British Mandate (1919–48) were of Ashkenazi origin. It was they who established the prevailing political, economic, social and cultural trends still observed in Israel (Agasy, 1991). Non-Ashkenazi groups were incorporated to the Jewish Yishov (Ashkenazi) community and to the Israeli society after 1948, using different means of incorporation, but still experiencing the same form of incorporation: officially, they were integrated into the new Israeli citizenship at the same formal level as the Ashkenazi founders. In practice, however, they were sent to live in peripheral communities where they continue to have fewer rights than the founding, dominant Ashkenazi group.

Oriental Jews, for example, were sent by the Ashkenazi elite to live in development towns that included the 27 urban centers built or significantly expanded during the 1950s to house new Jewish immigrants as part of the official *population dispersal* strategy. In 1998 these towns housed a population of 1.01 million, or 18 percent of Israel's population. About two-thirds of this number were Mizrahim (Oriental); most of the rest were recent Russian-speaking immigrants. During the 1950s and 1960s the towns evolved into a poor, isolated and distressed sector of Israeli-Jewish society. Over the years, these towns became subject to policies that enhanced their dependence on the central state apparatus (e.g. labor-intensive and economically insecure industries and the mass construction of cheap public housing were channeled to the towns). The result was social stigma and concentrated social problems and crime that caused a process of *negative filtering* and considerable population turn-over (Tzefadia and Yiftachel, 2004; Yiftachel, 2000).

The cooperation strategy affecting religious groups and the politics of demands

Religious groups, both Western and Oriental, chose to live in segregated towns and neighborhoods and were excluded from mainstream public life in Israel. These groups practice their social, cultural, economic and even political life at a distance from the Israeli Ashkenazi and the secular domain. As part of the Jewish community before and after 1948, they are struggling against Ashkenazi and Western dominance and have developed a strategy for achieving their demands. For example, as an Oriental and religious political movement that emerged during the 1980s, SHAS added significant value to the demands of Oriental and religious groups. Subsequent chapters will elaborate on the modes of political participation and protest of the Orientals and the religious groups against the Ashkenazi domination.

The multi-cultural policies affecting Russian immigrants and the politics of accommodation

Russians constitute the second largest group of immigrants (after the

Orientals) who will be discussed in this book. Russian immigrants attempted to enforce their collective interests through ethnic policies, but without changing the social-national structure of Israel as a Jewish state. However, the Israeli power structure, unlike in the case of the Oriental Jews, did not reject Russian culture. The character of the Russian immigrants, particularly their cultural character, made them a desired group, as manifested by their ability to communicate with the ruling groups in Israel. It is important to remember that Israel's founding group had deep roots in Russia. Although a hundred years separate Israeli founders from modern Russian immigrants, a longing for Russian classical culture remains a common factor between them. An additional cultural factor that the two groups have in common is their feeling of superiority, and a kind of hostility towards the Orientals.

In addition to their cultural advantage, the Russian immigrants have high professional abilities. For example, 60 percent have academic professions, compared to 29 percent of Israelis; the percentage of engineers among these Russians is very high – 11 percent of the total number of workers in Israel are Russian engineers (Central Bureau of Statistics, 2000). It seems that Israel convinced many to come to Israel and that the ruling group used their arrival as part of its demographic war against Arabs, against the Haredim (Jewish fundamentalists) and against the Oriental Jews (Kimmerling, 1998).

Israel accepted the legitimacy of political organization by the Russians and this eased their situation. The legitimacy of Russian political organization enabled the Russians to act both within the parliament and outside it. This legitimacy also enabled the Russians to provide strong support to Russian political parties. The district analysis for election results in the late 1990s clearly indicated that Russian political parties garnered 60 percent of the Russian immigrant vote. A transformation occurred in this trend during the last decade, when Russian parties became very similar to the other Jewish parties with a diverse membership and political and ideological agendas similar to other active powers in Israel. Subsequent chapters will present an elaboration of the demands of Russian immigrants and of the forms of political participation that they have utilized to further their interests.

In conclusion, if we limit our field of research to Israeli pre-1967 borders, we easily find a multi-faceted regime that functions in different ways towards the various groups that are officially considered as Israeli citizens. The intention of researchers to describe Israeli experience with marginal groups during the past two decades has created a cluster of models and alternative theoretical frameworks aimed at understanding the Israeli situation in its plural multi-group faces. It is my judgment that no one of the proposed models describes completely the multiple systems proposed to explain the various group situations that comprise the Israeli state and society. However, these models, considered collectively, do shed light on the different systems that were created by the "ethnic state" system.

The overall Israeli phenomenon can be best described using "ethnic state" concepts, where under the umbrella of an hegemonic ethnic state regime, different and complicated arrangements were created by the state to control ethnic diversity. This regime was created and managed by the Ashkenazi founding group and has changed gradually since 1948. Today it is clear that, under the Jewish ethnic state and as a bi-product of this state character, multi-faceted arrangements are still functioning that affect the main marginal groups in Israel.

The following chapters will explain and analyze the different aims, strategies and means used by the four main marginal groups – Palestinian-Arabs, Orientals, religious and Russian immigrants – to cope with and to resist the diverse "ethnic state" arrangements that affect them.

2 The Palestinian minority in Israel
Resisting the "ethnocratic" system

On the eve of the 1948 war and the establishment of the State of Israel, nearly two million persons lived within the borders of Mandatory Palestine, two-thirds of them Palestinian-Arabs and one-third Jews. The vast majority of the Palestinians (almost 940,000) and almost all the Jews, lived in the areas that became Israel. As a result of expulsions and mass flight, by the end of the war only about 150,000 Palestinians – 10 percent of all Palestinians – remained in the territory under Israeli control. After the war they were distinguished from other Palestinians by the fact that they had stayed on their land and become citizens of Israel. In the intervening six decades, the Palestinians in Israel have known many vagaries in their political, social, cultural and economic development.

The general sense among the Palestinians in Israel is one of neglect, omission from the regional agenda, and their own failure to win major achievements in the minds of Israelis, the Palestinians in general and the world at large. In general, the history of the Palestinian minority in Israel can be divided into two distinct periods, each with its own characteristics.

1948–66

During the first period, which lasted from 1948 until the abolition of the military government in 1966, the Palestinian citizens of Israel were the victims of severe discrimination in every sphere. Nevertheless, consciousness of this discrimination was not strongly crystallized or well developed; the demand for equality was voiced hesitantly and in limited terms, and there was no demand whatsoever for collective equality, including recognition of the Palestinians as a national minority. All the attempts to set up countrywide Palestinian political organizations failed. This situation produced diffident political participation and deterred the presentation of ideological alternatives that posed a challenge to the authorities.

1967 to the present

Beginning in the mid-1960s, a major change took place in the nature, level and scope of political activity by the Palestinians of Israel. This included political institution-building and participation, and a willingness to promote ideologies and positions that challenge the regime and the Jewish majority. One could witness an increased awareness of the issues of equality and of resolving the Palestinian problem, along with a willingness to make some active contribution on these fronts, generating a sharp increase in self-confidence.

Factors that influenced the development of Palestinians in Israel

In principle, one can sketch out three circles of factors that influence the political development of the Palestinians in Israel. Although these circles are interlocking, for the purpose of analysis I have tried to isolate them.

1) The internal circle encompasses the various factors associated with the internal development taking place among the Palestinians. They include processes of internal democratization and mutual tolerance, the status of the clan, the family, women, inter-confessional relations, level of development, processes of modernization and so on.

   Traditional Palestinian society is closed and rigid; in many senses intolerant both inwardly and outwardly. It discriminates against some of its members, particularly women, and rests on clan and confessional affiliations that leave individuals in an inferior position vis-à-vis the collective. The Palestinians in Israel, who after the birth of the country found themselves in an inferior position as a group and as individuals, experienced significant changes in these arenas under the influence of the majority, as modernization processes influenced their political behavior. In particular, there was a process of internal democratization and to a large extent an internalization of democratic norms and values. There was a change in the status of women, who started to go out to work and study in increasing numbers as the years passed. For example, in Knesset elections Palestinian voting patterns are influenced less and less by clan considerations; this is not so municipal elections, where clannish voting has actually gained strength in recent years (Rouhana and Ghanem, 1993).

2) The Palestinian circle includes everything relevant to the Palestinian problem and its influence on the political development of the Palestinians in Israel, including attempts by some of the Palestinian leadership in the occupied West Bank and Gaza Strip and Diaspora to influence this development. For example, in their election campaigns, lists that compete for Palestinian votes now emphasize the need to solve the *Palestinian problem*. This emphasis is a result of their belief that the Palestinians in Israel are very much interested in the Palestinian problem and in the establishment of an independent Palestinian state

alongside Israel. This is one point of consensus among the Palestinians in Israel. Accordingly, their political development is influenced by developments in the Palestinian arena.

3) The Israeli circle encompasses all of the factors associated with the relations between Israel and its Palestinian citizens. Specifically, it relates to Israeli policy towards Palestinian citizens and the Palestinians' position vis-à-vis the state and its Jewish-Zionist character.

Since its founding, Israel has conducted a discriminatory policy against its Palestinian citizens (Al-Haj and Rosenfeld, 1990; Benziman and Mansour, 1992; Falah, 1990; Ghanem, 1998; Rouhana, 1997). Israel, established as the state of the Jewish people, was concerned first and foremost with realizing the yearnings of the Jews. It existed to serve their interests. The Palestinians who became its citizens after 1948 were subjected to a regime directed against them by the state; even today they occupy an inferior position with regard to the government's scale of priorities. The political development of the Palestinians in Israel can be explained in the context of the mutual influence and relations between this minority group and the Jewish majority that dominates it.

The Palestinians in Israel: needs and requirements

In principle, Israel enables its Palestinian citizens to realize basic rights such as the franchise, the right to be elected to state institutions, freedom of expression, freedom of movement and freedom of assembly. On the other hand, the state retains a preference for Jews in all spheres, including the law (Kretzmer, 1990; Rouhana, 1997). On one hand, Israel observes the arrangements of a democratic regime in certain ways: (a) on the general institutional level; (b) in the conduct of periodic elections; (c) in the manner in which one administration succeeds another; and (d) with respect to separation of powers (e.g. separation between the military and politics, etc). On the other hand, Israel practices ethnocratic measures and arrangements at its most essential level: as a country it is identified with one ethnic/national group, the Jews, and many actions are taken by the state in order deliberately to exclude its Palestinian citizens as equals, entitled to the entirety of benefits enjoyed by Jewish citizens (Yiftachel, 2006).

In practice, therefore, Israel preserves the inferior status of Palestinians as compared to Jews through selective discrimination in various spheres and on various levels. Further, the Jewish majority: (a) is in favor of the ethnic state; (b) supports these policies and their continuation toward the Palestinian minority; and (c) treats Jews as superior and Palestinians as inferior.

The quest of the Palestinian minority for change has negligible prospects in the current demographic and political circumstances. This drives the minority ever closer to crisis, and/or to a quest for revolutionary solutions with respect to its status in the overall system.

The Palestinian minority in Israel 25

The diverse political activity undertaken by Palestinians in Israel to express their needs and demands is generally limited to bringing about meaningful change in their status and living conditions. This limitation arises from the impenetrable Jewish-Zionist nature of the State of Israel whose obligation is to advance the interests of Jews, even at the cost of the interests of Palestinian citizens. Thus, the basic character of the state is an impediment to real change in the situation of Palestinians who reside within it. This is clearly evident on three planes: the ideological-declarative level, the structural level, and the policy/implementation level (Ghanem, 1998).

Ideological-declarative level impediments severely thwart the Palestinian quest for change. The State of Israel was founded as the State of the Jewish people. It has a Jewish-Zionist character and goals, symbols and policies premised on denying the existence of the Palestinian national minority within it. The Palestinian situation deteriorated following an amendment to the Basic Laws of the Knesset in 1985 prohibiting election lists that do not expressly recognize the State of Israel as the State of the Jewish people. During debate on the amendment, MKs Tawfiq Toubi of the Israel Communist Party and Matti Peled of the Progressive List for Peace, proposed alternative wording. They suggested the amended laws should state that Israel is "the State of its citizens" or even "the State of the Jewish people and its Palestinian citizens." The suggestion, however was overwhelmingly voted down.

The consequences of ideological barriers are not limited to day-to-day discrimination against Palestinians nor to the improbability that Palestinians will achieve equality with Jewish citizens. Legally and formally, these barriers render their status ambiguous: Is this state also theirs, or not? What are their prospects for attaining equality in this state, under these circumstances? The situation is acutely distressing for the Palestinian population and for its leadership, and not solely on the emotional/affiliation level.

Palestinian citizens are also discriminated against with regard to the dominant symbols and values of the state and its institutions. In comparison with Jews, for whom such symbols and values comprise their tradition and the source of their identity, Palestinian citizens are estranged from these exclusively Jewish and Zionist symbols. Palestinians in Israel simply cannot identify with many of the symbols of the state of which they are citizens because these symbols are rooted exclusively in the religious and ideological heritage of the majority.

Structural level impediments also obstruct change for Palestinians in Israel. Against their will, they are excluded from Israeli institutions; these are considered to be the purview of Jewish citizens. They serve Jewish Israeli or Jewish goals and not necessarily goals relating to all Israeli citizens. The structural exclusion is many-faceted. It includes: (a) political exclusion, whereby Palestinians are kept at a distance from key centers of political decision-making; (b) non-conscription into the armed forces; (c) non-hiring for senior public positions; (d) the existence of special civil institutions serving Palestinians only; (e) the systematic under-funding and discriminatory structuring of Palestinian education; (f) discrimination against Palestinian citizens in the institutions of the mass media; and so on.

Policy or implementation level impediments exclude Palestinians from equal citizenship, through discrimination grounded in laws, in the allocation of funding and in the allocation of territory. Basic legalized discrimination involves the state's basic goals as they are expressed by the Jewish majority; it operates in favor of Jewish citizens and to the detriment of Palestinian citizens. For example, the Law of Return and the Law of Citizenship are intended to preserve and augment the Jewish majority of the state, with a clear aim of reducing the number of non-Jews, including Palestinians. Non-Israeli Jewish institutions have a special status (See Amendment 7A to the Basic Law of the Knesset, 1985). Further, a series of laws exists intended mainly to assure preferential status to Jewish religious and ethnic heritage, symbols and values.

In the realm of state funding allocations, Palestinians in Israel suffer ongoing discrimination in nearly every sphere of life. This discrimination has been documented in numerous studies and official reports and by a number of NGOs. Despite the positive changes noted by researchers in recent years, up-to-date comparisons of various indices indicate that the gaps arising from outright discrimination are still substantial and suggest that Palestinian citizens will probably be living with this situation for a good many years to come

The voice of Palestinians in Israel

This section of the chapter describes the opinions, positions and so on of Palestinian citizens in Israel. Survey data that were collected among the Palestinians in Israel during the past decade have been analyzed to provide answers to the following questions:[1]

- What is the current and future political orientation of the Palestinian citizens of Israel?
- What is their position on the existence of Israel as an independent state?
- What is their attitude to living inside the state or elsewhere?
- Who represents them?

Recognition of the state

An overwhelming majority of the Palestinian citizens of Israel recognize the state and its right to exist. In the 2001 survey, when asked whether they recognized or rejected the existence of the state, 50.7 percent of the respondents replied in the affirmative ("yes"); 33.7 percent replied "yes with reservations"; and the rest (15.6 percent) answered in the negative ("no" or "absolutely not"). Thus an overwhelming majority of the Palestinians recognize the state's right to exist. Similar figures were obtained in the 1995 survey: an overwhelming majority of the Palestinians (93.3 percent) accepted the existence of Israel without reservations or with certain reservations. Another index to buttress this figure comes from the data regarding a solution to the Palestinian problem or the conflict between Israel and the Palestinian people: only a tiny minority – 8.3 percent of respondents – favored a solution that essentially calls for the elimination of Israel from the region; the vast majority supported solutions whose practical import means solving the Palestinian problem while taking account of the present and future existence of Israel as a state. The results of the 1995 survey were similar: only 3.1 percent of the Palestinians responding supported a solution involving the liquidation of Israel as a political entity in the region.

A well-known statistic that does not require particular corroboration is that most Palestinian citizens of Israel support resolving the Palestinian problem – the core of the Palestinian–Israeli dispute – by setting up a Palestinian state alongside Israel. This position is reinforced by the answers to many questions in both the recent and past surveys. Results of the 1994 survey, which investigated support for the establishment of a Palestinian state in the West Bank and Gaza Strip alongside Israel, indicated that 75.1 percent responded in the affirmative, 18.6 percent responded affirmatively provided certain conditions were met; only 6.2 percent responded in the negative. Smooha's figures from a 1988 survey are strikingly similar: 76.5 percent of the Palestinians supported the establishment of a Palestinian state alongside Israel with no reservations, 17.4 percent had certain reservations, and 6 percent were opposed to the establishment of such a state (Smooha, 1992). According to the 1994 survey, the preferred route for achieving this goal is peaceful negotiations, involving mutual recognition by Israel and the PLO. The majority supported Israel's recognition of the PLO (79.6 percent) and the PLO's recognition of Israel (68.1 percent). Most respondents also supported a continuation of the peace talks, conducted since the 1992 Madrid Conference between Israel and representatives of the Palestinian people from the territories and, since mid-1993, between official representatives of the PLO and official representatives of Israel (89.4 percent supported or absolutely supported these negotiations; 10.6 percent were opposed or totally opposed to them).

Another important issue for the Palestinian citizens of Israel is the problem of refugees. Survey results indicated support for return of the 1948 refugees to their villages – both refugees who left Israel and those who were relocated to other places in its territory. Sixty-eight percent of the Palestinian citizens of Israel believe that Israel must agree to the refugees' return to their villages; 22.5 percent support this "in certain conditions"; only 8.7 percent believe that a solution to the conflict need not include Israeli agreement to allow the return of the Palestinian refugees to their villages. A small fraction (18.6 percent) of those who support the refugees' return as part of the resolution of the conflict expressed willingness to waive this demand if that were essential to achieving peace; 43.7 percent of the Palestinians were not willing to concede this demand, even if this refusal prolongs the conflict between Israel and the Palestinians. The remaining 37.6 percent of respondents had reservations on this count.

The Palestinian future

Survey results from past studies indicate most Israeli Palestinians see their future within the state and as its citizens (Ghanem, 2001b; Rouhana and Ghanem, 1998; Smooha, 1992) distinct from other groups of the Palestinian people. Most see their future as largely or somewhat different from that of their fellow Palestinians who would live in a political entity to be established on the West Bank and Gaza Strip, or in the Palestinian Diaspora.

The data indicate that most Palestinian citizens of Israel (77.2 percent) prefer to remain citizens of Israel and would not want to move to a state established alongside it and become citizens of that entity. This is despite the fact that in the 2001 survey 64.5 percent of the Palestinian citizens of Israel reported feeling closer to the Palestinians on the West Bank and Gaza Strip than to the Jews in Israel – only 35.5 percent felt closer to the Jews in Israel than to the Palestinians in the West Bank and Gaza Strip. In this question, one's national-emotional affiliation seemed to be the determining factor. (See Table 2.1.)

According to empirical and qualitative investigations of their political orientation, most Palestinian citizens of Israel rejected active participation in the Intifada that began in December 1987 against the continued Israeli occupation of the West Bank and Gaza Strip, and in the second Intifada that broke out in late 2000 (Ghanem, 1996a; Ghanem and Ozacky-Lazar, 2003). Most other Palestinians believe that their own position during the Intifadas was appropriate, including provision of moral support or material assistance for the Intifada and espousal of its goals – an end to the occupation and the establishment of a Palestinian state alongside Israel in the West Bank and Gaza Strip (Ghanem and Ozacky-Lazar, 1990; Rouhana, 1990).

In summary, analysis of survey data indicates that the Palestinian citizens of Israel see themselves and their future as citizens of Israel. They are not interested in moving to another country, not even to a Palestinian state

Table 2.1 National-emotional affiliation of Palestinian citizens of Israel (%)

Year	1995 survey	2001 survey
I feel closer to the Palestinians in the West Bank and Gaza Strip	50.4	64.5
I feel closer to the Jews in Israel	49.6	35.5

when and if it is established in the West Bank and Gaza Strip. Further, they do not believe that Palestinian institutions such as the PLO and PNC represent them. They see their place, their future and the organizational bodies that represent them, as distinct from those of the Palestinians in the West Bank, Gaza Strip and Diaspora.

Perceptions of collective-group status

In general, the Palestinian citizens of Israel are dissatisfied with the living conditions of their group, as well as with their collective situation and standing. This great dissatisfaction touches on all of the internal areas crucial for the advancement of the Palestinian citizens of Israel. The Palestinian citizens of Israel attach decisive importance to areas such as: (a) equality with the Jews; (b) proportional parity with Jews in government employment; (c) increased budgets and improved administration for Palestinian local authorities in Israel; (d) expansion of the powers granted to these local authorities; (e) the ability to plan their own future; and (f) an improvement in official policy toward them (Ghanem, 1996c; Ghanem, 2001a). Their extremely low level of satisfaction with their collective situation in these domains is quite conspicuous and substantiated by survey results. Specifically, when asked to rank the degree of disparity or equality between Jews and Palestinians in Israel in areas of life related to the state and influence on its organs, most Palestinians said that there are large and even huge gaps between Jews and Palestinians in these domains.

Results reported in Table 2.2 indicate that the Palestinians see their situation as a group as substantially different from that of the Jews in the areas of life presented. In their estimation, their group status in Israel is generally inferior and is characterized by radical disparities in power and benefits, as compared to the Jews.

In summary, the data indicates that an overwhelming majority of Israel's Palestinian citizens are generally unhappy with the progress of their group: conditions and achievements, ability to influence their own future, make decisions, achieve countrywide integration and attain an appropriate collective status. The gulf between satisfaction with individual modernization and dissatisfaction with collective modernization helps explain the nature and direction of the Palestinian political evolution in Israel.

Table 2.2 Perception of the disparity between Jews and Palestinians in Israel in key areas of life (2001 survey) (%)

	Large gap	Moderate gap	Small gap	No gap
Allocation of financial resources	81.8	14.2	2.9	1.1
Definition of the character of the state	76.4	17.2	3.7	2.7
Definition of the objectives of the state	75.7	17.9	4.2	2.2

Requirements of Palestinians in Israel

The requirements of Palestinian citizens of Israel revolve around two objectives. First, since the mid-1980s, broad consensus has developed among the Palestinian citizens of Israel to solve the "Palestinian problem" by establishing a Palestinian state alongside Israel on the West Bank and Gaza Strip with East Jerusalem as its capital. They desire the establishment of a Palestinian state not only because it would provide a national home for non-Israeli Palestinians, but also because it would improve their own situation (Ghanem, 1996c). Second, as noted previously, Palestinian Israelis have expressed a consensual demand for equality with the Jews in Israel. Studies have shown that a majority of the Palestinian citizens of Israel believe that their struggle must focus on advancing both of these objectives. Only a minority believe that the struggle of the Palestinian citizens of Israel should focus solely on one or the other (i.e. on peace or on equality). (Al-Haj, 1988; Ghanem, 2001a).

Table 2.3 presents survey data indicating Palestinian opinions regarding the degree of equality that should prevail between Jews and Palestinians in Israel. The chapter then addresses questions such as:

- What is the essence of the equality that the Palestinian citizens in Israel seek with the Jews?
- What factors impede its attainment?
- What changes are required in the state system to permit the realization of this aspiration?

Succinctly stated, Palestinians in Israel insist that the state: (a) serve them on an equal footing with the Jews; (b) provide them with equal resources; (c) ensure that their group receives equal public services; (d) allocate civil-service jobs fairly to members of their group; (e) permit them full partnership in government and governing coalitions; and (f) grant them parity in determining the nature and objectives of the state. In practice, they demand that the state function as a bi-national one, rather than one that favors a

Table 2.3 Opinions regarding desired degree of equality (2001 survey)

Area	Percentage of respondents favoring specified degree of equality			
	Full equality	Almost full equality	Partial equality	No need for equality
Allocation of financial resources	78.7	11.7	6.9	2.7
Definition of the character of the state	63.9	21.7	10.6	2.8
Definition of the objectives of the state	68.2	16.2	11.1	4.5

single group – Jews – over all others. These requirements reflect an overarching demand to change the character of the state (see Ghanem, 2001a).

Responses to direct questions about the nature of the state indicate that the Palestinian citizens of Israel are opposed to its Jewish-Zionist character, consistently expressed in a clear preference for Jews. Only 17.3 percent of the Palestinian respondents believe that "a Palestinian can live as an equal citizen in the State of Israel as a Jewish-Zionist state and identify with it." While they affirm the right of the State of Israel to exist, they take strong exception to the *nature* of the state; almost half (46.1 percent) hold that "Israel has no right to exist as a Jewish-Zionist state." Nearly three-fourths (72.9 percent) believe that "Israel should stop being a Jewish-Zionist state and Jews and Palestinians should be recognized as equal national groups, represented according to their weight in the population and full partners in running the country."

In alignment with these views, most believe that Israel has no right to pursue policies intended to "preserve a Jewish majority." This opinion is significant on two fronts. First, it indicates that Palestinian respondents reject the idea that the state should encourage only Jewish immigration. A practical outcome of this opinion would be repeal of the Law of Return for Jews and a halt to the policy of encouraging Jews to immigrate. Second, this opinion implies that no steps should be taken to stop or impede a process by which Palestinian citizens of the state (or any other group), might replace Jews as the majority. In sum, Palestinians in Israel maintain that Israel should not be an ethnic state preferring one group of its citizens over another. In practice, they demand the abolition of the ethnic-national character of the state and its transformation into a bi-national state with an egalitarian attitude toward its citizens.

There are two dimensions to the changes that the Palestinians desire for their group. On the one hand, they demand integration into the state and its institutions on an equal footing with Jews. On the other hand, they also demand institutional autonomy for their group. Their survey responses emphasize the importance they ascribe to state recognition of their group as an autonomous national minority. Specifically, they desire: (a) educational autonomy; (b) a Palestinian labor union; (c) a Palestinian health maintenance organization; (d) Palestinian administration of the waqf (the collective property of the Muslim community); (e) expanded powers for Palestinian local authorities; and (f) official government recognition of the present supreme monitoring committee as representing the Palestinian citizens of Israel. Respondents also emphasize the importance of direct elections to this monitoring committee, even though most of the Palestinian citizens of Israel are not happy with its functioning (e.g. only 42.6 percent expressed "great" or "very great" satisfaction with its performance). Similar findings confirming Palestinians' aspirations for cultural and educational autonomy were reported by Smooha in his earlier surveys in 1976, 1980, 1985 and 1988 (see Smooha, 1992).

In summary, the data indicate that most of the Palestinian citizens of Israel are dissatisfied with their collective status and aspire to integrate into the state and its institutions. However, they also want institutional autonomy – as part of Israeli citizenship – and equality with the Jewish majority. In practice, such autonomy within the state would produce a type of bi-nationalism as a solution to the presence of two national groups – Jews and Palestinians – in the country.

Political organization and mobilization among Palestinians in Israel

The main active political organizations among the Palestinian minority in Israel today are described in the following sections.

The Communist Party and the Democratic Front for Peace and Equality (DFPE)

The Communists began to organize in Palestine long before the establishment of the State of Israel. The Socialist Workers' Party, the first organized manifestation of Communism in the country, was founded in 1919; later, in 1923, it renamed itself the Palestine Communist Party (PCP), joined the Comintern, and began to accept Palestinian members, in addition to its Jewish founders. The party did, however, retain a Jewish majority (Rekhess, 1993: 25–26).

Intervention by the Soviet Communist Party to "Palestinianize" the Palestine Communist Party, and the dissolution of the Comintern in the early 1940s, led to a split in the ranks of the PCP. Most of its Palestinian members seceded to form their own national Communist organization, the League for National Liberation. The Jewish group, led by Shmuel Mikunis, Meir Wilner and Esther Wilensky, continued to be active as the PCP (Rekhess, 1993). The Jewish and the Palestinian Communist factions did not reunite until after the establishment of Israel. At a joint conference in October, 1948 they proclaimed the founding of the Israel Communist Party (ICP), known by its Hebrew acronym *Maki*. Maki immediately set to work to reorganize, to promote its platform and objectives, and to garner support among Jewish and Palestinian citizens of the state.

In the early years, most ICP/Maki members and voters were Jewish. This preponderance actually increased, at first, because of the good relations between the Soviet Union and Israel during the late 1940s. However, the Soviet attitude toward Israel became more hostile in the mid-fifties, especially after the rapprochement between Egypt and the Communist bloc and the first arms deal between Egypt and Czechoslovakia. Jewish support for the ICP then waned, accompanied by a gradual parallel increase in Palestinian support that slowly Palestinianized the party.

The party was able to attract Palestinians because it functioned as a legitimate political party represented in the Knesset and strongly defended the rights of the Palestinians For example, it opposed Israeli policies in both foreign and domestic affairs, demanding that Israel allow the refugees to return, stop expropriating land, make peace with the Palestinian states, and implement the other half of the 1947 UN partition resolution calling for the establishment of a Palestinian–Palestinian state alongside Israel (Jerais, 1973; Kahwaji, 1972; Rekhess, 1993).

The Israeli Communist Party experienced a grave crisis in the mid-sixties when it split in two. One faction, led by Mikunis, continued to call itself the Israel Communist Party (Maki). This faction consisted primarily of the Jewish members of the party and a handful of Palestinians. The other faction, led by Wilner and Tewfiq Toubi, called itself the New Communist List (known by its Hebrew acronym *Rakah*); its membership was predominantly Palestinian. In the elections for the sixth Knesset (1965), held after the split, Rakah came out ahead, winning three seats in the Knesset and garnering about 75 percent of its votes from Palestinians. Maki won only one seat, with negligible (less than 0.5 percent) Palestinian support (Rekhess, 1993). Maki, having failed to clear the threshold in the elections for the seventh Knesset (1969), disappeared from the political map, leaving Rakah as the only representative of the Communists in Israel in the parliamentary and public arenas.

The disappearance of Maki, the "Jewish" faction of the Communist movement in Israel; the status of the Palestinians in Israel; the status of the Palestinian national movement, in general; and changes in the tactics adopted by the Communist Party itself, were important factors in enhancing the position of the Communist Party among the Palestinians in Israel during the early 1970s. Rakah began garnering an increasing share of Palestinian support, with regard to membership and electoral results. In elections to the eighth, ninth and tenth Knessets (1973, 1977 and 1981), Rakah took a plurality of the Palestinian vote; the high point for the organization came in 1977, when it actually won an absolute majority of the valid Palestinian votes (see Table 2.4).

In his comprehensive book about the Israel Communist Party, Rekhess summarizes the chief factors behind the rise of the party:

> The explanation for the rapid consolidation of the Communist Party among the Palestinian minority is to be found on four levels: a political and ideological platform that suited the changing situation, the socio-political processes of change that ripened in the period in question, the strategy that the Communists developed in response to changing needs, and an excellent and effective party organization.
>
> (Rekhess, 1993: 219)

In fact, it can be argued that the period from the early 1970s through the mid-1980s was the golden age of the Communist Party among the Palestinians in Israel.

Starting in the early 1970s, the Communist initiatives reflected a profound change in perception vis-à-vis the Palestinians and other forces active in the political arena. The party launched activity based on the concept that the Communist party was the central force leading the Palestinian struggle. The search for ways to attract wider support led to the establishment of extra-parliamentary committees such as the Land Defense Committee. The party was active with other committees whose leadership it aspired to win (e.g. the National Committee of Local Authorities). It organized the successful candidacy of the chairman of the committee, Hana Mois – head of the Kafr Rama local council – for the Knesset on the list of the Democratic Front for Peace and Equality (DFPE – also known as *Hadash*) (Rekhess, 1993). The DFPE was, in fact, the pinnacle of the Communist party's efforts to broaden its influence.

The DFPE, established at the initiative of the Communist Party to serve as an umbrella organization, included, in addition to Communist party: (a) the Black Panthers, led by Charlie Biton; (b) representatives from committees of Palestinian university graduates, especially that in Nazareth; (c) some Palestinian local authorities; (d) students; and (e) other public committees and organizations. Even though the DFPE was essentially controlled by the Communists, they did not speak of "the realization of Communism in the country" in their guidelines. Rather, the DFPE settled for a number of points that constituted a minimum platform under which all the forces could unite:

- achieving a comprehensive and stable Israeli-Arab and Israeli-Palestinian peace,
- defending workers' rights,
- achieving equality for Palestinians in Israel,
- advancing the status of women,
- abolishing communal discrimination, and
- protecting the interests of the poor neighborhoods and development towns.

In the complex situation in which the Palestinians of Israel live, the DFPE, with the Communist party at its head, offered a platform on domestic and foreign issues that, for that period, met the needs and demands of the Palestinians in Israel and attracted Palestinians to it and the Communist Party. Perhaps the most important factor in strengthening and consolidating the Communist Party and the DFPE was the highly effective party organization. The Party worked meticulously to build an organizational pyramid rising from individual members to the central committee and supervised by the general secretary; this was an efficient organizational model (Rekhess, 1993).

Communist Party membership increased from 500 after the split in 1965, to 1600 Palestinian members in 1988 who lived in virtually every Palestinian town or village (ibid.: 5). Additionally, in virtually every community, dozens of activists who were not officially party members were prepared to work in all forums to promote its platform. These activists were generally characterized by initiative, good organization and a willingness to volunteer for the sake of Palestinian society.

Since 1984 there has been a significant retreat in Palestinian electoral support for the Party, a decline that continued until the elections for the fourteenth Knesset in the summer of 1996 (see Table 2.4). In those elections, the Communist Party, in cooperation with the National Democratic Alliance, received a significant portion of the Palestinian vote, winning five Knesset seats. This change did not necessarily indicate that the party is returning to its days of glory; the change was influenced by outside factors such as the change in the electoral system and the Communists' agreement with the National Democratic Alliance. In the fifteenth Knesset election (1999), support for the DFPE dropped to about 22 percent of the Palestinian votes – good for three Knesset seats. This result constituted a severe defeat in the eyes of party leadership and supporters, who had evidently expected to win at least four mandates. Although it is too early to eulogize the DFPE as the main political force in the Palestinian sector, the party has certainly become weaker. The decline in its strength and status has been reflected at the polls.

In the sixteenth Knesset elections (2003), the Communist Party entered into a coalition with MK Ahmad Tibi of "The Palestinian Party for Change." This joint bloc won three seats (Mohammad Barakah, Issam Makhul and Ahmad Tibi). It marked the first time that the Communist Party representatives in the Knesset did not include any Jewish MKs. In the general election of 2006, the Israeli Communist Party and the DFPE ran in a separate list and won three Knesset members including one Communist Jew.

The rise and fall of the Israeli Communist Party, particularly among the Palestinian citizens of Israel, is a fascinating historical topic, which has attracted the interest of a wide range of scholars. Perhaps the members of the ICP and DFPE themselves have still not managed to cope with the profound internal and external impacts of their movement.

The Sons of the Village (Ibnaa al-Balad)

During the years preceding the 1967 war, two Palestinian national organizations were established in Israel: the Palestinian Popular Front and al-Ard (see Ghanem, 2001a for details). The outcome of the war caused a momentary paralysis in the activity of the Palestinian national streams. For members the Palestinian organizations, Israeli victory over the Palestinian armies came as a great surprise. On the one hand, they were in a state of shock after the defeat; on the other hand, the results of the war led to renewed contact between the Palestinians in Israel and the main concentration of the Palestinian people in the West Bank and Gaza Strip, who fell under Israeli control. The war's outcome stirred a national awakening among the Palestinians in Israel. This awakening, along with exposure to various factors in the Palestinian national movement, provided fertile ground for the establishment of a Marxist Palestinian national group in 1972 – the Sons of the Village (Ibnaa al-Balad). The Sons of the Village was established in the village of Umm al-Fahm in the Triangle, under the leadership of a young attorney, Muhammad Kewan. The decision to set up a new local organization was spurred by the Communists' support for the incumbent Council and its head, who was identified with the Labor party (Ghanem, 2001a).

The Sons of the Village boycotted Knesset elections. In the 1973 local authority elections, however, the Sons of the Village won a single seat on the 15-member village Council and saw this as a significant achievement and as a launching pad for countrywide activity. The movement established branches in other communities under other names: the *al-Nahda* movement in Tayyibe and the *al-Fajr* movement in Ar'ara. In the 1978 local-authority elections, Sons of the Village doubled its representation in Umm al-Fahm to two councilors and also won single seats in Tayyibe, Kabul, Mi'ilya and Baqa al-Gharbiyya. In the 1983 local elections, the party won nine seats on various local councils (Landau, 1993). In 1989, however, the movement suffered a severe defeat, winning only three seats throughout the country and failing to win any seats in the Council of Umm al-Fahm, which by then had municipal status. In 1993, the movement regained some of its strength, winning a total of eight seats, including two in Umm al-Fahm and two in Makr-Judeida (Ozacky-Lazar and Ghanem, 1996).

The Sons of the Village was particularly active among Palestinian university students in Israel. Campuses provided fertile ground for the movement, which called itself the National Progressive Movement (NPM). It focused on student activity in the hope that the students would continue their activity in the movement at home after completing their studies. At the same time, the NPM worked to solve student problems and competed for control of the Palestinian student committees, which were not recognized by the university administration, and most of which were dominated by the Communist Party.

In 1976, the National Progressive Movement was at its zenith, winning a majority in the elections of the Palestinian students' committee at the Hebrew University (Rekhess, 1993). In the late 1970s and early 1980s, however, the NPM faltered and the DFPE recovered. After the appearance of the Progressive List, its campus supporters joined with other members of the NPM and set up a joint National Action Front that posed a more effective threat to the DFPE. In the late 1980s and early 1990s, the National Action Front made significant inroads into the Palestinian student committees.

The Sons of the Village were backed by a network of weekly and periodical newspapers including *al-Raya*, a weekly that was closed by a military order of the Israeli authorities, and then *al-Midan*, another weekly, published after the closure of *al-Raya*. In recent years the movement has stopped publishing a newspaper and has resorted to posters or articles placed in mass-circulation Palestinian language weeklies.

In 1982, the movement split following disagreements over participation in Knesset elections and stance toward the PLO. One faction, headed by the founder, Muhammad Kawan, adopted the name *Jabahat al-Ansar*. This faction favored Arafat's leadership, supported Fatah and advocated participation in Knesset elections. The larger faction retained the old name (Sons of the Village), supported the Popular Front for the Liberation of Palestine, and continued to call for a boycott of Knesset elections.

The Sons of the Village initially fought for "a democratic, secular Palestinian state on the territory of Palestine," and initially demanded equality with the Jewish majority in Israel. Later, however, and especially after the outbreak of the Intifada, the Sons of the Village reformulated its objectives. The movement's political program, drafted in February 1988 and approved at its conference in Nazareth in July, 1988, speaks of "the right to determine our destiny in the context of a Palestinian state," without defining the boundaries of such a state. It speaks of "equal rights without distinction of nationality, religion, sex, or color" (Landau, 1993: 80–81). Representatives of the movement have spoken of a willingness to implement Security Council Resolution 242 and voiced an explicit demand for the establishment of a Palestinian state in the West Bank and Gaza Strip alongside Israel. This 1988 policy represents a significant change in the attitude of the Sons of the Village toward the very existence of Israel and in their preferred solution for the Palestinian problem.

From within the Palestinian Israeli community, the movement worked to introduce changes into Palestinian society itself. For instance, it: (a) actively opposed clan domination in Palestinian local government; (b) opposed the traditional leadership and those who collaborated with the Israeli authorities and the Jewish political parties; and (c) emphasized the need to improve the conditions of Palestinian society in Israel (e.g. the status of women).

The 1990s marked the beginning of a general decline in the activity of the Sons of the Village and an advance of the elections to the fourteenth Knesset. In May 1996, in cooperation with other national groups, the Sons of the Village established a new party, the National Democratic Alliance, to which I will refer later.

The Islamic Movement

"Political Islam" began organizing in Mandatory Palestine before 1948. The Muslim Brotherhood, founded in Egypt in the 1920s, did not begin to take an interest in events in Palestine until the mid-1930s. After the eruption of the Palestinian revolt against the British and Jewish immigration in 1936, movement representatives came from Egypt to encourage the Palestinians in their struggle. The first local branch of the Muslim Brotherhood was founded in Jerusalem in 1946. During the 1948 war, three battalions of volunteers from the Brotherhood enlisted in the Egyptian army (Shabi and Shaked, 1994). However, the results of the 1948 war – the dispersal of Palestinians, and the establishment of Israel, which imposed a military government on the Palestinian communities – limited the activity of political Islam. In fact, one cannot point to any such organization by Palestinian citizens of Israel during the 1950s, 1960s or 1970s. After 1967, the situation changed as a result of renewed contact between the Palestinians in Israel and Palestinians in the occupied West Bank and Gaza Strip and existence there of fundamentalist organizations, and religious seminaries. New conditions were created for the development of political Islam among the Palestinians in Israel (Meir, 1989).

A number of young people who completed High School and were attracted to an Islamic environment continued their studies in the Islamic colleges and institutes that prepared them for the title of "Sheikh." These young men began unorganized activity to preach religion in their home communities and elsewhere in Muslim communities, including sermons in the Mosques and meetings held at Muslim festivals (Meir, 1989). Their activity paved the way for the Islamic stream to organize in the form of political and social associations.

The history of Islamic religious organization in Israel can be divided into two periods. The first period (1979–81) featured a semi-military underground organization composed of a small core of people who believed in armed struggle against the Jews and the State of Israel; they called themselves Asrat al-Jihad (The Family of Jihad). This group was apprehended by the Israeli security forces in 1981 and its leaders imprisoned, putting an end to this period. The second period, from 1983 through the present, began with the emergence of Sheikh Abdallah Nimr Darwish of Kafr Qasim-in-the-Triangle as the leader of a new organization, that called itself the "Young Muslims."

The Young Muslims began to organize in almost every community where there were Muslims, establishing voluntary associations both to promote social activity and to gather contributions for their financing. Its members also began to organize on a countrywide scale – where they could enroll new members and preach for a return to the sources. Until recently, the Islamic Movement did not participate officially in Knesset elections, even though it did not formally boycott them. Before election day it would call upon its members to act in accordance with their conscience. Before the elections to the fourteenth Knesset (1996), however, the Islamic Movement set up a joint list with the Arab Palestinian Party. Two of its representatives then won seats to the fourteenth Knesset (out of four seats for the joint list); likewise, two representatives won seats to the fifteenth Knesset (out of five seats for the joint list). Some members of the Young Muslims movement seceded in protest of the group's participation in these elections; these individuals established an alternate movement, led by Ra'ad Salah, Mayor of Umm al-Fahm (Ozacky-Lazar and Ghanem, 1996).

The Islamic Movement concentrates its efforts on the municipal level. This trend goes back to 1984, when the Movement ran for and won control of the local council of Kafr Bara-in-the-Triangle. In 1989, the Islamic Movement sought a number of local positions and managed to elect the head of five Councils – Umm al-Fahm, Kafr Bara, Kafr Qasim, Jaljulya-in-the-Triangle and Rahat-in-the-Negev – plus 46 Council members. A year later the Movement added the head of the Kabul local Council to this list. In the 1993 municipal elections, the Islamic Movement again won six places as heads of Councils. It lost Rahat, but won Kafr Qara-in-the-Triangle, as well as a rotation arrangement in Kafr Kanna-in-the-Galilee. The Movement also elected 50 Council members, including some in the mixed cities of Acre and Lyde (Ozacky-Lazar and Ghanem, 1996).

In addition to its responsibility for the local government in these communities, the Movement focused its effort on providing the services associated with the institutions of civil society and on propaganda. Ever since its founding, the Islamic Movement has provided essential services to the local population in every community in which it is active (see the list in Aburaiya, 1989). These services include an educational network to supplement the state system, libraries, computer centers, community centers, pre-schools, rehabilitation centers for ex-convicts and addicts, medical and dental clinics, and so on. These can be found all over the country, including towns where the Islamic Movement is not part of the governing coalition (e.g. Umm al-Fahm, Kafr Qasim, Kafr Bara, Kafr Kanna, Nazareth, Kabul, Nahaf and others).

The Islamic Movement employed various means to manage and fund these institutions. It focused on volunteer activity and on mobilizing its members, for example, in projects that addressed their communal needs. The Mosques, found in every community where there are Muslims, hosted these projects. The Movement also took control of the task of collecting the Zakat, the tax that every Muslim is required to pay to support the poor. These funds underwrote a large portion of the Movement's activities. In localities where the Movement could draw on other financial sources, including governmental sources – especially in places where it controlled the local Council – it did so.

Today, the Islamic Movement, firmly rooted and institutionalized, faces different challenges. Among these, special mention must be made of the hostility towards it both from Israeli authorities and the Jewish sector in general, and from the staunchly secularist streams among the Palestinians in Israel. The Islamic Movement is substantially different from fundamentalist movements in the Arab countries around Israel. One difference is its awareness of its limitations with regard to these two adversaries (i.e. Jewish Israelis and secular Palestinian Israelis). Specifically, the Movement is aware that: (a) its prospects for growing and attracting new members are slim, given the wave of modernization and secularization in the Palestinian population in Israel; (b) it is unlikely ever to become a dominant force among the Palestinians in Israel; and (c) it will have to find fewer religious allies in order to take a stand against opponents in the Israeli public and on the local Palestinian scene.

The Democratic Arab Party (DAP)

In January 1988, shortly after the start of the Intifada, Labor MK Abdulwahab Darawshe, from the Galilee village of Iksal, addressed a rally in Nazareth. Protesting the government's handling of the unrest in the West Bank and Gaza Strip, he announced that he was resigning from the Labor party and its Knesset faction. Darawshe immediately began to look into the options for continuing his political career. In consultation with a number of local council heads, academics and others, he decided to establish a new party that would be overtly Palestinian and aspire to represent Palestinians' problems and ambitions.

The founding conference of the Democratic Arab Party was held in June 1988, with the participation of approximately 600 prominent figures from the Palestinian society. Attendees included about 20 heads of local councils, 140 deputy heads and council members, and leading academics and clerics. This conference helped Darawshe and his associates demonstrate that they had broad support in the Palestinian society (Landau, 1993).

The DAP platform called for (a) equality for the Palestinians in Israel; and (b) the establishment of a Palestinian state alongside Israel. The platform also explained the logic behind the establishment of a Palestinian party to represent Palestinian interests in Israel; it accused the Jewish parties of exploiting their Palestinian voters without making a serious attempt to satisfy their needs. To help disseminate its platform and positions the DAP founded a weekly called *Al-Diar*.

In the 1988 elections, the DAP won only one seat in the Knesset – a good beginning nevertheless. Four years later, in elections to the thirteenth Knesset, the DAP increased its share of the Palestinian vote from 11.3 percent to 15.2 percent and doubled its representation to two seats (Ghanem, 1996c). The party also made significant gains in local elections. In 1989, appearing for the first time, it returned two local council heads and several council members. In 1993, the DAP elected six council heads and 47 council members, an impressive accomplishment by any standard (Ozacky-Lazar and Ghanem, 1996).

In 1996, the Democratic Arab Party formed an alliance and set up a joint list with the "southern wing" of the Islamic movement. Together they received 25 percent of the valid Palestinian ballots in 1996 – good for four Knesset seats. In advance of the elections to the fifteenth Knesset, MK Mahametd, from the DFPE, joined its list; the list won about 31 percent of the valid Palestinian ballots and five mandates. This was an excellent result from every point of view and was attributed mainly to solid organizational structure and the ability to express the ethnic-religious strivings of the Palestinians in Israel.

Striving for a large, active Palestinian grouping, the DAP attempted to form a "unified Arab bloc." This attempt failed; however, the party achieved a "minimized unity" with a number of independents and the southern wing of the Islamic Movement, led by Shiekh Abdullah Nimer Darweesh and MK Abdul Malek Dahamsheh. The coalition won four seats in the Knesset. In 1999, the joint bloc was joined by the National Unity Front, under the leadership of Hashem Mahameed. Mahameed had split from the Democratic Front for Peace and Equality which he once represented in the Knesset. The joint bloc won five seats in the 1999 election. In 2003, some party members split from the party to run independently in the sixteenth Knesset elections. The coalition won only two seats during this election – Abdul Malek Dahamsheh from the Islamic Movement and Talab Sani' from the Arab Party.

The National Democratic Alliance (NDA)

The NDA was the best organized movement in the history of Palestinian national organizations in Israel. It was composed of a number of small left wing political groups that had previously operated in Palestinian towns and villages. It included the Sons of the Village; the Equality Alliance, founded by Dr Azmi Bishara of Nazareth (a lecturer at Bir Zeit University in the West Bank and a researcher at the Van Leer Institute in Jerusalem); the remnants of the Progressive List; and various other local groups (e.g. the Socialist Party from the village of Maghar; the al-Ansar movement from Umm al-Fahm; the al-Nahda movement of Tayyibe; the Bni al-Tira movement; and numerous Palestinian public figures).

One of the NDA's central demands was that Israel redefine itself as a state for all its citizens, rather than as the state for Jewish people. The group also proposed that the authorities grant special status to the Palestinian minority, in terms of institutional autonomy. The NDA expressed clear criticism of the peace accords between Israel and the Palestinians and dissatisfaction with Arafat's regime in Palestine. This was a unique platform: the ideas it presented, although popular among the Palestinians, had never been advanced in the form of a political agenda backed by a significant bloc and demanding implementation.

In advance of the elections for the fourteenth Knesset, the NDA ran for the Knesset on a joint list with the DFPE. Its representative, Dr Azmi Bishara, received fourth place on the joint list. During the term of the fourteenth Knesset, profound differences emerged between Bishara and the other members of the faction; consequently, a split into two parties occurred. Attempts at reconciliation before the elections failed and the NDA ran alone for the fifteenth Knesset, reinforced by Dr Ahmad Tibi's movement. The party won about 17 percent of the valid Palestinian votes. This fine achievement provided the NDA with two Knesset members (Bishara and Tibi) and promising prospects. In 2003 and in 2006, the party ran independently in the Knesset elections and won three seats. Despite its promising prospects following the fifteenth Knesset, it appears that the party's conspicuous organizational weaknesses and its lack of a collective leadership ultimately prevented the NDA from realizing its full potential.

The Arab Movement for Change

The Arab Movement for Change party was established in 1996, after Dr Ahmad Tibi, Advisor to the late President Yassir Arafat, announced his intention to run in the Israeli parliamentarian elections. Although he was already well known in the Israeli media, before the fourteenth Knesset elections of 1996, he shrewdly declared that he was withdrawing his candidacy because he did not have a viable coalition with which to run.

In the fifteenth Knesset elections of 1999, the Arab Movement for Change built a coalition with the National Democratic Alliance and, consequently, won two seats in the Knesset. The coalition was dissolved one day after the elections. In the sixteenth Knesset elections of 2003, the Arab Movement for Change and the Democratic Front ran in a coalition that won three seats; Tibi obtained the third. In 2006, Tibi was integrated into the "Joint Arab List," and again was elected as a Knesset member.

Palestinians in Jewish parties

Before Israel was established, some elements of the Palestinian community developed ties with the Jewish leadership that was working, both openly and behind the scenes, to establish a Jewish national home. The establishment in 1948 of the State of Israel reinforced these ties, and tens of thousands of additional Palestinian activists found a place in Jewish parties. This trend was halting at first, but gained momentum over the years. Today there is a visible grouping of Palestinians who are members of, vote for or support Jewish parties.

Historically, this stream was represented chiefly by Palestinians directly associated with Jewish-Zionist parties – especially Mapam, Mapai and later, the Labor party. The direct support for the Jewish parties was in addition to the satellite lists that these parties initiated. Satellite lists lasted from the first Knesset elections in 1949 until 1981 (see Ghanem, 2001a), when the last of the satellite lists disappeared from the Israeli political scene.

Mapam

The new situation created in the wake of the 1948 war was extremely difficult for the Palestinians who remained in Israel. They were in shock at the

Palestinian rout, were forced to accept Israeli citizenship, and were subjected to a military government. Political activity among them was extremely limited and was manifested chiefly in the Israel Communist Party – although feelers were also put out by other Zionist parties. The first Zionist party that took a clear position on the matter was Mapam (the United Workers Party). As early as 1954 Mapam opened its ranks to Palestinians on an equal footing with its Jewish members. Since then it has maintained a network of activists to conduct vigorous activity among Palestinian youth and adults. It always insisted on having Palestinian representation on its Knesset list and has had Palestinian MKs ever since the elections to the second Knesset in 1951 (Landau 1971; Ozacky-Lazar 1996: 138–40).

Mapai and the Labor party

Mapai (the Eretz Yisrael Workers' Party), was led in the 1950s by David Ben-Gurion. Unlike Mapam, Mapai rejected the idea of opening its ranks to Palestinian members and continued to work in the Palestinian sector through satellite lists or through the traditional leadership that safeguarded the party's interests without becoming members. The heir of Mapai, however – the Labor party – changed its position beginning in 1970, when it agreed to accept as members, Palestinians "who serve in the security forces." Later, in 1973, the Labor party dropped this condition and began to enroll Palestinian members unconditionally. Subsequently, Herut and the other Jewish parties also began to accept Palestinian members (Cohen, R., 1985).

Palestinian electoral support for Jewish parties was influenced by many variables, associated with these parties' positions toward the Palestinians, the degree of control exercised by the heads of clans and communities, as well as the existence of satellite lists, which attracted most of the votes of this stream. Throughout the years in which the satellite lists were active (1949–77), most voters of the Israeli-Palestinian camp cast their ballots for the satellite lists; only about an eighth of their valid ballots were given directly to Zionist parties. But when the Zionist parties dropped their support for satellite lists and began to accept Palestinian members, they began to attract direct Palestinian support.

In the elections for the tenth Knesset in 1981, Palestinian support for Jewish parties jumped to about 40 percent and no satellite list made it into the Knesset. In the elections to the eleventh Knesset (1984), no satellite lists competed and the Jewish parties increased their direct support to about 50 percent of the Palestinian electorate. In the elections to the twelfth Knesset, the Democratic Palestinian Party (see below) appeared on the scene and cut into support for the Jewish parties, whose share of the Palestinian vote fell to about 40 percent. In the elections to the thirteenth Knesset in 1992, support for the Zionist parties rebounded to 52 percent, because of problems that beset the Palestinian parties. Most recently, in the elections to the fourteenth Knesset (1996) and to the fifteenth Knesset (1999), Palestinian support for Jewish-Zionist parties declined to only 37 percent and 30 percent accordingly. This was because of the change in the electoral system with the direct election of the Prime Minister, but also because of the Palestinian parties' improved performance (Ghanem, 1998; Ghanem and Ozacky-Lazar, 1999).

In recent years, this Palestinian representation is mainly found in three Zionist-Jewish parties: the Meretz "leftist" party, the Labor party and the Likud party. In the fifteenth Knesset elections of 1999, a number of Palestinian MKs were elected as part of the Zionist parties. For example:

- In the Meretz party, Husneya Jbara was elected as the first Palestinian woman member of the Knesset (Ghanem and Rouhana, 2001).
- In the Labor party, Nawwaf Masalha and Saleh Tarif were elected. Masalha was appointed as deputy minister for Foreign Affairs during the term of Ehud Barak – a matter that made him a subject for much criticism for representing Israeli foreign policy, including policy regarding Palestinians and the Palestinian world (Ghanem and Rouhana, 2001). Saleh Tarif, who occupied the Druze seat in the Labor party, was appointed Minister without Portfolio in the Likud–Labor government lead by Ariel Sharon. He became, therefore, the first Palestinian minister in an Israeli government (although he subsequently resigned because of rumors of corruption and other illegal activities).

Palestinian support for Jewish parties remains widespread. In this context, many Palestinian political activists have strengthened their self confidence over the years while changing their positions on key issues. This is a pragmatic stream that aspires only to limited changes. This Israeli-Palestinian stream recognizes the fundamental fact that Israel is a Jewish country with a Jewish majority. It accepts the existing order of "Israeliness" and Jewish-Zionist supremacy and does not demand a change in the character of the state. Instead, it focuses on improving the status of Palestinians with regard to civic issues such as equal allocation of resources, jobs and so on.

Consensus-based organizations among the Palestinian minority in Israel

In early 1974, the conclusions of a report on Palestinian local authorities, prepared by a committee headed by Dr Jeraisi, were published. The crux of these findings was that an immense disparity exists between the Jewish and Palestinian sectors with regard to government assistance and allocations. As a response to the report the national Committee of Heads of Arab Local Councils was established in June 1974.

The Committee of Heads of Arab Local Councils

The declared objective of the Committee of Heads of Arab Local Councils was to campaign at the local level to equalize the sums allocated by the government to local authorities in the two sectors (Cohen, 1985). The Committee elected Hana Mwies, head of the Rama local council in Galilee, as its chairman. He served until his death in 1981 and was succeeded by the head of the Shefar'am municipal council, Ibrahim Nimr Hussein.

The first Land Day (March 30, 1976), was a watershed in the history of the Committee, which, until then, had limited its activity to local matters such as budgets, health and education. The Committee began to involve itself in a host of issues affecting all Palestinians in Israel, including political and ideological issues and problems not associated with municipal affairs. After Land Day, the Committee sent an official memorandum to then Prime Minister, Yitzhak Rabin, in which it insisted on the right of Israeli Palestinians to be officially recognized as a *national minority* and as part of the Palestinian people, rather than merely as religious-cultural minorities (e.g. Muslims, Christians and Druze). The Committee not only tackled the daily problems of the population, but also raised purely political issues, such as the return of lands expropriated by the state (Al-Haj, 1988).

The Higher Arab Follow-up Committee

A significant change in history of the Committee of Heads of Arab Local Councils occurred against the backdrop of the Lebanon war in 1982, when its chairman, Ibrahim Nimr Hussein, originated an initiative that established the Higher Arab Follow-up Committee. The Follow-up Committee was an umbrella organization consisting of: (a) the heads of local councils; (b) Palestinian Knesset members; (c) members of the Histadrut executive committee; (d) representatives of the Islamic Movement and of the Sons of the Village movement; (e) representatives of the Palestinian student unions on university campuses; (f) representatives of the secondary school pupils' association; (g) a representative of the national Arab parents' committee; and (h) representatives of Palestinians living in the mixed cities.

Because of the broad representation of the Follow-up Committee, it came to be considered as the "parliament" of Palestinians in Israel, with overall responsibility for the conduct of their affairs, including the struggle for equality with the Jewish majority. The prestige of the Follow-up Committee peaked in the mid-1980s, with the zenith of its widespread activity. This activity was marked by the proclamation of two general strikes in 1987. The first, designated "Equality Day," was a protest against discrimination and a call for equality. The second, called "Peace," was initiated to protest the occupation in the West Bank and Gaza Strip and to demonstrate identification with the Intifada, which broke out at the end of 1987. In each case, response to the strike call was comprehensive and included the vast majority of public institutions in Palestinian localities.

The Follow-up Committee appointed sub-committees to deal with the status of the Palestinians in various areas of life, particularly education, social conditions and health. Each sub-committee, served by experts who were not necessarily from among its members, sought ways and means to pressure authorities into improving their effectiveness.

In the early 1990s, the status of the Follow-up Committee deteriorated. Numerous reasons accounted for this. First, the Committee of Heads, established to lead Palestinians' struggle for peace and equality, was meant to express their unity on this central issue. Unfortunately, the Committee became a platform for representatives of various political entities to squabble with each other, while failing to propose suitable ways to resolve the daily problems encountered by the Palestinian minority in Israel. Second, rather than majority votes, the Committee sought unanimous decisions, as a reflection of the will to maintain internal unity – often at the expense of real discussions on substantive issues. Consequently, the Committee was unable to make basic decisions. Third, most of the Committee members were heads of local councils, who had been elected to office because of their clan and family affiliation, rather than because of their qualifications for administering the affairs of their communities. This weakened the status of the Committee in the Palestinian community at a time when – unlike the heads of local authorities – that community was becoming more modernized and experienced.

Fourth, the Committee as a whole, and particularly its sub-committees, failed to improve its methods and upgrade its demands. The Committee should have taken measures commensurate with the substantive demands in the areas of education, society and health. It should have represented the Palestinians in Israel as Israeli citizens who constitute a national minority with the right to self determination in social and educational affairs.

Efforts have been made in recent years to institutionalize two committees: the Committee of Heads of local authorities, and the higher follow-up Committee. These efforts could mark a reactivization and vitalization of Committees that truly represent the interests of the Palestinian community in Israel.

Political participation among the Palestinians in Israel

The political participation of the Palestinians in Israel, as reflected by their voting behavior, reveals two main trends: (a) a general decline in participation in Knesset elections; and (b) fragmentation of the Palestinian vote.

One clear characteristic of Palestinian voting behavior in Israel is the persistent decline in turnout over the years. In the first seven Knesset elections (1949–69), the Palestinian participation rate was 80 to 90 percent. During this period, Mapai, the ruling party, used the military government institutions, in cooperation with the traditional Palestinian leadership, to guarantee a high voting turnout. The majority of Palestinian votes, under this tight system of control, went to Mapai and its affiliated lists (Lustick, 1980). A consistent decline in voter turnout began in the mid-1960s, corresponding to the relaxation of the military rule in 1964, and its total abolition in 1966. The participation rate hit 70 percent in 1992, before rebounding to 77 percent in 1996 and declining to 56 percent in 2006. During the elections of 1999 and 2003, the voting rate of the whole population in the country ranged between 75 percent and 62 percent.[2]

The steady decrease in Palestinian voting, especially since the 1970s, was caused by a growing awareness among many Palestinians that they were a marginal factor in Israel's political system and could never become full partners within it. In addition, came the realization that government policy, in general, and toward Palestinian citizens in particular, was not affected by their voting behavior. Their sense of marginality and exclusion was felt most intensely when possibilities for political influence evaporated just when they seemed about to develop. For example, when Labor leader Shimon Peres tried to form a Government in 1990, after the collapse of the National Unity government (comprising Labor, Likud and other parties), he calculated that the Knesset members representing the Palestinian parties would support him and give him a parliamentary majority without being members of his coalition. His attempt failed because a considerable number of Jewish Knesset members, especially from the religious parties, refused to join a government that would rely on Palestinian votes for its existence. This, and similar incidents, persuaded many Palestinians that their votes had limited influence; and by not voting they expressed their sense of marginality and limited political effectiveness. During the Likud Government of 1996–99, the Palestinians' sense of marginalization was heightened by the government's neglect of their needs.[3] Then, in their fierce competition for Jewish voters in 1999, both the Labor and Likud candidates for Prime Minister avoided discussing the concerns of Palestinian citizens, thus providing little incentive for skeptical Palestinian voters to go to the polls.[4]

A second cause for the decline in the Palestine vote is that Palestinian parties presented very few innovative ideas for resolving the predicament of Palestinians and their relationship with the state. They have repeatedly offered the same hackneyed and unsubstantial arguments. For example, until recently no party spelled out what it meant by equality between Palestinians and Jews in Israel, or examined implications of "equality" for the community and the state. No party has offered a vision of the appropriate relationship between the Palestinian citizens and the state. Zionist parties have promised improved services, but have avoided the fundamental question of the Palestinians' place within Israel and as a part of the Israeli polity. The Palestinian-dominated parties, especially the Israel Communist Party (ICP) and the National Democratic Alliance (NDA), turned the spotlight on discriminatory governmental policies. But Palestinian parties failed to present Palestinian voters with new ideas or tools to affect government policies towards Palestinian citizens. Because no party offered a way out of their predicament, many Palestinian citizens opted not to exercise their suffrage. When one Palestinian party, the NDA, presented its program for achieving equality by transforming Israel into the state of its citizens, many voters viewed it as far-fetched or unachievable.

Yet another explanation for the decline in Palestinian voting is that significant political forces and segments of the Islamic Movement historically opposed participation in national elections. Sons of the Village and the Islamic Movement argued, as a matter of principle, that Israel is a "foreign element" in the heart of the Palestinian and Islamic world and should be replaced in the whole area of historic Palestine by a secular-democratic state (Sons of the Village) or by an Islamic state (Islamic Movement). Consequently, these groups advocated avoiding the recognition of Israel implied by voting in its parliamentary elections.

Palestinian participation in the 1996 and 1999 Knesset elections was significantly higher than in 1992. This increase, not mirrored in any other sector of the electorate, can be explained by the unique characteristics of these particular two campaigns. For instance, in a significant departure from the past, the Prime Minister of Israel was elected directly by the voters. Political discourse, among both Palestinians and Jews, placed great importance on the Palestinian vote. Some asserted that the innovation of direct elections meant that Palestinian voters could determine who would head the Government of Israel and thereby influence the nature of policies adopted toward them and toward peace between Israel and the Palestinian world. This argument was reinforced by right wing Jewish political and intellectual leaders, who sought to delegitimize the Palestinian vote by playing on Jewish fears of the Palestinian preference for the Labor candidate. In addition, factions of two political movements that had previously boycotted Knesset elections (the Sons of the Village and the Islamic Movement) coalesced with existing parties in both elections. The participation of groups from these two movements added impetus to the campaigns and created an atmosphere that encouraged some voters to go to the polls.

In the seventeenth Knesset election (March 2006), the boycott reached 44 percent – the highest abstinence rate among the Palestinians since the first Knesset election in Israel. The boycott rate in 2006 was higher even than the rate in the previous elections of 2003, where it reached 38 percent. This extreme 2006 boycott of the parliamentary elections expressed the Palestinian political scene, in general, and the parliamentary scene, specifically.

Some people believe that the Palestinian vote in recent years was a protest vote. But the voting boycott was *also* a protest against the internal situation of Palestinians in Israel and against governmental policies towards the Palestinians (Ghanem and Mustafa, 2007). The boycott did not happen by chance; it arose from a sense of failure to influence on one hand, and a sense of political crisis, on the other. The feeling of being non-influential was prompted by the structural obstacles that the ethnic Israeli system raises against the Palestinian demands – both at the collective level and at the level of daily rights (Ghanem, 2001a; Ghanem and Rouhana, 2001). The sense of political crisis resulted from the fact that the Palestinian parties are unable to achieve their basic demands or to influence political decisions through parliamentary work (Ben-Eliezer, 1993;Ghanem, 1993). However, many Palestinian parties are noticing that non-parliamentary political programs can achieve more than parliamentary work.

The fragmentation and distribution of the Palestinian vote in Knesset elections, 1949–2006

Another important trend in Palestinian voting patterns, that reflects their relationship with the state, has been the distribution and increasing fragmentation of their vote. This fragmentation peaked in the last two or three elections. Ever since the elections to the first Knesset in 1949, all parties, including extreme right wing and Jewish religious parties, have competed for Palestinian votes, which accounted for 11 to 13 percent of the total electorate.

Several periods can be distinguished with regard to the distribution of Palestinian votes. The first period, spanning the elections of the first through the seventh Knessets (1949–69), coincides roughly with the period of the military government (1949–66). Most Palestinians voted for Mapai, either directly or through its satellite lists (66 percent in the elections for the second Knesset; 57 percent in those for the seventh Knesset).[5] This preference stemmed mainly from the fact that Mapai, which controlled the organs of government, wielded great power – including the machinery of the military government – to manipulate the Palestinians' political and electoral behavior.[6]

The second period (1970–81), which followed the abolition of the Military Government in 1966, and the war of 1967, continued until 1981. This period coincided with the rise of Palestinian nationalism. It was characterized by a gradual increase in the Palestinian self confidence which was reflected in their electoral behavior. The most conspicuous feature of the Palestinian voting pattern during this period, however, was the rise in support for the Israeli Communist Party. Beginning in 1977, the Israeli Communist Party ran for the Knesset as the main constituent in a broad coalition of smaller Jewish and mainly Palestinian groups, under the label of the Democratic Front for Peace and Equality (DFPE). The DFPE peaked at 50 percent of the Palestinian vote in 1977. Even after a precipitous drop to 37 percent in 1981, the DFPE remained a major political force in the Palestinian sector.

The third period in the distribution of Palestinian votes covers the eleventh through the thirteenth Knessets (1984–92) and marked the emergence of two new political parties in Palestinian society. Just before the 1984 elections, a group of Palestinian-Arab nationalists established a new party, the Progressive List for Peace (PLP). Four years later, before the elections of the thirteenth Knesset, the Democratic Palestinian Party (DAP) was formed. These three Palestinian and Palestinian-dominated parties – the DFPE, PLP and DAP – competed among themselves and against the Jewish parties – hence, the increased dispersion and fragmentation of the Palestinian vote. These three parties garnered half of the Palestinian vote in all elections during this period. The hallmark of Palestinian voting during this period was a sharp rise in Palestinian-Arab national awareness and greater readiness to fight for civic equality in Israel. Whereas the Labor and the Likud parties together received 70 to 80 percent of the vote in the Jewish sector, the strongest party in the Palestinian sector – the DFPE – received 32 percent of the vote in 1984, 33 percent in 1988 and only 23 percent in 1992.

The fourth period began with the institution of direct elections for Prime Minister in 1996. Subsequent elections witnessed the rise of what was termed the "ethnic vote," as voters cast two votes – one for a parliamentary list and one for Prime Minister. Ethnic parties such as SHAS and Russian immigrant parties benefited from this system and increased their representation in the Knesset. The same was true for Palestinian parties. In 1996, a record 63 percent of Palestinians who voted, cast their Knesset ballots for Palestinian or Palestinian-dominated parties. (That record was broken in 1999, when 70 percent of valid Palestinian votes went to Palestinian or Palestinian-dominated parties).

In 1996, the joint slate of the DFPE and the National Democratic Alliance received 37 percent of the Palestinian vote, up from the 23 percent received by the DFPE alone in 1992. The joint slate of the Democratic Palestinian Party and the Islamic Movement received 25 percent of the Palestinian vote, up from the 15 percent received by the DAP in 1992. These gains came at the expense of support for Jewish parties. Labor, which took some 20 percent of the Palestinian vote in 1992, fell to 16.6 percent, despite its efforts while in office to increase the allocation of resources to the Palestinian sector and its support for the peace process with the Palestinians. Meretz, the left wing Zionist party, preserved its strength – about 10 percent – thanks to the relatively aggressive policies adopted by its incumbent ministers in support of the Palestinians. Palestinian support for right wing Jewish parties almost disappeared. The Likud, SHAS and the National Religious parties, which had secured about 20 percent of the Palestinian vote in 1992, plummeted to 5.2 percent in 1996, first, because they were in the opposition during all or most of the thirteenth Knesset and thus deprived of patronage opportunities, and second, because they championed positions that the Palestinian sector perceived as incompatible with the Israel–Palestine peace process.

Paradoxically, despite the significant rise in support for Palestinian parties in recent elections, the fragmentation of the Palestinian vote increased. To summarize: The first period was characterized by the domination of the ruling Mapai party; the second by the domination of the DFPE and the third by rough parity between these two forces. The fourth period witnessed the dispersion of votes among three Palestinian and Palestinian-dominated parties, each of them a coalition of smaller parties and movements. These blocs were not formed on the basis of compatibility of views among the partners, but mainly for electoral considerations having to do with the Israeli electoral system.[7] Palestinians participating in the last general election in Israel (March 2006), can be divided into those who voted for Jewish parties and those who voted for Palestinian parties, including the Democratic Front and the Communist Party. The latter constitutes a Jewish–Palestinian party on the basis of a joint ideological and political stand by Palestinian and Jewish members. It is said that this structure has, in recent years, evolved for the benefit of the Palestinian minority among activists, members and even voters.

In the 2006 Knesset elections, the Jewish parties won 25 percent of the Palestinian votes, marking a decline in the percentage of support these parties received in the previous elections (29.4 percent in 1999 and 2003). The Palestinian votes were divided between the Jewish parties as follows:

- Labor, 12.5 percent
- Kadima, 6.5 percent
- SHAS, 2.8 percent
- Meretz, 2.7 percent
- Yisrael Beitenu, 1 percent
- others, 2 percent

Half of the Palestinian votes to the Zionist parties went to the Labor party, which became stronger in these elections than the previous ones.

The Palestinian parties that passed the threshold (and those which did not) won 75 percent of the Palestinian votes (256,721). This means that collectively Palestinian parties won fewer votes than the number of Palestinians who boycotted the elections (265,000). This marks the first time in the history of the Palestinian political behavior that abstainers were more numerous than voters, in general, and more numerous than voters for the Palestinian parties, in particular.

Three Palestinian lists passed the threshold. The United list obtained 3.1 percent of the votes and four seats; the Jabha won 2.8 percent of the votes and three seats; and the Tajammo won 2.4 percent and three seats. In the 1999 Knesset elections, the Palestinian parties (those who passed the threshold, and those who did not) won 61.7 percent of the votes of those who had the right to vote. In the 2003 Knesset elections, the Palestinian parties got 45.5 percent. In the seventeenth Knesset elections (2006), the support continued to decline: collectively, the Palestinian parties secured 41.9 percent of the vote from Palestinians who had the right to vote.

The voting patterns of Palestinians seem to reflect the failure of any one party to offer a truly attractive or persuasive escape from the dilemmas facing the Palestinian population. In fact, the intensified struggle for equality, waged in the face of Israel's entrenchment in its Jewish-Zionist character, has led to a proliferation of political streams that seek to extricate the Palestinians from their predicament. In practice, this means the frequent appearance of new political groupings – both parliamentary and extra-parliamentary – that advance their own ideas for solving the problem. The fragmentation is increased by the fact that Jewish-Zionist parties also compete for Palestinian votes.

Political achievements by Palestinian political parties: permanent exclusion and lack of effectiveness

Whatever influence the Palestinians have had on government policy toward them has been achieved through both parliamentary and extra-parliamentary means, although the effectiveness of the former has been extremely limited. I use the term "effectiveness" to denote civic competence as defined by Almond and Verba in *The Civic Culture* (1963) – the situation in which a group's political influence over a governmental decision is equal to the degree to which governmental officials act to benefit that group.

The Israeli electoral system encourages a proliferation of parties. Knesset elections are proportional, countrywide and free. A list that wins more than the threshold of 1.5 percent of the valid vote wins a proportional number of seats in the Knesset. Within the Knesset, factions seek to form a coalition that commands a majority in the parliament. The Knesset is the institution that monitors and supervises the Government; parliamentary activity is perceived by many MKs as a stepping-stone to a cabinet position. Until the 1996 elections, the Prime Minister was generally the leader of the largest faction in the coalition. Starting with the 1996 elections, the Prime Minister is now elected directly by the citizens. The Government (cabinet) has decision-making authority with regard to all matters of domestic and foreign policy and follows up the implementation of these policies at all levels. Every sector and organization aspires to be represented at the Government table, seeing this as the best way to reap benefits or advance causes it deems important.

Palestinian MKs affiliated with the Zionist parties (or their satellite lists until 1981) joined the coalition or opposition according to the position of their party (or the parent party). MKs representing the satellite lists held no independent position on issues related to coalition politics and obediently adhered to the parent party line (Lustick, 1980; Rouhana, 1986). Nor did they adopt any position contrary to the wishes of the Jewish majority in the party. The very participation of these MKs in Zionist parties reflected narrow interests that often focused on personal and parochial concerns. Except for the appointment of a Minister without Portfolio in charge of

Table 2.4 Distribution of the Palestinian vote in Knesset elections, 1949–2006

Year	Valid votes	Participation (%)	ICP and DFPE	PLP	NDA	DAP and Islamic movement	Palestinian lists	Labor party	Other Zionist parties
1949	26,332	79	22				28	10	40
1951	58,984	86	16				55	11	18
1955	77,979	90	15				48	14	23
1959	81,764	85	11				42	10	37
1961	86,843	83	22				40	10	28
1965	106,346	82	23				38	13	26
1969	117,190	80	28				40	17	15
1973	133,058	73	37				27	17	19
1977	145,925	74	50				16	11	23
1981	164,862	68	37				12	29	22
1984	199,968	72	32	18			–	26	24
1988	241,601	74	33	15		11	–	16	25
1992	273,920	70	23	9		15	–	20	33
1996	307,497	77	38			27	–	18	17
1999	315,201	75	22		17	31		8	22
2003	346,580	62	26		20	18		8	28
2006	620,000	56	26		18	26		12.5	17.5

Palestinian citizens' affairs – following the 2001 Prime Ministerial elections – Palestinian MKs, even those representing coalition parties or their satellites, have never attained a ministerial rank. Furthermore, while some Palestinian MKs have been appointed deputy ministers and put in charge of matters concerning "minorities," they have almost never been authorized to deal with issues of concern to the population as a whole.

In contrast, the Palestinian or Palestinian-dominated parties in the Knesset – the DFPE and its predecessor the Israel Communist Party, the PLP, the DAP and the NDA – took pride in their independent positions and outlook. Over the years, it became clear that these parties constituted a "permanent opposition" with no practical or even theoretical chance of joining a government coalition. This status derived from several factors, of which the foremost were that they were: (a) Palestinian (hence representatives of an untrustworthy and "hostile" minority); (b) non- or anti-Zionist; and (c) opposed, in various degrees, to many government policies in both domestic and foreign affairs. In other words, it was precisely the nature of the relationship between the state and its Jewish majority on the one hand, and the Palestinian minority on the other, that relegated these parties to the status of permanent opposition. Over the years, Palestinian-dominated parties have adopted a consistently anti-Zionist position that opposes the definition of Israel as the State of the Jewish people, deeming it "unfair" to the state's Palestinian citizens. They have stressed that Israel should be "the State of all its citizens," or at least, "the State of the Jewish people and its Palestinian citizens"(Ghanem, 1990). This position coincides with that held by the majority of Palestinian citizens of Israel, who reject the Jewish-Zionist nature of the state (Smooha, 1992).

In addition to the dispute over the country's character and purpose, the Palestinian parties and their Knesset representatives are firmly opposed to government policy on vital issues such as the distribution of resources within the state and the solution to the Israeli–Palestinian conflict, in general, and to its Palestinian component, in particular (Ghanem, 1990; Rouhana, 1997). This opposition exacerbates fears about the Palestinians among the Jewish public and decision-makers; it reinforces the notion that Palestinians constitute a "hostile minority" and potential fifth column. Anxiety in the Jewish community deters Jewish politicians from accepting Palestinians as full coalition partners, lest their own party's support within the Jewish sector suffer.

Thus, despite the improvement in attitudes toward the Palestinians over the years, Israel as a state continues to serve Jewish interests predominantly. One of its central purposes is to bring them from foreign countries to become citizens. By excluding the Palestinian parties and Palestinian citizens from full participation in the executive arm, the state has effectively kept them from having active and equal influence on decisions relating to momentous issues for the state and for themselves. Hence, the Palestinian Knesset factions have become a permanent opposition within the Israeli system of government. Accordingly, Palestinian parliamentary politics have failed to register any significant achievements for Palestinian society and have been unable to compel the government to redress any of the Palestinians' many complaints (even in cases that the Jewish majority considers to be legitimate and justified). I argue that this failure is inherent in the structural inequality of citizenship in an ethnic state.

The opposition status of the Palestinian-dominated parties has persisted since 1948 and has become even more prominent in recent years. Despite the fact that the left needs the Palestinian vote and despite the open support that some Palestinian parties expressed for its candidate for Prime Minister, the Labor party, after winning the elections in both 1992 and in 1999, insisted on setting up a pure Jewish coalition and leaving out Palestinian parties that expressed an interest in joining the coalition.

The predicament of Palestinian society and its parliamentary representatives is not limited to their inherent exclusion from government coalitions. Under the last two Labor governments they have even been deprived of genuine opposition status. In 1992, Labor and its allies counted 56 MKs, five short of a majority in the 120-seat Knesset. The Palestinian members could have provided the needed majority. However, Labor refused to accept them as partners in the coalition, while gladly accepting them as members of what became known as the "blocking majority." This situation made it impossible for the Likud to form a government by providing the Labor Government with support from the "outside" (Ghanem, 1996c). The MKs of the Palestinian factions found themselves in a "no-choice" situation; they were compelled to support the Rabin–Peres Government, although it did not respond to their demands in either domestic or foreign affairs, because the alternative was so much worse. Their best option was to support the Government because it appeared to be taking steps toward ending the Israeli–Palestinian conflict and resolving the Palestinian problem. This status deprived them of the many benefits of coalition membership, but also kept them from acting as a real opposition, since they could not present a credible threat to vote against the Government.

After the 1999 elections, the Palestinian Knesset members were not needed as members of the coalition but were still unable to play the role of opposition. The broad coalition of Jewish parties further marginalized the role of Palestinian parliamentarians and continued to deprive them of the benefits of coalition partners; further – because credible opposition to the Labor government emanates from right wing and anti-Palestinian parties – they were also deprived of the status of credible opposition parties.

A comparison between the achievements of Yisrael Ba'aliyah (the Russian immigrant party established in 1996) and the Palestinian-dominated parties highlights the marginality of the latter (Ghanem, 1996b). When the polls closed on election night in 1996, Israel Television announced that its exit poll indicated that Peres had defeated Netanyahu by a whisker. Peres' ostensible margin was clearly due to Palestinian votes. Labor leaders immediately began speculating, on live television, which parties would be included in Peres' coalition. One politician after another included the Jewish religious parties and Yisrael Ba'aliyah, but excluded the Palestinian parties. The same scene was repeated, for an even longer period, after Barak's victory in 1996. The media focused on potential coalition partners for more than a month, but never included any of the three Palestinian parties in their calculations. Both Yisrael Ba'aliyah and SHAS joined Netanyahu's Government in 1996 and Ehud Barak's in 1999, in return for enormous benefits in terms of access to power centers and other resources. This was despite the fact that SHAS had called on its supporters to vote for Barak's opponent, while Palestinian and Palestinian-dominated parties, on the other hand, had coordinated with Labor to calculate how to achieve maximum Palestinian support for Barak.

In conclusion, in terms of political participation, the Palestinian population of Israel has been portrayed as a minority within a liberal democracy (Avineri, 1995). This affiliation theoretically grants them free political participation. Indeed, many scholars have pointed out that Palestinian citizens enjoy substantial parliamentary political effectiveness in promoting their collective interests within the state (Lustick, 1987; 1988; Neuberger, 1993; Ozacky-Lazar, 1992; Smooha and Peretz, 1993). Some have even argued that the Palestinian citizens will come to wield political power because they will be in a position to tip the scales for or against either of the large parties. In this chapter I have maintained, however, that political participation and parliamentary politics are not as effective for Palestinian citizens as for Jewish citizens precisely because of their ethnic affiliation. In recent years, moreover, the voting behavior of the Palestinian citizens of Israel has reflected the deep-rooted predicament of their relationship with the state. The minority's potential for equal and effective political representation in the power centers of the state is thwarted by ethnic policies that give preference to the Jewish majority in the distribution of symbolic and material resources and in the state structure itself. These inherent policies, supported by the majority of the Jewish public, in turn lead to the existential predicament of the minority's relationship with the state (Rouhana and Ghanem, 1998). Not only does the minority have a limited "civic competence," but also its main goal – equality between Palestinians and Jews – seems unattainable. Voting behavior and parliamentary politics are inextricably related to this predicament.

Israel, as an ethnic state, is committed to serving the needs of the Jewish majority, instead of serving the needs of all citizens. Reviewing the inferior status of the Palestinians in Israel – as individuals and as a group – in light of the literature on democracy – supports my conclusion about the incompatibility of democracy with Israel's ethnic institutionalizing, structure and identity. The hope of Palestinian citizens for escaping their predicament lies in democratizing Israel for all its citizens – equivalent to changing Israel's Jewish-ethnic nature and ending the state's preference of Jews over other citizens. Although it seems dramatic, such a change is the only way to normalize Israel, the political condition of the minority, and the relations between them.

In order for the Palestinians to extricate themselves from the predicament, they must change their methods of political activity, including their voting patterns and parliamentary politics. The irony of their status is that their predicament is predicated, not only on the opposition of Israeli state and society to any meaningful changes in its ethnic superstructure, but also on their inability to take bold steps because of regional politicians whose calculations ignore their own interests. For example, a compromise solution between Israel and the Palestinian national movement that features a two state solution might contradict Palestinians' fundamental concern for equality. If the compromise recognizes Israel as the state of the Jewish people, the Palestinian citizens' case for full equality would be weakened. However, raising this concern openly adds to the complexity of the Palestinian–Israeli conflict and might harden Israeli positions in the negotiation process.

The limited success of conventional politics to achieve a breakthrough in Palestinians' relationship with the state and the majority, led them to consider alternative options, including open conflict with the state. In March 1976, the Palestinian leaders declared a one-day strike against the state policies in the land confiscation policy. During the day of the strike (March 30, 1976), six Palestinians were killed in a confrontation with the state police. The state blamed the Palestinian leadership for the escalation; Palestinians blamed the state for the over use of force – including military force – against the protesting Palestinians.

Relations between the state and the majority on one hand and the Palestinian minority on the other hand, continued to deteriorate during the next two decades. Relations were influenced by state policies towards the minority, the politicization process among the minority, and developments that shaped the general Israeli–Palestinian conflict. When the Oslo agreement was achieved between the PLO and Israel and the peace process began, the Palestinians in Israel were among the supporters; their political representatives in the Knesset gave full backing to Rabin–Peres' government. However, following the 1996 general elections and the election of Binyamin Netanyahu, the representative of the Israeli right, as the new Israeli Prime Minister, the state of the conflict and the relationship between the Palestinian minority and the state again deteriorated. This will be more elaborated in the post-1996 era in Chapter 6.

The future of the state–minority relationship

About 1.2 million of Israel's citizens are Palestinians. They constitute about 10 percent of the Palestinian people and 17 percent of the citizens of Israel. Their voting strength comes to about 650,000, or 13 percent of the Israeli electorate.[8] Formally, the Palestinians have the status of Israeli citizens, but in fact, their Israeliness is incomplete in a number of ways. They occupy the periphery of society; they are marginal in all spheres of life; and they have negligible influence on the decision-making process in most important areas. The main venue where they are represented, courted and heard is the political arena – especially during election campaigns. There too, however, they have also been on the sidelines, never included in government coalitions and never attaining senior positions (Ghanem, 1996c; 2001a). The overwhelming majority of Palestinian citizens take their citizenship seriously and exercise it by voting, active public and political participation, and in the struggle for civic equality. The struggle for equality is the greatest proof that the Palestinians wish to give real meaning to their citizenship and do not take it for granted. Their interpretation of the meaning of citizenship is at variance with most Jewish interpretations, which involve "loyalty to the state" (Ghanem, 2004). At many junctures in life, Palestinian citizens find that the establishment and the Jewish majority do not treat them as equal citizens and that the Jewish character of the state and its security exigencies, more than its professed democratic nature, determine its path and attitude toward them (Ghanem, 1998; Rouhana, 1997).

During the last two decades, there has been increasing delegitimization of the Palestinian population and its elected representatives. One of the most blatant expressions of this occurred during the years of the Rabin government (1992–96), when the term "Jewish majority" first entered the political lexicon. The Rabin government did not have "a Jewish majority" for peace and therefore was illegitimate; it maintained right wing circles, thereby asserting that there are two types of citizens in the country and two types of Knesset members – some more equal than others. Despite several feeble protests, the term penetrated the public discourse and became "legitimate" and widespread. When an attempt was made to bar Palestinians from holding the balance of power in a future referendum on withdrawal from the Golan Heights, the Golan Reinforcement law was born. Similarly, from time to time there are proposals to prevent the Palestinians from participating in referendums about questions of fateful import for the state, as if they are not part of it.

Israel has a democratic form of government on the institutional level – periodic elections, changes in government, separation of powers, exclusion of the military from politics and so on. However, its policy toward its Palestinian-Arab majority runs counter to the true essence of democracy, as measured by equality before the law, freedom and defense of minority rights. The state is identified with one ethnic and national group, the Jews, and adopts various means to avoid including members of the Palestinian minority as equal citizens eligible for all benefits. It preserves the inferiority of the Palestinians vis-à-vis the Jews while discriminating against them in many areas of life (Ghanem, 1998; Ghanem, Rouhana and Yiftachel, 2000; Yiftachel, 1998; 1999). Israel's ethnic policy toward the Palestinian minority is supported by a large majority of the Jews, who see the state as an instrument to serve the Jews in Israel and the world and advocate its absolute identification as a Jewish state with Jewish primacy in all spheres (Ghanem, 2004). The Jewish majority and its official representatives in the Knesset and government are not willing to surrender the privileges of "the state of the Jews"; they retain their dominance at the individual level and exclusivity at the group level. This majority is not willing to grant personal equality to Palestinians and preserves a unique and senior status as a group (see Smooha, 1989, 1992), and exclusivity in making fateful decisions for the state. Although this policy allows for some marginal reliance on the Palestinians, they are not equal partners, either on the personal or on the group level. In other words, the majority alone determines the boundaries of inclusion and exclusion for individuals and groups in society, on the clear basis of ethnic and national affiliation. On the other hand, the sophisticated policy of inclusion and exclusion creates existential dilemmas in the lives of Palestinians and pushes them in the direction of a major confrontation with the Jews and the state.

Most Palestinians advocate total equality and an unwavering anti-Zionist stance. They want group equality, manifested in equal treatment by the state, integration into the state and the abolition of the official state ideology, which, they believe, is the major cause of the discrimination against them. They also favor the granting of institutional autonomy to their group (Ghanem, 1996c; 2001a). In other words, they want Israel (within the Green Line) transformed into a bi-national state with a bi-national character, goals and objectives and a democratic regime that guarantees that the state does not intervene exclusively in favor of one group of its citizens. The Palestinians' distress over their continuing inequality is likely to worsen as they redouble their demands for significant changes in their status and in the character of the state. Many signs indicate that this demand will be accompanied by a hardening of the position of the majority and its representatives, leading to a confrontation and the emergence of a significant crisis in minority–majority relations in Israel (Rouhana and Ghanem, 1998).

In summary, the ethnic character of the state and the absence of an equal citizenship or territorial nationality to unite all citizens confront both the majority and the minority with a difficult choice concerning the nature of a partnership that would satisfy the desires of the majority and the aspirations of the minority. On the one hand, the state and the Jewish majority will find themselves facing a difficult situation if they continue to ignore the demands and aspirations of the minority. They will not be able to perpetuate the ethnic system and policy directed against the Palestinian citizens of Israel and will have to give serious consideration to instituting full equality among all its citizens. On the other hand, the minority, which over the years will become increasingly aware of the limitations imposed on it, might be impelled to consider unconventional means of achieving equality, including the resort to violence.

3 Mizrahi (Oriental) Jews and the Ashkenazi system
Incorporation versus separation politics

The State of Israel was established by Jews who immigrated from Europe and America (Ashkenazi Jews). The majority of Jews who immigrated to Palestine during the British Mandate (1919–48) were of Ashkenazi origin. It was they who established the prevailing political, economic, social and cultural trends which are still observed in Israel (Agasy, 1991).

During the 1950s, as a direct result of the establishment of the State of Israel, great waves of Jews arrived from Asia and Africa. They were called Sephardim, or Orientals, or *Mizrahim* in Hebrew. (The terms Oriental and Mizrahi will be used interchangeably in this chapter.) Because the Mizrahim constituted the majority of immigrant Jews in Israel, a drastic change took place in the demographic balance between the Ashkenazi and Mizrahi Jews. In the mid-1960s, the number of Orientals equaled that of the Ashkenazim and subsequently outnumbered them. There was concern over possible changes in the make-up of the society and the structure of the state, were the Ashkenazim to lose power. There were also fears about development among the Orientals of feelings of deprivation, injustice and discrimination. The seeds of strife between the Ashkenazi and Mizrahi Jews were sown in the 1950s with the immigration of the Orientals to the country. Smooha (1993a: 436–38, 1993b) maintains that three factors characterized the Mizrahi immigration and led to the creation of the Ashkenazi–Mizrahi gap:

1 Israel's immigration policy

Unlike the Ashkenazi immigration, which was neither limited nor monitored by the authorities, the immigrant Jews from Islamic countries – Asia and Africa – were required to meet criteria (e.g. as skilled laborers), if they were to be admitted to Israel. Though the criteria were not strictly observed in practice, they created a feeling that Orientals as such were unwanted and were needed only for the development of the country.

2 Israel's absorption policy

This policy was based on two main pillars. First, was to prevent any change that might be caused by the Orientals to the Israeli-European culture and the socio-political system established by the Ashkenazim. Second, was to use Mizrahi manpower to serve the ends of the well-to-do Ashkenazi strata. Mizrahi immigrant Jews were sent to temporary transit camps or "Ma'abarot" before they were taken to settle in development towns built in geographically and economically marginalized areas of the state. These towns did not enjoy the same standard of services as did Ashkenazi towns in terms of housing, education and other basic services. The degradation and disrespect practiced by the ruling establishment in Israel toward the Mizrahi Jews drastically affected the Orientals' ability to respond and negatively affected their self-esteem, dignity and ability to take initiatives.

3 Demographic vulnerabilities of the Mizrahi Jews

A number of demographic vulnerabilities also affected relations between the Mizrahi Jews and Ashkenazi Jews in Israel. Specifically, the Mizrahi Jews, upon arrival, generally had poor education, large families and no relatives in the country from whom to seek support. In addition, they had little political experience to call upon in pursuit of their interests.

These Jews were absorbed in the peripheral areas, creating a number of underdeveloped towns, compared to other towns and cities in Israel. Research on the socio-economic gaps among different communities in Israel revealed that most of the inhabitants of these "development towns" were of Mizrahi origin; in some cases, Orientals constituted 90 percent of the inhabitants (Tzefadia and Yiftachel, 1999).

In the development towns, a new identity emerged among Mizrahi Jews characterized by feelings of discrimination and alienation from the Ashkenazi Jews and the Israeli center. These feelings were coupled with a growing perception of the Ashkenazi role in creating the development towns and the deterioration of living conditions in them (Tzefadia and Yiftachel, 1999). Although the processes of assimilation and intermarriage between the Ashkenazi and Mizrahi Jews reduced the number of Jews who say that their ethnic identity is of prime importance, a majority of Israelis still identify themselves as affiliated with one of these groups.

This ethnic loyalty became linked with the Orientals' feeling of discrimination and injustice against them as a group. This is a matter that could consequently become an incentive for taking collective political action, including violence (Bernstein, 1984).

The experience of Mizrahi Jews

Attempts to eliminate the Arabic culture of the Mizrahi Jews were accompanied by discrimination against them in the distribution of resources, employment, housing and education. They qualified only for low standard jobs compared to the veteran Ashkenazi Jews who were trained for high status white collar administrative positions in the administrative and economic systems (Swirski, 1989). Geographically, the Orientals were directed against their will to rural suburbs (development towns and agricultural villages) and poor city suburbs (Kemp *et al.*, 2004; Tzefadia and Yiftachel, 2004). In many cases they were directed to take over vacant Palestinian houses and villages. These policies and practices pushed Mizrahi Jews to urban and border suburbs and villages, often close to Palestinian communities, and revealed their designated role in the national settlement module. The policies fostered Jewish territorial control, alienated Orientals from the country's financial and power centers, and separated the poor Mizrahim from the better established Ashkenazi citizens. Additionally, they facilitated control of confiscated Palestinian property and monitoring of the remaining Palestinians within Israel. The outcome of these policies was the creation of a society with three main divisions: Ashkenazim, Orientals and Palestinians. Ashkenazim and Mizrahim constituted an entity called Israeli Jewish "nationality," from which the third division – the Palestinians – remained excluded. This division is manifested in the similarity between geographical ethnic limits (territorial-geographical division) of each division and the lack of cultural and political equality as a unifying factor (Yiftachel, 1996).

Defining the limits of status, ethnic origin and areas of inhabitance created a feeling among the Mizrahi Jews of injustice done to them by the authorities and the absorbing society (Hertsogh, 1986).

It is no coincidence that the educational gap and the income gap between the second generation Mizrahim and their Ashkenazi counterparts have widened (Cohen and Haberfeld, 1998). The widening of these gaps is due to unjust geographical distribution of resources; areas inhabited by Mizrahi Jews receive smaller allocations of land and housing resources than areas inhabited by Ashkenazi Jews (Yiftachel and Kedar, 2000; Youna and Sporta, 2000).

It is interesting that the anger of Mizrahi Jews is not directed against Israel or the Zionist movement, but rather against the political leadership that ruled Israel during the first three decades and was responsible for the absorption of Mizrahi Jews. Leadership at that time was the Zionist "Mapai" (Labor) party, headed by prominent leaders such as David Ben-Gurion, Moshe Sharet, Golda Meir, Yitzhak Rabin, Shimon Peres, Ehud Barak and others. Thus, the Mizrahi protest was directed mainly against the Mapai party.

Political participation and organization among the Mizrahi Jews

If one asks what is behind Mizrahi Jewish ethnic political identity with regard to institutionalized political frameworks (parties) or protest movements – the answer would include the following factors: their feeling of cultural alienation; their economic weakness; their living in the geographical periphery; and their feeling of anger toward Mapai. Yet, attempts by Mizrahi Jews in Israel to achieve their aims through political organization in Israel in the 1950s, 1960s, 1970s and to date have been rejected by the leadership of the state. They were accused of dividing the people and acting against the so-called 'Merging of the Exiles" – a Zionist slogan referring to integration within one people or the merging of different tribes. These negative responses blocked the Mizrahi's chance of utilizing their ethnicity to gain political power (Hertsogh, 1986). Thus, instead of struggling to change central concepts in Israeli society, they campaigned for representation and for equal distribution of resources.

The large political parties were open to including Mizrahi representatives in their lists as a means of attracting voters (Hertsogh, 1986). However, the parties did not allow Mizrahi representatives to make it to high ranking positions – these remained under Ashkenazi control (Grinberg, 1998). Mizrahi representatives, in Parliament or other frameworks, came from the poor neighborhoods in or near large cities. Those living in the peripheral development towns, especially in the Northern and Southern parts of the country, were hardly represented in the Knesset and their voice was rarely heard. During the Mizrahi protest movements of the 1950s (especially those in "Wadi Salib," a Haifa slum area, and in the temporary transit camps (or Ma'abarot), the Mizrahi demonstrators only demanded a fairer allocation of material resources; they did not suggest any structural change in Israeli society. Likewise in the 1970s when the "Black Panthers" organization launched widespread protests against ethnic discrimination and the socio-economic gap, the Mizrahim sought full acceptance in Israeli society, rather than a fundamental alteration of that society (Cohen, 1972; Shitrit, 2001).

Residents of the development towns depended for their living on the Labor party institutions that governed, not only the state, but also the Histadrut, which was often the main employer in these places. This dependence was manifested everywhere – in employment, in the distribution of housing, in education and in social welfare allocations. For many years, it forced development town residents to support the Labor party. However, this dependence disappeared in the 1970s, amid new local political developments in the towns and growing Jewish ethnic and cultural consciousness. Youth began to find work in the open job market that was not dependent on the ruling party. Protests started against the Labor party's favoring of Ashkenazim and discrimination toward the Mizrahim (Ben-Zadok, 1993).

Mizrahim political approaches

In light of these developments, two different approaches to political struggle appeared in the development towns and the poor neighborhoods in Israel. First, the Mizrahim began to vote for the Likud party. This approach can be understood by comparing voting trends in the development towns during

Knesset elections of 1965 and 1988 (before the arrival of Russian immigrants to the development towns). In the interim between these years, the Likud party doubled its support in the development towns. For example, in 1988, the Likud secured 40.8 percent of eligible votes, compared to only 20.1 percent in 1965. The Labor party, on the other hand, received 53.8 percent of these votes in 1965, but only 27.4 percent in 1988. These reversals were a major factor in the Likud party winning power in 1977.

In their second approach to political struggle, the Mizrahim, during the early 1980s, began to vote for ethnic parties that emphasized ethnicity in their political message and called for the revival of a separate Jewish Mizrahi cultural and social identity. These trends, strongly felt in the development towns, were less evident in the coastal cities and the middle class areas, where living with Ashkenazim tended to obliterate Mizrahi ethnic perceptions and their related political implications (Benski, 1993; Grinberg, 1998).

Each of the Mizrahi political approaches is discussed in greater detail in the following sections of this chapter.

Mizrahi support for the Likud

The political organization (both parliamentary and non-parliamentary) of the Mizrahi Jews started mainly in the poor neighborhoods in the large cities and suburbs in Israel. The citizens in the development towns and in concentrated immigrants' communities, especially in the Southern and Northern areas, had practically had no effect on Israeli politics or on the Knesset during Israel's first 20 years. They had strong ties with the Labor party and its institutions which controlled employment as well as housing affairs, education and social welfare.

Labor's ties with the Mizrahi communities in the development towns, were bound to be challenged with the emergence of local political leadership there. Thus, the citizens' economic ties with the Labor party in the development towns gradually started to weaken, parallel to the growing understanding of the ethnic needs of different Jewish communities in Israel. Finally, after an unchallenged 30 years in office, the Mapai party had to step down following the 1977 elections, when the Likud party, headed by Menahem Begin, won a clear victory against it. The Likud victory was attributed to the strong support of the Mizrahi Jews, among whom the Likud party doubled its support between 1965 and 1988.

Israeli sociologists have explained this phenomenon in different ways. It is worth noting the arrogance and racial discrimination against the Mizrahim that is inherent in some of the explanations, several of which are provided below:

1) The Mizrahi Jews were inclined to rely on force and to distrust the Palestinians: Since its establishment, the Likud movement symbolized

the extremist national wing in the Zionist movement, calling for enforcement of Israeli sovereignty over large Palestinian areas and considering eastern Jordan, which is now the Kingdom of Jordan, as an integral part of the "Land of Israel." Throughout the years the Likud movement opposed any regional settlement, and supported Jewish settlement in the West Bank and Gaza Strip. Sociologists believed that the Mizrahim's support for the Likud is based on their desire to take revenge against the Palestinians in light of their treatment as a minority in the Palestinian states, where they were treated as a minority and lost their status and possessions. This change in position, following the transition from minority into majority, matched the Orientals' view of the Palestinians as people that can't be trusted and who understand nothing but force (Hertsogh, 1986).

2) Mizrahi were in competition with Palestinian workers: According to this explanation, when Palestinian workers from the West Bank and Gaza Strip entered the Israeli labor market, they posed competition for the Mizrahi Jew, whose position deteriorated. They hoped that rightist-national parties would prevent the Palestinian workers from entering the Israeli labor (Peled, 1998). So, since the Likud movement was the arch opponent for the Labor party, it was expected that the Orientals would support the movement (Smooha, 1993b).

3) The Likud allowed the Orientals to assume high ranking positions within the party (Grinberg, 1998), David Levy providing a good example: the Orientals looked at the Likud as a party that allows them to climb up the leadership ladder, thus warranting their support.

4) Mizrahim believed that, "Only the Likud can make peace": this explanation says that the Orientals understand that the injustices they suffer are a result to the ongoing conflict between Israel and the Palestinians, in which from a cultural point of view they are considered to be like Palestinians. The longer the conflict continues, the more budgets are diverted to the military and security operations and settlement in the occupied Palestinian territories, instead of allocating these budgets to the meet the needs of the Orientals. Therefore, out of the belief that unlike the Likud, the Labor party wasn't capable or interested in making peace, part of the Mizrahi public supported the Likud (Smooha, 1993b).

5) The head of the Likud Party, Menahem Begin, was a charismatic leader: Begin, despite being Ashkenazi, stressed the Mizrahi's affiliation with the state and the Jewish people. Begin supported the Mizrahi protest movements even during the Wad al Saleeb events. He openly declared his objection to ethnic discrimination before the Knesset. Thus his personality and views on the Orientals granted his party much support from them (Hertsogh, 1986). It is true that the Orientals' support for the Likud has weakened over the years. Nevertheless, a large part of Likud's support still comes from this sector. Why did this support

become weaker, as in the 1980s many of the Orientals concluded that the Likud used them? There are many reasons.
6) The Likud adopted a free market policy and reduced taxes: as a rightist movement, the Likud's adoption of a free market policy and reduction of taxes resulted in inflation and economic instability (Nitzan and Bichler, 2002). It deepened the gap between the rich, most of whom were Ashkenazim, and the poor, most of whom were Oriental and Palestinians.
7) The Likud allocated huge funds to the settlements instead of allocating for the welfare of the under-privileged sectors of the population.

The impact of Likud Mizrahi leaders was limited: Few of them had the opportunity to be decision-makers like the Ashkenazim. Most of the Mizrahi never rose above the role of second-line Likud leaders. For these reasons, the Mizrahi support for the Likud, though still strong, was reduced. Part of the lost support went to Tami; in the 1980s, part went to SHAS.

I now turn to the second approach the Mizrahi adopted to their political struggles – separatist ethnic voting. This separatist trend is more fully described in the following section where I have chronologically reviewed the parliamentary and extra-parliamentary political organization of the Mizrahim. The review covers the following major phases of Mizrahi political organization: (a) party organization during the early years; (b) non-parliamentary political action and major demonstrations; (c) Mizrahi parliamentary activities; and (d) political and social organization in the parliament in the 1980s and 1990s.

The early years – Mizrahi Jews within the large political parties

Most activists during the early years of the Jewish immigration from North Africa and Asian Jews invested their efforts in supporting candidates of Mizrahi and Yemenite origin within the representative bodies of the Jewish community in Palestine. There were also spontaneous local demonstrations in immigrant camps, before the old Knesset building in Tel Aviv and outside the offices of the Jewish Agency in Haifa. There was no one leader or organization behind these activities and these protests against the humiliation of the immigrants in the camps were not widely reported in the media. However, the leaders of the state did not underestimate the tension that was felt in face of a potential Mizrahi "uprising." (Shitrit, 2001).

The Yemenite Union

In light of the injustice done in Palestine to the Jews of Yemenite origin, the Union of Yemenite Jews was established in 1923 to represent the community before Zionist institutions. In the first Knesset elections on January 25, 1949, the Yemenite Union won 4399 votes and a seat in the Knesset. The

Union was divided into two factions, but, in any case, Zionist leaders did not want to concede any of their power to it. Thus, they resisted any independent initiative by the Union. Moreover, the movement was on the opposition side in parliament (Diskin, 2001). In the second Knesset elections, the Yemenites won one seat and joined the General Zionists, remaining in the opposition (Diskin, 2001). In the third Knesset elections, held on July 26, 1955, the Union failed to secure the necessary votes to win a Knesset seat. This pattern was continued until the 1960s when the movement's activities stopped completely following a court case.

The Mizrahim and Mizrahi factions

In light of differences within the Mizrahi community, a national Mizrahi representative body was established in early 1948. The new body included representatives from Tel Aviv and Haifa, but not from Jerusalem. After the establishment of Israel, the Mizrahim demanded a representative in the State Council and Ben-Gurion nominated Bechor Shitrit to the position. The Mizrahi representative body was divided in November 1948 into two factions, led by Shitrit (who was close to the Labor party) and Elyahu Ben Elishar.

Before the first Knesset elections, these two factions merged to create a new Mizrahi bloc called "The National Mizrahi and Mizrahi Bloc." In the first Knesset elections held on January 25, 1949, the group won 15,287 votes, 3.5 percent of the eligible votes, and four Knesset seats. They joined the Mapai government coalition and their leader Shitrit was appointed Minister of Police. However, internal differences developed, with Elishar objecting to the Mapai orientation, and the group split. In the second Knesset elections (1951), having won the support of 12,002 voters and two seats in the Knesset, this bloc worked as a united bloc with the General Zionists. They continued during the terms of Israel's first three governments, all led by Mapai. In June 1955, the bloc left the Sharett government coalition (Diskin, 2001) and aligned with the General Zionists, who offered them improved status in the Knesset. In the elections to the third Knesset, the General Zionists failed to secure a single seat and in 1959, prior to the fourth Knesset, the alliance between the Mizrahim and the General Zionists ended.

The emergence of Mizrahi and Yemenite factions worried the major Ashkenazi parties, who saw a united Mizrahi bloc as a regrettable sign of sectarianism. The larger parties, especially Mapai and Mapam, defamed the Mizrahi leaders, accusing them of creating obstacles to forming a united people in the new state. Perhaps this explains the Mizrahi failure to convert ethnic into political affiliation. Yet, the objection of the larger parties did not hinder the establishment of competitive Mizrahi organizations, bodies and parties, alongside the ethnic presence which existed in all the large parties. However, the Mizrahi groupings were generally manipulated by the

Israeli parties. Thus the "Independent North African bloc," which ran in the 1959 Knesset elections, was supported by Mapam, whereas the Mizrahi Jewish bloc, "For Justice and Brotherhood – Religious Mizrahim" (1958), was backed by the NRP. Both failed to enter the Knesset.

The other Mizrahi lists that appeared at that time did not fare any better and for years they too failed in Knesset elections. In 1955, for instance, one was led by Ben Harush, who led the Wadi Salib riots and was imprisoned during the election campaign. Over the years, the larger parties did their best to persuade leaders of these blocs to leave them and join their ranks. This was especially true of Mapai (Ben-Zadok, 1993). Consequently, until the mid-1950s, the only Mizrahi Jews in the Knesset were there as part of the large parties; they did not represent specifically Mizrahi parties. However, the Mizrahim constituted 50 percent of the Jewish population at that time and 55 percent in 1967 (Central Bureau of Statistics, 2000), and although they were not directly represented in the Knesset, they made their voice heard in extra-parliamentary protests.

Mizrahi non-parliamentary action and major demonstrations

The "Wadi Salib" protests provided the momentum for development of a new collective Mizrahi consciousness, which, in turn, provided a base for subsequent establishment of the "Black Panther" movement.

During the 1960s, there were no legislative successes or attempts at political organization by the Mizrahim. Following the 1967 war, Israel was so involved in celebrating its victory that attention was distracted from the broadening gap between Mizrahim and Ashkenazim with regard to educational achievements, income and general living standards (Cohen and Haberfeld, 1998). The Musrara neighborhood on the Jordanian border with Jerusalem had remained, from 1948 until the 1967 occupation, one of the poorest Jewish areas, inhabited by Mizrahi and neglected by the authorities. The housing units were old and crowded compared to the new apartments in Jerusalem; the population had a one-third employment rate; families were large; income was low; and education was poor – indicators of the stark discrimination Musrara suffered compared to the prestigious Ashkenazi Rehavia and Beit Hakerem neighborhoods of Jerusalem. Against this backdrop, the Black Panther organization emerged in the 1970s, led by Reuven Abargil, Sa'adya Martziano, Charlie Biton, Udi Malka and Kochavi Shemesh. The movement signaled an awakening of Mizrahi cultural consciousness.

The "Black Panther" movement

Initially the Black Panther movement resembled street gangs. However, with the help of professionals from radical leftist movements (e.g. Matspen and Siah), there emerged, in spite of internal difficulties, an elected leadership and an organizational hierarchy. From Jerusalem the Black Panther movement spread all over the country. Committees were established to deal with finance, the media, public announcements, logistics, protests activities and mobilization.

The "Black Panther" movement did not make extremist demands; rather, it called for elementary justice in the allocation of public resources. On the other hand, the movement adopted a radical tactical approach and initiated violent protests in pursuing its demands. The message, proclaimed in radical language, was that, "We want our share of the cake, or else there won't be any cake!" (Bernstein, 1979: 69). The Black Panthers was the first movement that linked the suffering of the Mizrahi and that of the Palestinians. The movement, was able to move beyond the Oriental-ethnic level and succeed in mobilizing even non-Orientals – including people from the universities and from leftist circles (Bernstein, 1984).

The Black Panthers opposed the myth that "Security has priority" and, unlike other Ashkenazi and Zionist groups, saw the encouragement of Jewish immigration and the Law of Return as lies and myths. While attacking Zionism abroad, they, nevertheless, demonstrated no objection to the Zionist idea and supported no demands for changing the nature of the state. Bernstein (1979; 1984), Cohen (1984) and Shitrit (2001) have described the activities of the Black Panther movement. A chronology of the movement's history is delineated in the following box.

Chronology of the Black Panther movement

3/31/1971 – First demonstration. PM Golda Meir denied the Panthers a license and some leaders were arrested but the movement demonstrated peacefully outside a meeting of the Municipal Council, along with some Ashkenazi supporters.

4/13/1971 – PM Golda Meir met with representatives of the Black Panthers. The meeting did not yield results, but was good publicity for the Panthers.

5/18/1971 – Around 5000 to 7000 people demonstrated in Jerusalem. The police used excessive violence in dispersing them and they responded by throwing stones and Molotov cocktails at the police. Dozens of the demonstrators and policemen were injured and about a hundred demonstrators arrested. The event received strong media coverage and strengthened the movement's motivation and public sympathy.

1971 – Peaceful demonstrations were conducted in Jerusalem. The Panthers started publishing their own paper. In that year a demonstration in Jerusalem, the last of its kind, was met with violent police opposition and arrests continued for a week. There was a feeling that the

Panthers were losing public support. They established connections with the "Black Panthers" in the USA.

1972 – The budget ratified by the Knesset reflected a major achievement for the Black Panther movement. Compared to former budgets, larger sums were allocated to housing, education and so on.

1973 – Divisions occurred within the movement. Along with Shalom Cohen, a movement called "Black Panthers – Israeli Democrats" ran in the Histadrut elections and won three seats (1.6 percent of votes). This result encouraged the leaders to prepare for the Knesset elections. However, one faction supported and another faction opposed participating in these elections (Shitrit, 2001). Ultimately, several blocs affiliated with the Black Panthers ran for the eighth Knesset elections. The Black Panther movement was torn apart by internal splits; different factions appeared speaking in its name.

August 1973 – Cohen and his colleagues left the movement to establish a new bloc called "Israeli Social Struggle." However, some of those who broke away returned to the original movement (Hertsogh, 1986). Some Panthers established contact with radical leftist movements; others, without abandoning their ethnic commitment, considered themselves as Zionists. Some even proposed a separate state for the Mizrahi Jews (Hertsogh, 1986). None of these groups was able to secure the necessary votes to enter the eighth Knesset in December, 1973. The movement entered a long process of collapse.

1977 – In the ninth Knesset elections held on May 15, 1977, four blocs representing different leftist and Panther factions ran for election, without success (Hertsogh, 1986). It was said that the majority of Mizrahim in Israel, at this point, considered the leaders of the Black Panthers as criminals, or people with criminal records (Bernstein, 1979).

Despite their failure to attract the majority of Mizrahim in Israel (Cohen, 1972), the Black Panthers were able to claim a number of achievements. In terms of bridging the gap between the Mizrahim and Ashkenazim, they enhanced public awareness that the official establishment, rather than the Mizrahi, were responsible for the inequality. Also, the Panthers were the first to make a connection between the struggle of the Mizrahi in Israel and that of the black minority in the USA or the situation in Apartheid South Africa. The Black Panthers were also among the first to link the crisis of the Mizrahi in Israel with the occupation and subjection of the Palestinians. The collective Mizrahi consciousness fostered by the Panthers paved the way for the establishment of new Mizrahi political movements such as Tami and

SHAS. Following the decline of the Panthers, Mizrahi Jewish leaders – such as Rafi Edri, Avner Shaki and David Levy – gained prominence in the large parties. In addition, an immediate consequence of the Black Panthers was the establishment of the "Ohalim" (Tents) movement.

The "Ohalim" movement

As the Black Panthers movement disappeared, the new Ohalim movement emerged. This movement was established by a group of youths from Jerusalem's Katamon neighborhood who studied theater and produced works addressing their social and economic problems. In 1978, Yemin Suissa joined this group and, until 1981, led its protest activities as a direct extension of the Black Panther movement. Like the Black Panthers, the group understood that investments were going to the settlements rather than to the poor neighborhoods, and called attention to the housing crisis of the Mizrahi. Ohalim was not countrywide, but was a regional grassroots movement of Jerusalem neighborhoods that also provided education and social services for the community.

Among several protest activities, in December 1979, the movement staged a demonstration to protest the government's increase of basic foodstuff prices. The demonstration became violent and dozens were injured. In June 1980, the movement erected the "Ohel Moreh" tent to resemble the "Alon Moreh" settlement established in Nablus by the extremist Gush Emunim movement. The protest tent in Katamon encouraged the erection of similar projects elsewhere. During the tenth Knesset elections, Yamin Suissa failed to win a seat in the Knesset and joined the Mapai party, ending the protest activities (Shitrit, 2001).

In spite of the short period during which the movement was active, it recorded a number of achievements. First, it maintained the continuity of the radical Mizrahi protest movement, though its clashes with the police were milder than those of the Black Panthers. Second, though Zionist, the movement helped dispel the Mizrahi's illusion that they would benefit from Likud rule. Though it maintained its relations both with Likud and Labor, the group remained totally opposed to investments in the settlements rather than in the poor neighborhoods.

The Mizrahi non-parliamentarian movements failed to achieve the central goal of reducing the gap between the Mizrahi and Western Ashkenazi communities in Israel. Nevertheless, the extra-parliamentary protest activities of the Mizrahi movements indirectly paved the way for a few Mizrahi leaders to assume prominence within the larger parties and subsequently for the reemergence of Mizrahi political parties. These developments – that is, inclusion of Mizrahi leaders in the larger parties and the renewed assertion of Mizrahi political parties – will now be addressed.

Mizrahi parliamentary activities

Mizrahi leaders generally did not make it to the top of the larger parties they joined. However, Moshe Katsav became the President of Israel while David Levy was one of the foremost leaders of the Likud.

Mizrahi leaders in large parties – David Levy[1]

David Levy was born in 1937 in Morocco where he was educated at the "Alliance" schools. He obtained a religious education at a Jewish school. At the age of 18, while continuing his studies, Levy worked at his father's carpentry workshop. In 1956, at the age of 19, Levy immigrated to Israel and settled in Beith Sha'an. Even during his early days in Israel, he took a critical view of the official Israeli establishment. Watching his father lose his job, Levy broke into the Labor office in protest more than once and was detained for 12 days. Following a lengthy period of unemployment during which he was dependent on his wife's meager income, Levy obtained work in construction. He was then elected a member of the Construction Workers Union, representing the Mapai party. Levy subsequently left the party in protest against Mapai's "dictatorial regime"; he returned to work in construction.

The Herut movement offered Levy membership and nominated him for the post of Mayor of Beith She'an. He was elected Deputy Mayor. In 1965, Levy headed the Herut (Gahal) bloc in the Histadrut elections. He boosted support for the bloc from 15.2 percent to 22.7 percent. At the age of 31, Levy was elected to the Knesset, maintaining his Histadrut and municipal posts. In 1977, with the Likud election victory over Mapai, Levy was appointed Minister of Absorption, and two years later, was appointed Minister of Housing and Construction. In the Histadrut elections he, once again, boosted support for his party.

As a party leader, Levy struggled against capitalist economics and voted against the government's economic plans. He sought to implement practical steps to improve the lives of the Mizrahi Jews (e.g. reforming procedures for making housing loans to young couples). During his first year as Minister of Housing, Levy also succeeded in building 20,400 new housing units in development towns, Jewish population centers and the occupied Palestinian territories. In the tenth Knesset elections (June 30, 1981) Levy led the Mizrahi in the Herut movement; this shift from local to national politics became a precedent for other Mizrahi leaders (e.g. Moshe Katsav, Meir Shitrit, David Magen).

Following the 1981 elections, the first difference between Levy and the Likud party surfaced when he declined to enter the government without having his demands met. He was pacified by appointments as both Minister of Housing and Construction and Deputy Prime Minister. Levy decried the degraded status of the Mizrahi within the various parties and was among those expressing reservations about Ariel Sharon's adventures in Lebanon. However, Levy failed to be considered as the successor to Menahem Begin after Begin resigned as leader of the Likud party; Begin relinquished his position to Yitzhak Shamir in the 1983 Likud primaries. The unity governments of 1984 and 1988 checked Levy's high ambitions, however, in the Shamir government of 1990, Levy was appointed Minister for Foreign Affairs. In March 1992, Levy again lost to Shamir in the Likud leadership elections and none of his supporters won high places on the Knesset list. Levy accused his opponents of discriminating against him because of his ethnicity.

While in opposition, following the Likud defeat in the thirteenth Knesset elections (June 23, 1992), Levy again competed for the Likud leadership in the 1995 primary elections, this time facing Netanyahu, the Ashkenazi candidate. Levy was defeated by Netanyahu. Following this loss, Levy left the Likud. In March 1996, two months before the fourteenth Knesset elections (May 29, 1996), Levy established his own faction, "Geher," and, given the good conditions his faction received, he abandoned plans to run independently in the elections.

Following the 1996 elections, Levy was appointed Minister of Foreign Affairs and acting Prime Minister during Netanyahu's term. Yet, the coalition was short lived. In early 1999, because of personal differences with Netanyahu, Levy quit the government and, in preparation for the fifteenth Knesset elections (May 17, 1999), joined the "One Israel" bloc, led by Ehud Barak. A year later, Levy left "One Israel" in protest against Barak's performance. During the early 2001 elections for Prime Minister, Levy supported Ariel Sharon. He avoided joining the government then, but did so later on.

Throughout his years in politics, Levy, although he denied it, actually projected himself as a "Mizrahi leader." Yet, despite his many political achievements, politicians looked at him with suspicion, Furthermore, in the media, he was the butt of innumerable degrading jokes.

Reassertion of Mizrahi political movements – the "Tami Movement" (Mesoret Yisrael)

Although I believe political and economic interests were paramount in the rise of the Tami (Traditional Israel) Movement, many observers consider the movement's rise as an expression of dissatisfaction by the Israeli-Swiss businessman, Nissim Gaon, with governmental support for his business. For years, Nissim Gaon had supported the Likud and Mapai parties. Members of his family married relatives of prominent Israeli politicians. In fact, Gaon also stood by Menahem Begin when the latter received the Nobel Prize for peace. However, in 1981, Gaon failed to receive a license to operate the first private TV station in Israel. Thus, it is said, he established a new political party – Tami – and provided it with immense financial support. In turn, its leaders arranged for the government to support his business (Nitzan and Bichler, 2002).

Tami, led by Aharon Abu-Hatzeira, was established in spring 1981, just before the elections to the tenth Knesset. Abu-Hatzeira was a prominent NRP activist and Mayor of Ramleh during the 1970s. Benefiting, among Mizrahi Jews, from his ancestral links to a Morrocan Rabbinical dynasty and his charismatic personality, Abu-Hatzeira had gained appointment to the post of Minister of Religions in 1977. In July 1980, malpractice in the Ministry was reported and the police indicted Abu-Hatzeira and his close allies on charges of corruption and financial mismanagement. Abu-Hatzeira's friends considered his indictment as part of an internal struggle within the NRP and a conspiracy designed by the Ashkenazim against the Mizrahi leader (Grienstien, 1984). Rich Sephardi Jewish leaders from abroad, including Nissim Gaon and Leon Taman, paid the expenses of the court case.

Unhappy with the NRP and now enjoying other financial backing, the Mizrahi – including the Labor Minister of Agriculture, Aharon Ozen – founded Tami while Abu-Hatzeira was awaiting the court's ruling on his indictment. Tami also included a movement called "Oded," established by educated youth from the impoverished neighborhoods and development towns. (Oded later became part of the "Dash" movement). When Abu-Hatzeira was acquitted, Tami registered as a party for the coming elections.

The 1981 elections were among the most significant in Israel's history; the political struggle was characterized by ethnic-cultural propaganda. The Likud, headed by Begin, orchestrated an all-out campaign against Labor party institutions, the Histadrut and Kibbutsim. Violent incidents occurred in development towns. During Labor's final campaign in Tel Aviv, the comedian, Dudu Topaz, referred to Likud supporters as "Tshachshachim" – a degrading description of Mizrahi Jews. This term typified the use of ethnic incitement during the campaign. The "Tami" movement was no exception; it, too, focused on ethnic and religious factors.

The Tami election campaign stressed a return to Jewish spiritual roots, the unity of the Jewish people, and educating people to love the Land of Israel (Grienstien, 1984). In addition to these themes, Tami spoke of the ongoing injustice against Mizrahi Jews. For example, Abu-Hatzeira noted that 95 percent of prison inmates were Mizrahi as evidence of the decline in the status of Mizrahi Judaism (Grienstien, 1984). The Tami movement succeeded in mobilizing Mizrahi, religious and traditional sectors that previously had lacked proper political organization. In fact, it was difficult to distinguish between one sector and another – Rabbis and spiritual leaders were held in high regard by all. During the tenth Knesset elections, held in late June 1981, Tami was successful in winning three seats. Party electees joined the Likud government and received appointment to important Ministries, including Labor, Welfare and Absorption.

A variety of sectoral and religious factors, as well as feelings of discrimination and injustice, can be found behind the rise of the Tami movement. It would be difficult to define the nature of the movement precisely as religious, social or sectarian. Tami struggled for the welfare of Mizrahi Judaism by enforcing Jewish traditions in Israel and by redressing social injustice. These different missions and visions of the movement help to explain its sudden rise during the 1981 elections and its downfall three years later. Though Tami ceased to exist in its second election term, the party, nevertheless, left lasting effects on Israeli politics. Perhaps the rise of SHAS in 1984 can be seen in the context of the fall of Tami.

The decline of the Tami movement

Following the tenth Knesset elections when Tami was well integrated into the Israeli political system, negative developments began to appear. New accusations against Abu-Hatzeira's integrity finally led to his trial, indictment and, in May 1982, resignation from his government post. Though Abu-Hatzeira's prison sentence was changed to community service, his return to Begin's government was blocked by public pressure. The party embarked on a campaign to return him to office, supporting new elections after PM Begin's resignation in 1983. However, Tami, once claiming to defend the unprivileged, had now lost its moral integrity and began to forfeit its former supporters.

Other reasons also explain the decline of Tami:

- There was some improvement in the real status of Mizrahi Jews.
- Mizrahi representation in senior positions within the large parties (e.g. Labor and Likud) grew as prominent Mizrahi leaders joined these parties. For example, the Army Chief of Staff at that time, Moshe Levy, being of Iraqi origin, was a Mizrahi Jew.
- Certain developments worked against the arguments for a sectarian party and thus weakened Tami – a wholly sectarian party. For example, following the 1982 Israeli invasion of Lebanon and the implementation of the Sinai withdrawal agreements, the division between "doves" and "hawks" replaced the previous sectarian divisions in Israeli public opinion.
- Serious differences emerged between Tami leadership and voters. For example, while the majority of Tami leaders, including those who came from the NRP, were centrists, their voters were clearly rightist. When discussions became heated in Israeli society regarding the future of the West Bank and Gaza Strip or regarding Lebanon, the party became alienated from its voters. Moreover, the Likud government's catastrophic economic policies encouraged fake economic growth, in which nobody wanted to be considered poor. This made Tami's policies sound anachronistic.

Finally, the existence of SHAS was a central factor in the downfall of

Tami, whose representation in the eleventh Knesset fell from three to one. For example, SHAS enjoyed the support of many Rabbis, unlike Tami's one family. During the eleventh Knesset, Tami was almost non-existent. Its only Knesset representative did not join the unity government and many Tami members left the party to join others. Tami institutions ceased to operate and the party became a thing of the past in Israeli politics. Nevertheless, Tami was a significant phenomenon in the early period of Israeli politics, not so much because of its traditional religious path but because it was pledged to represent the North African Jews and redress the social and cultural injustice that they suffered in Israel. The Tami movement spoke not of religion but of tradition. For instance, the group never demanded a radical "religious revolution." Stressing cultural-sectoral identity allowed Tami to enjoy support outside the purely religious sector. Unfortunately, it also weakened the movement's long term internal unity. In a sense, Tami paved the way for SHAS, proving that a sectarian party could be successful in Israeli politics (Grienstien, 1984).

Mizrahi political and social organizations

The failure of Mizrahi politicians, and the public support for the extremist religious SHAS movement, led in the 1990s to the emergence of a wave of Mizrahi non-governmental organizations (NGOs) striving to fill in the gap left by the politicians (see Yishai, 1998; Ben-Zadok, 1993). Whereas 1970s non-parliamentary Mizrahi activity began at the grassroots level, such activity during the 1990s came from the heart of academic institutions and elite social and cultural organizations. One of these organizations was the "Democratic Mizrahi Rainbow."

The Democratic Mizrahi Rainbow was established by a limited group of nine members: Eli Hamu, Elly She'a, Moshe Karin, Shosh Gabbai, Dr Vicky Shiran, Dr Henrietta Dahan-Kaleb, Dolly Bin-Habib, Dr Sami Shalom-Chitrit and Professor Yehuda Shenhab. The nine tried to establish an alliance with David Levy's Gesher movement. However, when he returned to the Likud, they decided to leave him. The founding members of the Democratic Mizrahi Rainbow held a series of meetings over six months, organized a successful conference, and established an interim forum – "Israel 96" – in a preparation for founding a new Mizrahi social movement. In December 1996, 100 members elected a founding council; in March 1997, the movement held its first large conference with participation from 300 members, including academics, businessmen, workers, teachers, artists, scholars, university students and local activists from cultural and social organizations.

According to its website, the Democratic Mizrahi Rainbow works on exposing the deepening economic gap and cultural oppression from which the Mizrahi Jews in Israel suffer. It strives to eradicate stereotypical images adopted by educational and cultural institutions in their dealings with

Mizrahi Jews and their culture. The movement believes that these social problems undermine the stability of the Israeli society.[2] Furthermore, the movement claims that improving the social, cultural and economic status of the Mizrahim in Israel can serve as a first step toward realizing a stable and lasting peace in the region.

The movement's first success was recorded in the struggle over the status of families living in public housing, most of whom are Mizrahim. The group expressed solidarity with the homeless citizens in Mevaseret Tzion, who stormed flats belonging to the Jewish Agency and took them over. However, the Democratic Rainbow observed the rule of law and had no part in the violence that was committed there. Thus, its members, unlike those in former protest movements, were not arrested by the police. Nevertheless, despite the significant success attained by the movement in the struggles over public housing and the distribution of land resources in Israeli society, when it attacked the Kibbutz system (see The Mizrahi Democratic Rainbow against the Israel Land Authority – the ruling of the Supreme Court 244/00) the movement was still considered leftist and could not claim sweeping Mizrahi support.

Conclusion

Israel was founded by Jewish immigrants from Europe and North America (Ashkenazim) who came to Palestine during the period of the British mandate (1919–48) and founded and consolidated the political, economic, social and cultural systems that dominated Israel after independence and that continue to do so. Large waves of immigrants from Asia and North Africa (Mizrahim or Sephardim) altered demographics in Israel, inspiring Ashkenazim fears about the character of society and state and about potential loss of their hegemony.

Three factors characteristic of the Mizrahi immigration to Israel helped create the Ashkenazi–Mizrahi fissure:

1) immigration policy restrictions for the immigrants from Islamic countries in Asia and Africa that left "a vague sense that the Mizrahi immigrants were essential for developing the country but not really wanted";
2) an absorption policy that (a) aimed at keeping the Mizrahi immigrants from damaging or undermining the European Israeli culture and sociopolitical order constructed by the Ashkenazim; (b) used the Mizrahi labor force to serve the economic and military objectives of the well-to-do Ashkenazi strata; and (c) steered Mizrahi immigrants to sub-standard housing in development towns established on the geographic and economic periphery of the country;
3) Mizrahi vulnerabilities, such as (a) poor education, (b) large families, (c) lack of family networks to help them get started following their

arrival, and (d) lack of the political experience to help them organize and conduct successful campaigns to promote their own interests.

State policies produced a dramatic rise in the self awareness of the Mizrahim, sharpened their feelings of discrimination, and sparked a desire to work a change in the power relations between the two groups. Mizrahim political behavior designed to effect this change was influenced by (a) being part of the Israeli historical opposition party – the Likud – on one hand; and (b) support for Mizrahi movements and political parties, on the other hand. Parliamentary and extra-parliamentary movements that represented the Mizrahi appeared in different forms: public movements, political parties, and social and political non-governmental organizations.

Mizrahi Jews play a critical role in the stability of the Israeli political system. Ethnic consciousness among the Mizrahim has not weakened over the years and is still accompanied by a sense of discrimination and vulnerability (Shitrit, 2001b). There is still strong and deep resentment of the discrimination against Mizrahim as a group – a situation that could catalyze their collective political behavior and could include the possibility of recourse to instability. The politics launched by the SHAS movement and the demands raised by SHAS are bold proof of this possibility (see Chapter 4).

4 Jewish religious groups and the politics of identity in the "secular-Jewish" state

Conflict between religion and the state has always been a subject for debate in the country. Since Israel's establishment (Ravitsky, 1998), religion has established political parties and coalitions, caused governments to collapse, played a central role in all public discourse and constituted the essence of the state cultural as well as religious identity. This conflict has many different facets, including philosophical, theological, social, economic and political aspects. This chapter is intended to provide a general framework for discussion of the relations between the religious and the secular in Israel.

It is not only in Israel that there has been tension between religion and state. For the past 500 years, religion has fought a retrieval war against the growing powers of the state. Since the establishment and emergence of the modern state and institutionalization of the separation of church and monarchial authority, the clergy has been occupied with studying the significance of the state. Clerical, political and economic control, based on spiritual authority, no longer exists; the clergy finds itself compelled to struggle for resources and influence against leaders who base their rules on Machiavelli's book *The Prince*. The state won total power by stripping away the authority of what had been a monopoly for countless years – the Church.

The emergence of the national state in the nineteenth century posed a double challenge to the religious institutions. The national movement projected itself as a better alternative than religion and as a new base for the significance of the individual's life and affiliations. The national identity incorporated individuals of different religions and so contributed to obliterating the status of the Church. The nationalist wars that raged between followers of the same religion were sad proof of the rift between religion and the state.

This change made the state a constant subject of suspicion for clerics, who considered the state a materialistic attempt to build an agenda lacking any mission from the heavens. The liberals believe that all religious efforts by citizens are futile and that declaring a "state religion," as was done in many Catholic states, does not help. In addition to these aspects of the conflict, the Jewish people developed their own characteristics during the recent century, in interaction with the international community. These characteristics include:

1) The absence of legitimate political authority. The national political authority developed relatively recently, as the Jewish reality was characterized by political submission to the different regimes existing in the various countries where they lived, coupled with attempts to sustain religious independence. As for the emergence of Zionism in Europe, its rapid world-wide political and cultural expansion among the Jewish communities forced the religious leadership to react immediately and sharply to the situation.

2) The material crises that accompanied the development of the national movement. Jews in the Diaspora frequently fell victim to violence and religious oppression, in addition to suffering from much oppressive legislation and regulations. Along with their perception of failure, there was a growing national feeling among Jews to merge with the emancipation project as Europeans belonging to the religion of Moses. All of this created a sharp existential crisis. Incidents such as massacres perpetrated in south Russia in 1881 and 1903 and the trial of Dreyfus in France (1894) led many of the Jews, religious and secular alike, to seek a comprehensive solution for the crises of the Jews.

3) The significant status of the "Land of Israel" (Palestine). The "Land of Israel" (Eretz Yisrael) was seen by the majority of Jews as the cradle of the Jewish people's existence. It was the place where the Jewish people exercised sovereignty in the first century BC. It occupies a special status in Jewish religious doctrine. Longing for this land had a deep religious meaning and Jewish prayers, festivals and the coffins of the dead were directed to the Holy Land. Throughout the years in the Diaspora, the Jewish religious pilgrimage to Palestine never ceased. Also, every Jewish groom said on his wedding night, "If I forget thee o Yerushalayim, let my right hand forget its cunning."

The Jewish national project did not limit itself to fostering a public that agreed with its established values; rather it imported this public from the different Diaspora countries to the Holy Land, where conflict erupted between these Jews and the original inhabitants. The project mobilized great material and spiritual resources and shaped the psychological relations between every Jew and the "Land of Israel" – a feature that was to constitute a central factor in the success of the great emigration project.

The theological dimension

Against this backdrop, the rift between religion and the state in Israel widened. Lingental (2002) described three theological beliefs regarding the

Zionist concept: Zionism was seen as a sin by ultra-orthodox Jews; as a fulfillment of Jewish prophecy by some religious Zionists; and as an emancipation movement by others. The religious public and parties in Israel generally act in accordance with these theological viewpoints. Political demands and coalitions, in addition to creating political crises, are characterized by these beliefs, which underline the significance of the existence of the state.

Zionism as a sin

The "Haredim," ultra-orthodox Jews, considered Zionism to be a great sin and a form of sacrilege. A Haredi Jew was prohibited from seeking the redemption of Israel through political settlement or military means. It can only be attained through prayers and doing one's duty to God. The Haredim considered the secular leadership of the Zionists, who oppose the Torah, as a doubly grave sin. They also perceived the catastrophes that befell the Jewish people in Europe from the late nineteenth century to the twentieth century as a direct result of this disbelief in God. The classic orthodox Haredim refused to acknowledge any political authority for Zionism and boycotted it. However, the security and political situation in Israel forced the "Agudat Yisrael" (see below) to take a realistic stand towards increasing engagement in the political system; their adoption of the concept of a "Jewish state" as a symbol reflects such changes in their position.

Zionism as fulfillment of prophecy

The second belief is that of the religious Zionist stream, adopted in the early days of Zionism. This belief distinguished between Zionist realism and speeding or impeding the return of the Messiah. Its dealings with Zionism were based on the belief that Zionism was a means of salvaging the Jews and solving the problem of their existence. Representatives were elected within the Zionist movement to ensure that political existence for the religious Jews would be a Palestinian one. Religious Zionism depended on universal Jewish values that were based solely on the prophecy of the prophets of Israel. Incorporating these ideals into the Zionist movement was a preferred strategy for the religious Zionists.

Zionism as emancipation

The third widely accepted belief among religious Zionists was that Zionism was a movement of emancipation. These Zionists believed that the establishment of a Jewish state constituted a religious phenomenon and a stage of emancipation that comes from God. They felt, therefore, that every religious individual has a role to play and in a secular state this will be the substance upon which the religious soul is based. Rabbi Abraham Yitzhak Hacohen Kook (Greenberg, 1951: 8–9), who was considered an outstanding representative of religious Zionists, alleged that the "Land of Israel" could not be differentiated from the nation. He maintained that, "The land of Israel is tied to the nation with the ties of life." The idea of endowing the secular Zionist movement with a religious mission encouraged the religious public and institutions to participate voluntarily in the Zionist project, thereby bridging the gap between religion and the state to some extent.

The legal dimension

For the religious, defining the State of Israel as a "Jewish democratic state" constitutes the framework for conflict between religion and state. I am not now going to discuss the democracy of the state or the discrimination against its non-Jewish citizens (Palestinians and others) that is caused by the dual definition of the state. Rather, I am going to note the religious nature of the state as reflected by religious Jews (Agasy, 1991). The Declaration of Independence (a document that is not a law) refers to "the establishment of a Jewish state in Eretz Yisrael, to be known as Israel." The relevant questions, therefore, are, "What is a Jewish state?" "Can a political authority be Jewish, like an individual?" These questions can be approached from the perspective of: (a) regulations that force the Jewish individual to act according to the Jewish religion; (b) laws and regulations that force Jewish institutions to act according to the Jewish religion; and (c) definitions that indicate who is a Jew. The laws that impose limitations on Jews are much less onerous than is thought. They are generally concealed within social legislation and find their way to the auspices of local authorities, documented within larger social understandings.

The Labor and Rest Law of 1951 starts as follows: "It is prohibited to make a laborer work on the weekend day of rest." The law defines Saturday as a day of rest for Jews. It embodies a social significance that is deeply rooted in Judaism. This social dimension avoids dictating the law and focuses on leisure time issues, such as the closing on Saturday of malls, cinemas, theaters and restaurants. State institutions are forced to stop working on Saturdays and to act according to the "Kosher" dietary laws. Needless to say, the Israeli army generally observes the Shabbat; many orders issued by the Israeli army High Command clearly necessitate observing the holiness of Saturdays. This is also the case with other official state occasions defined by the Knesset as full rest days. In the coming pages I discuss, in detail, the struggles conducted in light of the Labor and Rest Law.

Other legislation relates to the powers at the disposal of religious courts over the life of the individual. The Religious Code Law, 1953 states that, "Matters of marriage and divorce for Jews and other Israeli citizens or residents shall be within the exclusive jurisdiction of the religious courts" (article 1). It also states that, "Marriage and divorce shall be conducted according to the Torah law code" (article 2). This legislation, which obligates almost every Jew, constitutes a constant source of conflict between individuals and the state law. The monopoly of the fundamentalist religious establishment over matters of marriage and divorce has resulted in the establishment of alternative marriage frameworks and has led to marriage ceremonies being conducted abroad. This, too, has stimulated a heated debate regarding the authority of the religious streams – especially the Reform and Conservative – pertaining to marriage and divorce.

The demands of the religious

The demands of the religious sectors frequently confuse secular analysts. Since the Israeli stand on the future of the West Bank and Gaza Strip is seen as either "dovish" or "hawkish," the demands of the religious parties sometimes seem illegitimate, narrow, sectarian or even contrary to the national interest. Understanding the policies adopted by the religious parties in Israel requires grasping the basics of the Jewish political structure. The Jewish religion, unlike other religions, is not evangelistic. Thus, Jewish believers need a certain religious environment that they believe should be provided by the state.[1]

Researchers hold differing opinions about the ultimate goals of the religious parties; the parties themselves also differ on this subject. Party policies change with time. However, some say that the ultimate end of the religious parties is to provide minority rights for the religious sectors in a national secular state. Others see the goal as providing a contemporary understanding of the Jewish state by intelligently incorporating the Torah laws into those of the state. Some interpret the aim of the ultra-orthodox Sephardi party, "SHAS," which joined the political system in 1980s, as a full-scale religious revolution, calling for establishing Israel as a State of "Halacha" (Tessler, 2003). Around these ideas the religious parties take their stand on the Zionist, political, economic, social, security and sectarian identity issues. It is not a coincidence that religious laws regarding the nature of the state are the most constant factor in the demands of the religious parties.

Critical issues on religious party agendas

A number of basic issues consistently stand out in the agendas of the religious parties. Among these issues are: (a) the nature of the educational system; (b) the Military Service Law; (c) the status quo in observing Shabbat and Kashrut; (d) the Law of Return; (e) Judaization according to Jewish code law ("Halacha"); the structures and powers of the religious councils; and the powers of the religious courts.

Nature of the educational system

The education of children is considered one of the substantial issues on the agenda of the religious parties. In a religion like Judaism, where the number of followers is relatively limited, and where Jews were persecuted and attempts made to force them into conversion, the educational struggle over every "Jewish soul" gains supreme importance. The huge resources required for the educational system makes controlling this system an important political issue. Until the establishment of the State of Israel, the majority of the Jewish community in the country was secular, seeking to provide their children with "Western liberal" or "socialist" education. At that time, there were three different Zionist educational schooling systems: the official schooling systems, where the majority of pupils were city inhabitants; the official religious schooling systems of the "Mizrahi" movement; and the Labor schooling system teaching children of the "Kibbutz" agricultural settlements, and some city dwellers.

These different schools were only financially dependent on the Zionist organization. The official religious schools fought an easy battle for independence and won a good margin of freedom for designing programs and even hiring teachers. Due to the lack of educational monopoly by the state, there was no struggle regarding programs and curriculum. This changed after statehood and the passing of the official government Education Law of 1953. Then schooling streams (including the orthodox religious "Agudat Yisrael") which had received government subsidies since 1949, were brought under the jurisdiction of the Ministry of Education. The Labor education stream was also abolished and a new basic educational system was drafted for all schools. Additional educational material could be added by the different streams. In 1983, following the establishment of "SHAS" as a strong political faction, the "Ma'ayan Hachinuch Hatorani," the SHAS educational system, joined the educational streams that receive government subsidies.

After 1948, following the increase in immigration to Israel, the struggle over the educational system reflected demographic changes in the community. The majority of immigrants came from Islamic countries and were either religious or traditional, so that the European liberal or socialist ideologies were strange to them. The struggle over the nature of the educational system remained on the agendas during the 1950s.

The domination of the "Mapai" (Labor party – later the Labor Alignment) over the Ministry of Education ensured, at least superficially, a status quo for the first three decades after the establishment of the state. Yet, the political reversal and the defeat of Labor in 1977 constituted a landmark, with control of the education portfolio passing into new hands. The Nationalist Religious Party (NRP or Mafdal) took over the Ministry of Education; SHAS and Agudat Yisrael demanded Deputy Ministers of Education.

Military Service Law

According to the system implemented in Israel, every citizen above 18 years old must serve in the army, although the Military Service Law grants the Minister of Defense the power to release citizens from this duty. (For example, Palestinians in Israel are exempted from military service.) Among the many problematic issues related to compulsory military service was the issue of enlisting students of the religious schools and colleges (Yeshivot) in the army. A struggle ensued between those who opposed conscription – the ultra-Haredim – and those who supported conscription – the secular and the National Religious Party.

Controversy also raged in Israel regarding the military service of women, who had served in different capacities in Zionist military militias that existed prior to the establishment of the state (e.g. the Hagana and Etzel). Consequently, after the establishment of the Israeli Defense Force (IDF), it was natural to have women joining the army units, particularly in view of the army's role as a social tool. A rift deepened between Haredim, who unequivocally opposed female military service, and those who supported it and called for special arrangements enabling women to serve. The crisis among the Haredim was so acute that the Minister for Social Affairs from Agudat Yisrael, Isaac Meir Livneh, tendered his resignation in September 1952; the effect was the collapse of Israel's third coalition government.

Religious parties had to accept a compromise that reaffirmed compulsory military service for women, with the exemption of anyone declaring herself as "religious." This mandate served as a reason for exempting students of religious schools and colleges. The rabbis had two goals behind their stand on this issue. First, they aimed at salvaging the "religious student community," that had existed in Eastern Europe (Elan, 2000), by consecrating a continuous educational track for Torah studies that was not interrupted by military service. Second, the rabbis expressed strong reservations about the secular licentiousness to which religious recruits could be exposed. According to the original arrangements of 1949, about 400 religious school students were exempted from military service (Cohen, 1993). In 1957, Ben-Gurion expanded the concept of "Turatam Emunatam" (those dedicated for Torah learning), so that those studying at a religious school could be exempted from military service, including those who also worked for their living. In practice, these students are granted a delay in their military service, which is renewed automatically until they pass the age of compulsory service.

Nine years later, a ministerial commission, headed by Defense Minister Moshe Dayan, limited the maximum number of beneficiaries to this exemption to only 800 youths a year.

An important change occurred after the Likud assumed office in 1977: government coalition agreements signed by the Likud with "Agudat Yisrael" abolished the annual quotas for military service exemption. This agreement also allowed religious high school graduates to be exempted from military service provided they continued their studies at a Haredim higher education institute. In 1981, Defense Minister Ariel Sharon exempted religious youths from having to renew their exemption annually by granting them a status of fully exempted at a certain age. Sharon also helped solve the problem the exempted and the demobilized faced of earning a living by allowing them to learn and receive salaries in return after the age of 30. Today, about 4000 "Haredim" students enjoy this exemption every year. The total number of the exempted is estimated in the tens of thousands. The expansion of the government funded Yeshivot system contributed to the emergence of the Haredi "student community" (Horowits, 2002) which is based on the observation of religious duties and devotion to religious education and depends on government subsidies and state welfare programs. This student community is the source of the political strength of "Yahadut Hatorah" (see below) (Elan, 2000).

The struggle for the status quo – observing Shabbat and Kashrut

One of the terms used to refer to the relations between the religious and the secular in Israel is the "status quo." Specifically, the term refers to preserving the religious character of the Jewish community as it existed before the establishment of the state. Maintaining the status quo remains an important political demand even today (Friedman, 1988).

Perhaps the most important and substantial components of the status quo are the Shabbat and Kashrut (dietary laws). The Jewish conception of the Shabbat (Saturday) is far stricter than any other religious "day of rest." The first Commandment calls for observing Shabbat; this means, for religious Jews, fully desisting from any work. The holiness of Shabbat is a concept of such importance that it cannot be violated for any reason but to save a human soul and life. According to this concept, once the Shabbat starts, until it ends, Jews are not allowed to perform any work, to write, to make business deals, to use electrical appliances or to travel in a vehicle. Shabbat – the core and symbol of Jewish life throughout the years – is characterized by synagogue attendance, family gatherings for Shabbat meals and overall quiet and calmness in Jewish neighborhoods.

Kashrut refers to the rules and regulations regarding the kinds of food Jews are allowed to eat. Only authorized Kosher food can be eaten. Related dietary laws include: (a) separation of meat and milk (dairy products); (b) a ban on consuming the meat of certain animals, reptiles and agricultural products unprocessed according to the Torah canon law; (c) the banning of various items of non-Kosher food; and (d) prohibition against eating bread or foodstuffs containing yeast during the Passover (Pesach) holiday. A system was devised for monitoring the planting and processing of Kosher food, with some differences occurring among religious communities. This led to having rabbinical authorities make rulings qualifying food products as Kosher.

In 1935, the Zionist Executive adopted a binding decision for all Zionist institutions to observe the sanctity of Shabbat and the laws of Kashrut

(Hason, 2001). Despite the fact that most members of the Zionist movement were secular, they nevertheless acknowledged the religious character of their movement, and wanted to enable the religious members to participate in the movement's activities. The coalition between the Mapai and Mizrahi parties held together until the 1970s, allowing Mapai to enjoy political supremacy, while meeting the religious needs of Mizrahi.

Most of the problems concerning Shabbat observation were associated with the status quo agreement set forth in a letter sent by the Jewish Agency to the "Agudat Yisrael" on December 19, 1947 (Cohen and Susser, 2000). In this letter, it was agreed that: (a) Shabbat would be observed as a day of rest (and would include inactivation of the transportation system on Saturday); (b) Kashrut would be observed in government departments; (c) the ultra-orthodox Haredi educational network would be autonomous; and (d) religious authorities would maintain the power to rule on marriage issues.

Many struggles related to observing the status quo took place at two levels. The first level concerned the behavior of government institutions and branches that had inherited the pre-state Zionist institutions as official Jewish state symbols. The second level concerned the nature of cultural, business and individual life. I believe that the status quo has been observed at the government level, but not at the individual level, where social and economic dynamics have weakened the religious character of the state.

The struggle for the "Law of Return"

An additional issue consistently on the agenda of the religious parties is the "Law of Return," best known as the question of "Who is a Jew?" This issue has involved many conflicting national, religious and social considerations. Issued in 1950, the "Law of Return" is considered one of the bases upon which Israel was established as a Jewish ethnic state. This law ensures Israeli citizenship for every Jewish individual upon his arrival in Israel, except in exceptional cases involving people posing a danger to public safety or with criminal records.

The complex nature of the relations between Jewish nationality and the Jewish religion creates a structural conflict of interests. On the one hand, the Zionist movement aspires to grant Israeli citizenship to every individual Jew, as a way of supporting its conflict with the Palestinians. On the other hand, orthodox Jews are concerned about over registering non-Jews as Jews, which could adversely affect Jewish ethnicity. The generous Israeli absorption policy adopted by the Israeli Ministry of Absorption is directed at tempting Jews from countries suffering crises to accept Israeli offers and immigrate to Israel.

Debate concerning interpretation of the "Law of Return" has taken different forms at different times. In the early 1950s, Israel had to absorb hundreds of thousands of Jews, most of whom immigrated from North

Africa, the Fertile Crescent, Syria, Lebanon, Jordan and Palestine, and Yemen. The country's economic absorption capacity was in question and debate revolved around functional issues such as, should the number of absorbees be reduced and according to what criteria? The religious Zionists argued that, come what may, every Jew should be brought to the country, rather than remaining in the Palestinian countries. In the following years, the debate centered around the question of registering immigrants as Jews in the population records (Elan, 2000). According to Jewish canon law (Halacha), a Jew is anyone born to a Jewish mother or properly converted to Judaism. However, in order to avoid dissension, the law, when drafted, did not include a clear definition of who is a Jew. In the first population census conducted in the aftermath of the 1948 war, the nationality and religion of citizens was registered according to their documents. In practice, registration teams decided based on their whims and political beliefs about an individual's right to be registered. An attempt made by the Minister of the Interior to devise criteria to regulate citizens' registration resulted in the NRP's withdrawal from the government.

Nowadays, the debate centers on the issue of conversion to Judaism. Religious Jewish factions that include the Haredim and the NRP are waging a war against the Judaization process conducted by non-orthodox Reformist and Conservative factions. In Israel, religious councils dominated by orthodox Jews monopolize Judaization, while among Jewish communities abroad, especially in the USA, these functions are exercised by Reform and Conservative Rabbis. The unwillingness of the Israeli religious establishment to recognize the authority of Reform and Conservative Rabbis has caused serious damage to Israel's relations with Diaspora Jewry. Even today, the problem remains unsolved.

Judaization according to Jewish code law

The issue of Judaization, which is related to the "Law of Return" and the authority of the religious powers, is considered a basic factor in defining religious identity. The desire to define Judaization suggests that the basis of political conflicts and distribution of resources is religious. One has to be born a Jew to be considered a Jew. This cannot be changed except by a person's being properly Judaized, regardless of how fervent he/she may be in observing religious rituals. Individuals who are born Jewish can even shun religious duties and consider themselves atheists and still be considered Jews because they were born so. There is a great significance in defining who can be considered a Jew. Many privileges in Israel, the most important of which is the right to citizenship, are conditioned on one's Jewish identity. Anyone who wishes to convert to Judaism must pass a lengthy process of education and preparation before declaring his Judaization before the Rabbinical Court and showing confirmations and documents signed by the Rabbis who tested him in advance.[2]

In Israel, the Judaization process has always been monopolized by the extreme orthodox faction. Conversions conducted by Reform or Conservative Rabbis – moderate religious groupings with influence in the Western Diaspora countries – have never been recognized as a basis for registering citizens as Jews (Cohen and Susser, 2000). Although Israeli religious parties and most of the secular parties agreed with this situation, it seems that the increasing influence of moderate streams in Israel and the rising influence of American Jewry in Israeli affairs, resulted in mounting pressure to change the status quo. In the early 1990s, the Israeli High Court ruled that non-orthodox Judaization conducted abroad could be accepted as a basis for registering citizens as Jews. Furthermore, Reform and Conservative stream appeals to the High Court to acknowledge Judaization conducted in Israel by their Rabbis were accepted by the court, which further stated that it had no power to decide who was qualified for citizenship. In a reaction to the growing interference of the High Court in issues of Judaization, the religious parties drafted a law for amending religious conversion. The law mandated that only orthodox Judaization was to be recognized. This initiative resulted in a crisis between Israeli and US Jewry and prompted the search for a compromise settlement on the issue of Judaization.

The Neeman commission, headed by Professor Yaakov Neeman, and established in 1998 to find such a compromise settlement, recommended establishing a Judaization Institute in which representatives of the different Jewish streams would participate.[3] The commission further recommended that ratification of Judaization should come under the authority of Judaization Courts appointed by the Chief Rabbinate. In spite of all reservations, there seemed to be adequate points of agreement.

Powers of Rabbinical Courts and the issue of authority over religious councils

A religious Jew needs a supportive socio-ethnic system to facilitate his observance of religious rituals; this observance of rituals is the connection point in relations between the individual and the religious establishment. The state funds the institutions of the religious establishment – the religious councils, the Rabbinate's religious courts, Synagogues and religious schools. Needless to say, the authority over these bodies constitutes a major factor in the political struggle.

The nature of services offered to religious individuals is a very important factor for two reasons: first, services can constitute a resource for political mobilization – the religious institutions are model authorities within the state, where different factions engage in political activities; second, the nature of services can be a source of religious influence – differences between Jewish religious factions manifest in the nature of religious services they offer.

Religious councils constitute the authority responsible for providing religious services in the local authority (Don-Yihya, 1988). This authority was established before the establishment of the state, with the consent of the Chief Rabbinate for the "Land of Israel." After the establishment of the state, the legitimacy of their authority was discussed and the Jewish services budget law of 1949 stated that these Councils were to be appointed by the Ministry of Religion and local councils. However, the law did not define their authority. In the 1960s, laws were drafted that were supposed to ratify the positions of the majority of the pre-state religious councils. In 1971, the Jewish Religious Services Law (Warhaftig, 1973) was adopted to consolidate all understandings and arrangements that accumulated with the passing of this law.

Nevertheless, three problematic issues related to the existence of religious councils have persisted – the issues of their authority, their status and their structure. The authority of religious councils has been the cause of differences which to this day have obstructed the ratification of an official law to organize the subject (Don-Yihya, 1988). Officially, the task of religious councils is limited to providing important religious services to concerned citizens, including monitoring Kashrut services, providing assistance to Synagogues, overseeing burial procedures and registering marriages. Yet, many religious Jews in Israel considered the religious councils as an extension of the traditional communal society that existed in Jewish communities. Accordingly, they felt that the Councils should assume most of the duties of the community. Hence, the Council extended its authority to include activities such as education, cultural and spiritual activities, religious conversion, intervention in political struggles, and involvement in choosing city Rabbis, local authorities and representatives of the major Synagogues.

The lack of a clear definition of the status of religious councils has left most arrangements for legislation within the power of the Ministry of Religions and thus, subject to the whims of the Minster. Adding to the confusion, the religious councils fall within the jurisdiction of the Municipal Councils and the Minister of Religion. In fact, the religious councils are considered an almost independent instrument for the Ministry of Religious Affairs. Ministers from the NRP and SHAS parties have sought to strengthen the religious councils by increasing their budgets and financial independence and by trying to ratify laws and regulations favorable to them.

The structure of religious councils, which is renewed every four years, is a political issue. Appointments to the Councils are theoretically predicated on local and national negotiations. However, in practice, members represent three political factors: the religious community of the city, the Local Council and the Ministry of Religious Affairs. The municipal Rabbi, who represents the religious community, enjoys the authority of appointing 10 percent of the religious council members; the Ministry and the Municipal Council share equally in appointing the remaining members of the Council.

Until the emergence of the SHAS party, the Agudat Yisrael and NRP parties shared responsibility for making council appointments and balanced power between them. In their harsh criticism against the religious establishment, SHAS insisted that their members be appointed to religious councils.

The Rabbinical Courts – unlike the religious councils, which are essentially administrative and rule on basic issues – assume powers that are part of the Israeli judicial apparatus. These powers essentially relate to issues of marriage, adoption, inheritance, divorce and so on (for example, "women whose husbands are absent, left them, or did not get an official divorce" (Warhaftig, 1973). Although their authority is taken from the civil law, the Rabbinical Courts follow the Torah court law (Shitrit, 1999). Their status and powers as spiritual religious authorities were emphasized when Jews brought lawsuits against other Jews. For example, in 1972, a lawsuit was brought against NRP Knesset member, Michael Hazani, when he acted in the Knesset to ratify a special law on Army service for girls in contradiction to the Torah ruling that opposes such a law. The government legal adviser said that the Religious Courts were not respecting the powers mandated for them by the state. This issue ended with a compromise solution. Yet the status of the religious code has remained.

The Jewish Religious Code Law "on the marriage and divorce issue," issued in 1953, stated that only the relevant Rabbinical religious Courts could conduct matters of marriage and divorce by Jews in Israel. It is well known that Judaism places various limitations on the right to marriage; for example, a marriage between a Rabbi who is the son of Rabbinical family and a divorced woman is prohibited according to the religion. Additionally, the marriage of a Rabbi to a converted woman or a non-Jewish woman is forbidden, according to the rules and regulations of the Rabbinical Courts. In the case of such a prohibited marriage, the couple is deprived of future religious services, for example obtaining a permit to adopt children or to divorce. This is a violation of freedom of belief.

Matters become particularly complicated when problems – such as an impending divorce – arise within a marriage. According to the Jewish code law, the only procedure that enables a religious court to ratify a divorce is the indictment of one of the two parties. Many couples seeking divorce are reluctant to accept this condition. Further, in many divorce cases, the courts drift into discussing actual details of relations between a couple. Men, because they are preferred according to Torah Court law, can withhold divorce from their women, causing them much suffering. This can result in many situations where men are considered married according to Halacha laws, but do not live with their "wives" or, in some cases, are already married for a second time.

This situation has resulted in attempts to circumvent the system by: (a) petitioning the Supreme Courts to apply the partnership laws in the case of divorce;[4] or (b) seeking alternative non-religious ways to contract marriage. Official marriage certificates issued for civil marriages in foreign countries are accepted in Israel as proving the legitimacy of the marriage. This includes marriages conducted by Reform Rabbis. Civil marriage has been a demand of many Israelis to counter the growing powers of the religious establishment in Israel. Yet to this day, religious services such as Judaization, marriage and divorce are accepted in Israel only if orthodox Rabbis conduct them.

The religious monopoly that prevents many Israelis from realizing and enjoying basic rights, constitutes a major source of strength for orthodox Judaism in the country. The fact that the majority of secular citizens show a lack of interest in religious services makes the subject a secondary one on the agenda of secular parties. However, the religious parties consider the subject of primary importance and the issue serves as a major goal of religious politics.

In sum, this section has sought to explain fundamental issues that constitute the bases for the demands of the religious parties. Although these issue could be viewed as expressions of restrictive sectarian interests, I believe their context or backdrop is an ethical-religious one that is influenced by religious beliefs, a certain vision of God, traditions and the role of the family. The emergence and establishment of religious parties confirms the observation that, in the eyes of orthodox Jewish citizens, basic religious-ethical issues justify relevant political action.

Political organization among the religious groups

A number of external and internal factors underlie the emergence of the religious parties. The internal factors are reflected in the struggles between religious factions over both spiritual and material resources. The external factors include the emergence of Zionism and the Enlightenment movement whose ideas presented a challenge to the orthodox Jewish citizenry and the religious community. In addition, the establishment of Israel as a secular national state with its particular cultural character, may be considered as a development that compelled the religious forces to react.

Following the institutionalization of the official state "establishment" in different areas of life in Israeli society, a new struggle for influence was initiated – the struggle by religious institutions for control of their budgets and funding. This struggle was in addition to those they conducted over their judicial status and on the vital subject of religious education provided by the state. The struggles by religious elements of the country were waged by religious political organizations. In this section of the chapter, I survey the main Israeli religious political organizations. Religious parties are not an exclusive Israeli phenomenon; there are many countries where various parties project themselves as religious ones (e.g. Protestant or Catholic Christian). However, the vociferous divisions and controversies between Israeli parties that present themselves as representing religion are among the most distinguishing characteristics of the Israeli political system.

The National Religious Party (NRP or Mizrahi)

The history of the National Religious Party (formerly the Mizrahi and Hapoel Hamizrachi movements) is a story of continued crises (Owna, 1984). The Mizrahi, as a religious national-Zionist movement, dates back to nineteenth century Europe, where it embraced ancient Jewish traditional values. The movement has been through numerous political crises and, though loyal to a religious Zionist ideology, it presents an indistinct political platform. The original Mizrahi movement was established in 1902, following the breakaway of religious members from the Zionist movement in protest against the decision of the Zionist institutions to include education within their area of work. The breakaway Mizrahi group argued that the role of the Zionist movement should be limited to politics only. In other words, they felt that the movement should focus solely on a political solution to the Jewish crises in Europe. Secular leadership of education was not acceptable to the Mizrahi, who opposed placing such an important subject in the hands of a secular Zionist movement. In 1911, following the establishment, within the Zionist orbit, of an independent education commission specializing in religious education, a compromise agreement was reached. This compromise enabled most of the Mizrahi members to remain within the Zionist faction. On the other hand, it encouraged some members to leave the Zionist organization and join other factions outside the movement – hence, the establishment of the party called Agudat Yisrael.

The most significant activity of the Mizrahi movement was the establishment of the Mizrahi education network, with an independent status within the Zionist movement. The Mizrahi likewise initiated the establishment of the "Chief Rabbinate for Eretz Yisrael" which considered itself as the supreme religious authority for the Jewish community. The Mizrahi was an integral part of the Zionist organization, despite differences regarding women's right to vote within the Zionist movement. The political stand taken by the Mizrahi reflected pragmatic inclinations similar to those of the Mapai party, with an extremely right wing line. Most Mizrahi members supported offensive activities against the Palestinians during the widespread civil disobedience of 1936–39. Most members also rejected the proposed British partition plan of 1937. This did not, however, affect the coalition between the Mizrahi movement and the Mapai party, which was so strong that it eventually (1953) won total control over the Zionist organization.

The Hapoel Hamizrahi Movement was established in 1922 by groups of religious Jewish workers in Palestine. The Hapoel Hamizrahi adopted a Labor oriented religious vision – a synthesis between modern socialist views and Torah laws. Members did not find it easy to merge either with the bourgeois Mizrahi movement or with the secular Zionist organization. Nevertheless, the Hapoel Hamizrahi engaged in the main projects of the Zionist movement in the country, including involvement in organized agricultural settlement and in the Haganah – which saw itself as responsible for

Jewish self-defense. Because of its involvement in these activities, the Hapoel Hamizrahi resembled the secular Zionist movement. This resemblance helped the movement establish itself as an influential political entity; it also aroused the envy and anger of the Mizrahi movement. The political stands taken by the Hapoel Hamizrahi became more moderate in light of its affinity with the secular Zionist left. In the 1930s, the influence of the Hapoel Hamizrahi increased and it won stronger representation within the Zionist movement.

From the early 1930s through the 1940s, circumstances were more amenable for ending the British Mandate and establishing an independent Jewish political entity in Palestine. Internal discussion and debate on the nature and character of the forthcoming Jewish state increasingly occupied the Mizrahi and Hapoel Hamizrahi movements (Owna, 1984). Differences of opinion on these issues emerged between the religious Zionists and the Agudat Yisrael. The latter focused their efforts on achieving the status of a religious minority in a secular state, while the religious Zionists sought to establish a Jewish state. These and other issues/disputes – see the section above on *Critical issues on religious party agendas* (p. 83) – have long been subjects of controversy and political crises in the State of Israel. Answers to some of the issues were defined in the status quo agreement, others are still subjects for political negotiations that have continued since the establishment of Israel.

Since the first Knesset elections, the Mizrahi and Hapoel Hamizrahi movements worked together within the "Religious Front" – the first coalition that included all religious parties. The view of these religious elements was that the character of the state is molded within the government not outside it; this view motivated a historical agreement among the orthodox religious parties that involved compromises by the different streams. This agreement enabled the religious Zionist parties to secure about half of the total 16 seats won by the Religious Front party, as a whole. The religious Zionist parties joined the Ben-Gurion coalition during the period of the first Knesset since the Prime Minister preferred a coalition with the religious party rather than with the leftist Mapam party.

The first Israeli government experienced bitter disputes over a range of religious matters that remain unsolved and continue to cause conflict and tension. These disputes occurred on two fronts: between the religious parties themselves and between the religious parties and the ruling Mapai party. The following are a few examples of the foci of these disputes – each was addressed in greater detail earlier in this chapter:

- conflict on ratifying the Shabbat (Saturday) Observation Law countrywide. Attempts at an agreement enforcing this law on the national level did not succeed;
- differences over the Labor and Rest Law, adopted in 1951 to deal with prohibiting the employment of Jews on Saturday;

- the struggle over the nature of education provided to the children of Jewish immigrants in the temporary transit camps in the early days of the state;
- the issue of mobilizing women for military service.

In the second Knesset election, the different religious factions ran separately. The Hapoel Hamizrahi party established itself as the dominant stream in the religious community when it won eight seats in the Knesset. The Mizrahi, who enjoyed a close relationship with the Jews in the Diaspora, secured only two seats in the election. The orthodox religious parties did not join the fourth coalition government. In 1956, the National Religious Party (NRP) was established. The NRP subsumed both the Mizrahi and Hapoel Hamizrahi factions. In a joint bloc called the "National Religious Front," the NRP won 11 seats. Hapoel Hamizrahi, the youngest of the religious Zionist streams, should have been capable of addressing socio-political as well as religious issues. However, in addition to religious subjects, it preferred to focus on foreign policy and security, rather than on social issues.

While in office, the NRP underwent many ideological changes.[5] The major change occurred with the June 1967 war: the NRP was transformed from a movement focused on preserving the Jewish character of the state into a pioneer of Israeli settlement policy in the newly occupied territories. The party was vehemently opposed to any political solution based on Israeli withdrawal from the West Bank and Gaza Strip.

The younger, Israel-born members of the religious Zionist movement developed the opinion that the NRP was not preserving the Torah laws (Israeli, 1990). These youths rejected the status quo agreement regarding the Shabbat. For example, they argued that there was no justification for violating the holy Shabbat by using a car on that day. Groups of young NRP members – graduates of the "Gahalit" forum (Oren, 1987) and the Merkaz Harav Institute – a stronghold of Rabbi Tsvi Neria – learned the theory of Rabbi Abraham Kook that, "there can be no separation between the land and the people," and that Messianic salvation would follow the establishment of the secular state. The ideological influence of these young NRP members began to be felt clearly in the late 1960s, particularly following the Israeli occupation of the West Bank and Gaza Strip. From that point on, the NRP became more important on the Israeli political scene.

The NRP rejected the concept of a secular national state, arguing that the time had come for a period of national salvation. In practice, this was manifested in the NRP's commitment to settlement activities over the "green line" (1967 borders). A political resolution adopted by the party in 1969 stated that, "The political and security developments witnessed by our generation in the Land of Israel are the beginning of the realization of the divine wish ... on the way to the full salvation of the people of Israel in the Land of their ancestors" (Ferber, 1973). This resolution called on the Israeli government to immediately act for the (Jewish) settlement of all the "liberated" lands in the West Bank and Gaza Strip. The resolution is considered a milestone in the development of the NRP's political and religious vision.

The establishment in 1974 of the religious Zionist settler movement, "Gush Emunim" – many of whose activists came from the NRP – posed a challenge to party leadership. Following the October 1973 war, Gush Emunim members embarked on the establishment of new settlements in the West Bank and Gaza Strip. The NRP's open support for this project and full participation in it came at the time when the party was a member of the government coalition led by the Labor alignment, under the leadership of Yitzhak Rabin. Conflict within the NRP between veteran and younger members was intensifying. Tension existed between those with more pragmatic and those with more extreme outlooks. The younger elements demanded the enforcement of Israeli sovereignty over the West Bank and Gaza Strip. There was also controversy over a demand in Rabbinical circles, supported by young NRP members, to amend the "Who is a Jew?" law in an orthodox religious spirit (Israeli, 1990). However, when the NRP received the Ministry of the Interior portfolio (which had authority over the registration of citizens), NRP Minister, Yosef Burg, did not agree to deny citizenship to Jews who had not been Judaized according to the orthodox Jewish tradition. Thus, the NRP was transformed, within the right wing of the Israeli political system, into a totally pro-settler party. The party became an important and highly influential player in successive Israeli governments and functioned as the mouthpiece of the settler movement in both the Rabin and Begin governments (Owna, 1984). The NRP continued until 1976 as a reliable partner in the governments of Mapai, and later of the Labor alignment (Mapai and Mapam).

As a result of political upheaval in 1977, the rightist Likud Party was elected to office. The NRP won 12 seats in the Knesset and joined the rightist Likud government coalition led by Menahem Begin. The strong political influence of the party was manifested in its assuming two Ministerial portfolios: Interior and Education. It was the first time in the political history of Israel that the party received the education portfolio. This was an indication of the strength of the NRP. It was also the cause of its downfall; participation in a government that signed the peace agreement with Egypt resulted in an internal rift with which the party was hardly capable of coping. The old political leadership of the party, headed by Yosef Burg and Zevulun Hammer, supported the stand of Prime Minister Menahem Begin which differentiated between the importance and significance of the West Bank and Gaza Strip territories on the one hand, and Sinai on the other hand. However, in Rabbinical circles, objection to giving up any settlements was accompanied by wholesale support for the settlers and an extremist and fundamentalist ideology. During voting on the peace agreement with Egypt and the withdrawal from the Yamit settlement strip in Sinai, seven (i.e. more than half) of the NRP Knesset members voted against the agreement or abstained from voting. This outcome signaled strong opposition within the religious Zionist movement to the political positions of its leadership.

In the 1981 elections, the NRP suffered a setback; its former 11 to 12 seats declined to six. Several reasons accounted for the NRP's loss of votes:

1) the establishment of the radical rightist Techiyah party, which received support from former NRP supporters, including Gush Emunim supporters (Pedahzur, 2000). Rabbi Tsvi Yehuda Kook also backed the new political movement (Israeli, 1990);
2) the establishment of the Tami party headed by Aharon Abu-Hatziera, who had broken away from the NRP. Tami was a list of Mizrahi (Sephardi) Jews protesting what they saw as ethnic discrimination;
3) the increasing electoral power demonstrated by the Likud in the elections.

The NRP was able to sustain its status in the Likud government coalition, with three portfolios: the Ministries of Interior, Education and Religions. The moderate stand adopted by the NRP over the Lebanon war and its support for establishing a Commission of Inquiry to investigate the Sabra and Shatila massacre did not strengthen the party base. In the 1984 elections, it lost two additional seats. Perhaps former NRP voters were moving to the right or to the ultra-orthodox Sephardi SHAS party.

Under the circumstances, it is not surprising that the NRP strongly supported a national unity government and played a central role in its formation in September 1984. However, the appearance of parties such as Tami and SHAS was causing much damage to the traditional constituency of the NRP. The party was losing what had been its natural status as a national party able to tackle the problem of state–religion relations (Israeli, 1990).

The second Rabin government, established in 1992, was the first government in Israel without the participation of the NRP (with the exception of the 1984 crisis and a short break in 1974). Despite the success of the NRP in winning six seats in the Knesset, Rabin preferred a coalition with the SHAS party, regardless of its smaller number of MKs. This, of course, weakened the NRP as the traditional representative of the religious sector in the government.

As an opposition party, the NRP focused on strong protests against the central project of the Rabin government – the Oslo accords. The NRP, thus, achieved some success as a political movement with a clear line combining a religious and a political message. This stand benefited the party in the 1996 elections where it won nine seats and became a major partner in Binyamin Netanyahu's government coalition. The return of Zevulun Hammer as Minister of Education was necessary for the government as a counter balance to SHAS's educational network, which had flourished under the former Labor government. The NRP now supported Netanyahu's policies – including the Hebron agreement of 1997 and the Wye River agreement of 1998. This left a political vacuum on the right (Pedahzur, 2000) and explains the role of the new political organization that had emerged – the Techiyah. (The Techiyah consisted of politicians who had broken away from the NRP and the Likud when they were not included in the list of party nominees for the 2000 elections.) The subsequent decline of the NRP (with only five Knesset seats, one Minister and two Deputy Ministers), compared to the unprecedented success of the SHAS movement (with 17 Knesset seats, three Ministers and two Deputy Ministers), indicated a new balance of power between the religious parties.

The NRP constituted the right wing of the Barak government. When the government voted in the Fall of 1999 for the peace initiative called the Sharm el Sheikh Memoranda, four out of five NRP MKs voted against the government initiative. Barak's subsequent participation in the Camp David summit of July 2000 provided the pretext for the NRP to withdraw from the government. SHAS and the Russian immigrant bloc, "Yisrael Ba'aliyah," later followed suit and withdrew from the government coalition.

The Al-aqsa Intifada broke out in September 2000, resulting in the adoption of an increasingly right wing political stance by the Israeli public. In early 2001, a new government was established without the NRP. These events forced the party to re-evaluate its internal situation and its political stance. The extremist political positions of the NRP were being adopted by large circles in the Jewish public. Moreover, the extremist National Union party, which included religious personalities such as MK Beni Alon, was gaining in strength. The choice of Efraim Itam, a former army general, to lead the NRP, was a good yardstick for the party's political line. The political position of Itam – who for a few months was the government's Minister of Infrastructure – was so extreme that he supported the "transfer" out of the country of all Israeli Palestinians.

The second Sharon government, formed in 2003, was considered, from an economic perspective, to be one of the most extreme right wing governments in the history of Israel. The NRP was the only representative of the religious community in the second Sharon government where it held two portfolios: the Ministries of Housing and Social Welfare. The party's position provided some worthwhile political privileges. The inclusion of a woman – Gila Frankenstein – in the party's Knesset list, also constituted a precedent for the religious party.

In addition to the coalition agreement signed with the Likud, the NRP signed a separate bilateral agreement with the secular Shinui party. This agreement was reminiscent of the coalition between the Religious Front and the General Zionists in the governments of the 1950s. In each case, the religious party joined a coalition that mainly represented the secular middle class. The NRP–Shinui coalition might have signified a moderate and flexible stand by the NRP, or it might have become a point of internal and external friction for the party. In reality, the Shinui Ministers set out to fight what they saw as religious coercion and a coalition crisis broke out over the right of Jews to work on Shabbat. During the period of this government two NRP Ministers voted against plans that would harm the interests of the poorer sections of the population. Here, it appeared in the spirit of Hapoel Hamizrahi as a social-oriented party.

Finally, the history of the NRP bears witness to many fundamental changes, both in the religious and in the political spheres. These can best be understood in the context of the party's approach to the relationship between Church and state. This approach is what distinguishes the NRP both from other Zionist parties and from the orthodox religious parties. It is this approach that shaped the NRP's historical path. For instance, the NRP created political crises within the government around issues such as education, the Shabbat, Kashrut and so on. As long as problems of religion and state continued to be priority subjects on the Israeli political agenda, the NRP retained its significance. The stability of the political system in Israel was contingent, to a considerable extent, on the NRP's readiness – or lack of readiness – to create such crises.

The character of the state has been constantly in flux as the result of immigration and globalization processes. Given the threat this flux is thought to pose to what is called Israel's "Jewish character," the possibility of future crises based on religious issues is worth mentioning.

Agudat Yisrael (Yahadut Hatorah)

The Agudat Yisrael party, recently called "Yahadut Hatorah Hameuhedet," is considered a veteran player on the Israeli political stage. Nevertheless, only a limited number of academic research works have attempted to analyze the orthodox Ashkenazi religious parties (Horowitz, 2002). Orthodox individuals in Israel are considered as "others" or "outsiders" due to their traditions, dress and geographical distribution; this and other factors might explain why the secular community does not view the Agudat as a subject for comparative political study.

The following discourse proceeds from the assumption that: (a) Agudat Yisrael is a legitimate party participating in Israeli political life and undergoing constant political and organizational changes; and (b) the essence of the party's existence is its opposition to accepting the Israeli Zionist movement as representative of the Jewish people. This opposition, though it appears futile in light of the situation in "Eretz Yisrael" during the present century, is based on thousands of years of traditional belief in the Torah and divine law.

Agudat Yisrael was established in 1912 as a reaction to the enlightened secular and Zionist movements that were increasingly dominating the Diaspora Jewish communities. Thus, even from its early days, Agudat Yisrael constituted a reaction to secular Zionism; it was a meeting ground for different religious Jewish streams that had in common a fear of losing Jewish tradition. Agudat Yisrael opposed the cooperation between the Mizrahi members and the Zionist movement and attempted, in its founding conference, to find common ground between East and West European Jews. The same conference (Owna, 1984) addressed relations between the Rabbinate and the political sphere by establishing a Commission of prominent Rabbis to provide both spiritual and political guidance to the movement (Horowitz, 2002). The problems of establishing the spiritual leader's authority over political issues will be discussed later.

Following World War I, the movement established a stronger presence among the veteran Jews in pre-Zionist Palestine, especially the orthodox Jews living in the four "Holy cities" of Hebron, Jerusalem, Safed and Tiberias (Fond, 1989). The immigration of Rabbis from Poland, Lithuania and Germany in the 1920s and 1930s also strengthened support for Agudat Yisrael.

Some of the Agudat leaders favored giving priority to the "Land of Israel" in the party's platform. However, there were differences within the movement about the appropriate degree of cooperation with the Zionist movement, which was gaining strength in Palestine. The Agudat leadership adopted varying positions regarding the relationship between the "People of Israel" and the "Land of Israel."

Just as a labor wing of Mizrahi was established, a new movement of Agudat Yisrael workers (Poalei Agudat Yisrael) was established in the early 1920s. This movement set up agricultural villages and schools and workers' neighborhoods (Tellme and Tellme, 1982). In the mid-1930s, the Agudat, as a national party, competed with the Zionist movement in claiming to represent the Jewish people before the British authorities. At the third conference of Agudat Yisrael, held in 1937, a major discussion occurred on the issue of Jewish statehood. Some opposed the establishment of such a state; others supported it on the condition that it be a Torah state; still others supported the establishment of a Zionist state. The question remained whether senior Torah scholars could rule and make decisions on decisive issues regarding Zionism.

The political Agudat leaders established good relations with the leadership of the Zionist settlement community. The most prominent leader at that time was Rabbi Yitzhak Meir Levine, who – with his special understanding both of political affairs in Eretz Yisrael and the situation of European Jewry – was considered the grandfather of Agudat ideology.

The Mizrahi and the Agudat clearly differed with regard to their policies on statehood (Owna, 1984). Mizrahi attempted, not totally successfully, to draft a Torah-based code of constitutional laws for the future state. Perhaps mistakenly, Agudat ignored this issue and focused, instead, on ensuring the rights of ultra-orthodox (Haredi) Jews in the upcoming secular state. However, the holocaust in Europe transformed the map of the Jewish people. One of its consequences was to make the population in which

Agudat Yisrael functioned a minority among the Jewish people. Thus, the previous orthodox majority became a minority, struggling against the political hegemony of Zionism. In fact, among the Haredim, a stereotype was disseminated that the Zionists had abandoned them in face of the Nazi holocaust.

With the termination of the British Mandate in Palestine, just before the establishment of the State of Israel and the development of state institutions, representatives of Agudat Yisrael participated in the interim State council. This period in Agudat was characterized by a positive attitude toward the Zionist movement, by the silence of Torah scholars, and by the granting of autonomy to the Agudat political leadership (Horowitz, 2002). Vague talk persisted about the possibility that the establishment of the state indeed heralded the long-awaited salvation of the Jewish people.

In the first session of Israel's Interim State Council on May 16, 1948 (Owna, 1984), the representative of Agudat Yisrael announced that, in spite of the despicable secular nature of the Declaration of Independence and its failure to address the religious nature of the Land of Israel, Agudat would sign the document. The party explained that not signing might be interpreted as verifying the differences among the Jews concerning the Land of Israel. After the establishment of the state, the movement gained strength, though it did not abandon its opposition to Zionism. Agudat Yisrael was a full partner in the process of establishing Israel's governing institutions. It participated in the first Israeli government as part of the Religious Front and Rabbi Isaac Meir Levine assumed the post of Minister of Social Affairs.

However, there were grave differences between the religious Zionists and the ultra-orthodox Jews. For example, mainly because of problematic relations between the state and the Jewish religion, no constitution had been adopted for Israel. However, unlike the Mizrahi, the Agudat, in 1950, categorically rejected the idea of a secular constitution that organized the life of the society and the state on a non-Torah basis (Owna, 1984). Controversy over compulsory military service, particularly for women, was another issue that highlighted internal differences within Israeli society. The Rabbi known as "Hazon Ish," the supreme spiritual authority in Agudat Yisrael, considered the issue of mobilizing women in the Israeli army (IDF), as well as an alternative suggestion for religious girls called "national service." Activists in the Agudat Yisrael believed that enlisting women in the IDF totally contradicted the role of the woman in Judaism according to the Halacha. On the other hand, Hapoel Hamizrahi people supported the idea as long as there would be a suitable framework for religious girls. Ultimately, Ben-Gurion's concept of gender equality prevailed and the Military Service Law was adopted despite the reservations of the Religious Front.

Mobilizing men for IDF service was a different issue. Release from the army was granted for about 400 students from Yeshivot – followers of Agudat Yisrael. This decision by the authorities to allow evasion of army service in certain circumstances created a gap between Hamizrahi and Agudat members. The Mizrahi struggled for the rights of religious soldiers, either in regular military units or in special military units established for the religious. The Agudat, on the other hand, rejected military service altogether, considering it irrelevant to the religious way of life. They believed that all Jews who carried out their religious duties served the Jewish people no less than IDF soldiers.

Ideologically, Agudat Yisrael was not enthusiastic about unity with other religious streams. Nevertheless, the party had an interest in preserving the parliamentary framework of the religious bloc. Yisrael won three seats, while Poalei Agudat Yisrael won two seats. The two parties joined the government coalition and served in the Ministries of Social Affairs and the Ministry of Education (as Deputy Minister). The party made two major demands: that the adoption of the official Education Law and the adoption of the National Service Law for girls be postponed (Fond, 1989).

Agudat Yisrael opposition to the Education Law and the National Service Law for Girls

Education was always a major concern of the Agudat; it strongly opposed the government's proposed Education Law because of its secular and national concepts. Although Agudat Yisrael was outside the government when the Education Law was adopted in 1953, the Law took into consideration the party's demands. Accordingly, the government acknowledged, in its legislation, two official education frameworks: the official and the independent. The latter catered to Agudat Yisrael schools. The Agudat schools did not have to follow the Ministry of Education curriculum. Winning autonomy with regard to the curriculum and to government subsidies (Warhaftig, 1973) was certainly an achievement for the movement and bolstered its strength. However, the Agudat Yisrael movement remained adamant in its opposition to adoption of the National Service Law for girls.[6] In the summer of 1952, following passage of the Law, Agudat Yisrael withdrew from the government. Interestingly, this was the last time that Agudat Yisrael had a Minister in the Israeli government.

Government involvement of the Agudat Yisrael

Although it did not have another Minister, the Agudat Yisrael maintained its involvement in the government. For example, in the third and fourth Knesset elections of 1954 and 1959, the Agudat Yisrael and the Poalei Agudat Yisrael, under the authority of senior Torah scholars, ran together in a bloc called the Torah Religious Front (Fond, 1989). In 1960, Prime Minister David Ben-Gurion included representatives of Poalei Agudat Yisrael in his government.

In an important conference of all Agudat Yisrael representatives held in

Jerusalem, most of the speakers, in light of the bitter struggle over the nature of the state, called for the party's continued participation in Israeli political life (Fond, 1989). This Haredi conference also affirmed the movement's Zionist spirit when it called upon ultra-orthodox Jews throughout the world to immigrate to Israel. In effect, discussions about rejecting the concept of the state or of rejecting Zionism became more marginal in Agudat and the movement's participation in the Knesset and in government came to be taken for granted. Agudat and Poalei Agudat Yisrael joined the national consensus in calling for Jewish immigration and supporting settlements (Fond, 1989). Thus, Agudat Yisrael, which had originated in European countries of immigration and its sectarian Ashkenazi character were to provide the basis for formation of the Sephardi SHAS movement.

When political change in 1977 brought Menahem Begin to power, the new Prime Minister invited representatives of the Agudat to participate in his government coalition. They did so; however, it is important to point out that they did not assume any Ministerial portfolio in the government. To do so would have signified their acknowledgment of the Zionist state. In a tradition established in the eighth Knesset and maintained in the ninth, the representative of Agudat Yisrael assumed the post of Chairman of the Finance Committee. From this vantage point, the Agudat strove to promote the demands of the ultra-orthodox Haredi Jewish communities. Participation in the government coalition allowed the party to enjoy many benefits – particularly with respect to budgetary allocations. Specifically, the movement's religious schools and institutions began to obtain funds and large subsidies from the state. Additionally, the custom of postponement, and eventually exemption from military service for religious youths was widely practiced during those years under Ministers of Defense Ezer Weizmann and Ariel Sharon. Also worthy of note was the decision, made during the period of the ninth Knesset, to stop flights by El-Al, the Israeli airline, on Saturdays. Finally, having been led by Ashkenazi leaders since its establishment in Western Europe, Agudat Yisrael continued to practice ethnic discrimination in its educational apparatus. Although some Jewish students from Islamic countries were allowed to study in its schools, the immigration from Islamic countries was not well represented in the institutions of the Agudat Yisrael.

During the 1980s, the ultra-orthodox communities witnessed unprecedented internal divisiveness involving, among others, the Chief Sephardi Rabbi, Ovadiya Yosef, and the powerful Ashkenazi Rabbi, Elazar Schach. Rifts were grounded both in personal struggles over their status and in longstanding historical religious differences (Rahat, 1998) and were reflected in the relations among these representatives of the different factions in the Knesset. One result of the complicated relations among the ultra-orthodox communities, where competing factions regularly made and broke coalitions, was the appearance, in the eleventh Knesset (1984) elections, of a new Sephardi party, SHAS. SHAS became increasingly associated with the name of a charismatic Rabbi, Ovadiya Yosef. Agudat Yisrael received only two seats in these elections while the SHAS movement won four seats. Two more seats went to smaller religious factions.

In another surprise move, before the elections to the twelfth Knesset, Rabbi Schach initiated a new Ashkenazi Haredi election bloc called "Degel Hatorah." Using his influence among the graduates of Ashkenazi and Mizrahi (Sephardi) religious schools, the Rabbi's faction was able to win two seats in the Knesset. This achievement, however, did not weaken the Agudat Yisrael, which won over former members of Poalei Agudat Yisrael and extended its influence to new communities, including development towns. The three parties – Degel Hatorah, Yahadut Hatorah and SHAS – received 13 Knesset seats in the twelfth Knesset (Don-Yihya, 1988)

During the coalition negotiations with the Likud party, representatives of the Agudat presented their demands for amending the, "Who is a Jew?" Law so as to acknowledges Jews only according to the orthodox "Halacha" (Don-Yihya, 1988). However, the Likud leader, Yitzhak Shamir, decided to renew his national unity government with the Labor alignment, forcing Agudat Yisrael to accept the role of marginal partner in the extended government coalition.

The group's partnership in the government of national unity ended in November 1989, following a year of deteriorating relations with Prime Minister Shamir because of his unwillingness to change the "Who is a Jew?" law. Strong influence was exerted by the orthodox Haredi parties as a balancing factor between left and right factions in the Israel political arena. Political instability reigned. However, "partnership" of sorts existed between the Likud and the Labor alignment in the national unity government, although they could not agree on the procedures or the goals of the peace process. This situation encouraged implementation of Shamir's favored policy of procrastination.

The 1990s witnessed a tangible change in the trends of Agudat's political activity. In the spring of 1990, the Labor party leader, Shimon Peres, planned – along with the SHAS leader, Arye Deri – to bring about the collapse of the national unity government in which both were members. Their intent was to gain the support of the ultra-religious parties for a government in which they would serve alongside the Labor party. At that time, the Rabbis were considered "dovish" concerning the future of the West Bank and the Gaza Strip, based on the religious precept that preserving Jewish lives was more important than retaining territories. In March 1990, the national unity government collapsed following a vote of no confidence in the Knesset – a first in the history of Israeli governments (Rahat, 1998). Peres then embarked on negotiations with SHAS to form a new government. However, Rabbi Schach sabotaged the idea of a Labor and ultra-religious coalition by withholding the support of his Degel Hatorah party, whose participation was crucial for the formation of a governing coalition headed by Peres. Disgusted with the secular liberal character of the Labor party, the aged Rabbi delivered a famous anti-secular speech at the Yad Elyahu stadium in Tel Aviv. He launched an all-out attack on "those who eat pig meat and rabbits" and castigated secular culture, which he accused the Kibbutzim and the secular Jews of cultivating.

Peres then began to negotiate with Agudat Yisrael (Rahat, 1998), whose many demands in all fields of life were accompanied by the demand to control two important ministries: Housing and Social Welfare. In spite of the willingness of senior Torah scholars to join the government, not all of the movement's MKs agreed. Agudat demanded increased state subsidies for its schools. It also demanded funds to meet the housing needs of young religious couples who could not live in secular neighborhoods – a demand that later led to the establishment of "orthodox cities" in the West Bank (e.g. Betar Elite and Emanuel). In the 1990s, Agudat adopted outright right wing political positions and spoke out against the Oslo accords (Horowitz, 2002).

When it was decided that the Prime Minister would be chosen via direct election, the ultra-orthodox Jews found it difficult to recommend a secular candidate – whether he was from the left or right. Nevertheless, despite Rabbinical reservations against such voting, the 1996 orthodox vote went overwhelmingly to the rightist Binyamin Netanyahu. When Netanyahu formed his government, Yahadut Hatorah received the post of Deputy Minister of Housing and thus, the chance to cater to the housing needs of the orthodox community.

In spite of its clear right wing inclinations, the Yahadut Hatorah (Agudat Yisrael and Degel Hatorah) joined the government coalition formed by Ehud Barak in 1999. This participation was to be short-lived because the SHAS party was stronger and much more important in the coalition. In 2001, Yahadut Hatorah representatives returned to assume the posts of deputy ministers in the Ministries of Housing and Education.

In sum, Yahadut Hatorah (Agudat Yisrael) shifted over the years from opposition to the Zionist movement to accepting representation in the Israeli government. It changed from the party of a Rabbinical Ashkenazi "elite" into a party with supporters throughout the country and in many sectors of Israeli society (Horowitz, 2002). Yet, the party retained its belief that while the Jewish Torah was eternal, the Jewish national movement – Zionism – was merely a temporary phenomenon. As a result of its need for budgets from the state, however, the orthodox community became more open to the secular world and had to recognize the daily authority of the state. The Agudat Yisrael or Yahadut Hatorah movement had to fight for votes in the elections and there was no longer any possibility of its abandoning the political arena.[7]

SHAS movement[8] *– Sephardi Torah guardians*

The emergence of the SHAS movement on the Israeli political arena can be considered as one of the most important developments in the state's political history. It changed the religious "balance of power" and rules of the game in the political life of the country. SHAS emerged, not only from a religious backdrop, but as an outcome of the socio-economic rift in Israeli society. In projecting itself as representing oppressed Jewry (mainly Oriental or Mizrahi), SHAS set a precedent and presented a formerly unheard-of socio-political platform.

The establishment of SHAS[9]

SHAS was officially established as a political movement in 1984, following an agreement between two senior Israeli Rabbis: Rabbi Ovadiya Yosef and Rabbi Eliezer Schach. Rabbi Yosef was a highly popular personality among the Mizrahi Jewish communities. He developed feelings of sectarian prejudice following difficulties he encountered during his youth in efforts to win recognition for Sephardi orthodox institutions. In the 1960s he was appointed Chief Rabbi for the city of Tel Aviv. Rabbi Yosef's writings and religious rulings gained much popularity, particularly because of his readiness to make the Halacha compatible with modern times.

In 1970, Rabbi Yosef was awarded the Israel Prize and embarrassed Prime Minister Golda Meir by refusing to shake hands with her. In 1972, Rabbi Yosef was elected to the position of Chief Sephardi Rabbi (alongside Rabbi Shlomo Goren, Chief Ashkenazi Rabbi). Since the law prevented him from a second term of office, Rabbi Yosef decided to capitalize on the respect he had won and break away from the Rabbinical "establishment." He saw systematic discrimination against Sephardim in the independent religious educational system. Rabbi Yosef was admired as a spiritual leader, but was being drawn into the political arena. His major long term plan became to revive Mizrahi Jewish traditions, under the slogan of "restoring the crown to its old glory."

Rabbi Eliezer Schach was the leader of the orthodox Ashkenazi camp of the "Lithuanian" community. This community had struggled since the nineteenth century in Europe against so-called "Hasidim." However, the Knesset had equal representation of "Hasidim" and "Lithuanians"; thus, in spite of internal tension between these factions, Agudat in Israel, united by its anti-Zionism, sought to bridge the division. When Rabbi Schach decided to withdraw from the Torah Scholar's Council of Agudat Yisrael and to seek support in wider circles that included traditional Mizrahi and even secular Jews, Agudat, which had represented the orthodox Jewish world for so many years, faced major internal divisions.

SHAS involvement in the government

Thus, both these influential Rabbis – Yosef and Schach – shared some common ground in their political activity. In the eleventh Knesset elections in 1984, the SHAS party list included, for the first time, supporters of both

Rabbis. The movement surprised everyone when it won four seats (compared to only two seats for Agudat Yisrael). An analysis of the voting trends showed that about one-third of those voting for SHAS had supported Agudat, one-third had supported the Likud and one-third had supported the NRP and the Mizrahi "Tami" lists (Dayan, 1999). The SHAS movement joined the national unity government of 1984, as a marginal partner for the Likud; Agudat Yisrael rejected participation in the government. After receiving the Ministry of Religion, SHAS finally won the more important and influential Ministry of the Interior, which, among other things, controlled municipal affairs. Thus, the party began to realize the Mizrahi religious "revolution" of which Rabbi Ovadiya Yosef had always dreamt.

SHAS spokesmen were wont to make provocative statements in the Knesset that aroused stormy responses. For example, one SHAS MK blamed the high Israeli casualties in the Lebanon war on the IDF's acceptance of women for military service. Another SHAS MK attributed a fatal road accident to permitting the opening of cinemas on Saturday in Tel Aviv. Everything in secular Israeli life was subject to the party's criticism.

The appointment of SHAS leader Rabbi Peretz as Minister of the Interior was unprecedented insofar as it was the first time that this post, with its sweeping powers, was occupied by a non-Zionist personality. Secularist fears that this could lead to an orthodox-oriented change in the very character of the state were exaggerated; SHAS representatives did not attempt to change the status quo with regard to relations between religion and state. Instead, they set about building a social and organizational base for a popular movement motivated by the vision of Rabbi Ovadiya Yosef. The organizational tool for the realization of this concept was the movement called "Hama'ayan" (Hebrew for "the Spring"). Hama'ayan was actually a network of popular centers that provided a variety of services. There were centers for teaching Torah (and other subjects), clubs for pensioners, and other educational and cultural projects. The aim of Hama'ayan was to revive Mizrahi Jewish tradition and culture and to tackle the financial and economic crisis they faced. Rabbi Yosef sought to end dependence on the government establishment through fostering an autonomous organization promoting his vision of traditional Jewish values, respect for the family and respect for the religious culture of the Jewish people. The Hama'ayan movement was run by the dynamic young Director-General of the Ministry of the Interior, Arye Deri.

The spiritual ascendance of Rabbi Schach was taken for granted in the orthodox community; even Rabbi Yosef did not publicly challenge it. Nevertheless, Rabbi Yosef's host of supporters still considered him their real leader. Over the years, SHAS also established itself within the religious establishment, winning growing support from neighborhood Rabbis and in religious councils. Toward the twelfth Knesset elections in 1988, Rabbi Schach surprised Rabbi Yosef by declaring the establishment of a new orthodox party, Degel Hatorah. Degel Hatorah was an Ashkenazi party, whereas Rabbi Schach had formerly encouraged his Mizrahi supporters to vote for SHAS. His break-away, made without discussions with Rabbi Yosef, harmed the Sephardi Rabbi. Nevertheless, the orthodox parties won an unprecedented 13 Knesset members; SHAS increased its seats from four to six. The election results reflected the growing strength of ultra-orthodox Jewry. SHAS, in spite of its ideological opposition to Zionism, now appeared as a broadly based orthodox national movement. SHAS joined the Likud-led national unity government and Arye Deri did not hesitate, as Minister of the Interior, to cater for SHAS's interests (Dayan, 1999). For example, he increased the branches of the Hama'ayan school system throughout the country. Although devoted to Rabbi Yosef, Minister Deri also enjoyed good relations with secular politicians and with the media. SHAS, unlike Agudat Yisrael, had no ideological scruples that kept it from maneuvering in coalition party negotiations.

In mid-1989, Shimon Peres and Arye Deri embarked on a plan to bring about the collapse of the national government in which they were partners. They declared that they were opposed to Yitzhak Shamir's policy toward the Palestinians. Cooperation between SHAS and the Labor party was politically possible (Corney, 1994) given Rabbi Yosef's dovish statements in the late 1980s (when Rabbi Schach had shown no interest in the issue of the West Bank and Gaza Strip). Deri demanded from Peres increased budgets for SHAS, three SHAS Ministers (including Deri as Finance Minister), more finance for Hama'ayan, more jobs for SHAS people in the Rabbinical establishments and so on (Rahat, 1998). However, it seems that Deri had gone too far in agreeing to join a leftist government. As noted previously, at the rally held in the Yad Elyahu stadium, Rabbi Schach made his famous "rabbits speech" in which he defended " the Jewish nature of the state," named the secular camp as the primary enemy, accused the Kibbutzim and the left parties of denying Judaism, and ignored the issue of the West Bank and Gaza Strip. In the end, the SHAS–Labor plan failed and Shamir formed a rightist government, with the participation of SHAS. Thus began another stage in the development of SHAS; under the leadership of Rabbi Yosef and Deri, the influence of Rabbi Schach began to wane and it was now Rabbi Yosef who constituted the supreme religious authority. Yosef and Deri set out to establish an educational apparatus that incorporated Mizrahi Jewish values and enjoyed the support of the state.

In the 1992 elections, SHAS attained six Knesset seats but could do no better against the united Ashkenazi Degel Hatorah and Yahadut Hatorah group, which won back the supporters of Rabbi Schach. SHAS was the only religious party to join the leftist government coalition established by Yitzhak Rabin following the 1992 elections. Rabin's government declared its readiness to reach a peace agreement with the Palestinians and make "concessions" over the territories that had been occupied in 1967. The government needed the support of SHAS, which was able, in the coalition agreement, to establish an orthodox Education Department as part of the

Ministry of Education. The Education Department enjoyed considerable authority and was directed by a SHAS representative. I noted previously that the injustice done to the Mizrahi students in the education institutions of Agudat Yisrael was one of the major factors behind the establishment of the SHAS movement. Now the tables were turned and the Agudat Yisrael educational institutions came under the authority of SHAS representatives (although this plan was aborted following an appeal by Agudat Yisrael to the High Court).

The Hama'ayan educational apparatus was established in 1998 (Elan, 1999). By the end of the period of the Shamir government (Elan, 1999), Ma'ayan was granted recognition equal to that of the Agudat's educational network in terms of funding, recruiting students and so on. A SHAS Deputy Minister of Education received virtual autonomy in planning and running the network. It was responsible for some 3000 teachers and many thousands of students. While the Agudat Yisrael educational institutions targeted orthodox boys following in the path of their parents, the Ma'ayan Hachinuch network sought to allow every Jewish boy to register. The pupils enjoyed a long day in smaller classes than in the official educational institutions, in addition to free meals and transportation to and from school.

The leftist Education Minister, Shulamit Aloni – leader of Meretz and a champion of civil rights and pluralism – was a source of unease for Rabbi Yosef, who demanded and eventually received Aloni's removal to a different Ministerial post. Prime Minister Rabin was busy lobbying to ensure a majority in the Knesset for ratifying the Oslo agreements. This subject posed a difficult challenge for SHAS. Opposition to the SHAS's support of the Oslo agreements came from orthodox and rightist circles and included many SHAS voters – some with extreme right wing and racist leanings.

Leading orthodox Rabbis, led by Rabbi Schach, strongly opposed returning the West Bank and Gaza Strip to the Palestinians. The religious Zionist representatives and especially the Jewish settlers in the occupied Palestinian territories, waged a vicious media campaign against the government and put strong pressure on SHAS to withdraw from the government. In the 1990s, a cult of nationalist orthodox Jews developed as part of the public that supported SHAS.

In effect, as of September 1993, when the Gaza-Jericho agreement was signed, the SHAS movement was not part of the government. In the summer of 1993, following a criminal investigation begun in 1990, the Attorney General formally charged Arye Deri, who tendered his resignation and withdrew from the government in hopes that SHAS would continue obtaining government subsidies for its institutions without having to shoulder any responsibility for the Oslo agreements. Yosef and Deri were cautious in the political sphere and refrained from voting for or against any important political agreement (Dayan, 1999). On the issue of the Golan Heights, SHAS supported the right wing. Perhaps more important, the movement continued its day-to-day work with the under-privileged sectors in Israeli society.

In the 1996 elections – the first direct elections of the Prime Minister – Deri, feeling that the traditional and religious public had clear right wing inclinations, called on SHAS voters to vote for Netanyahu. Agudat did the same. Meanwhile, the lengthy trial of Deri prevented his election to the thirteenth Knesset and he was replaced in the SHAS leadership by Eli Yishai. With 10 Knesset members, two Ministers and two deputy ministers,[10] SHAS continued to appear as a champion of the oppressed Mizrahi in Israel (Dayan, 1999) and to strengthen its own educational and social institutions.[11] During the 1990s, SHAS was broadcasting on dozens of unlicensed radio stations, challenging the "Ashkenazi monopoly over the media." Rabbi Yosef's weekly sermons were broadcast from his Synagogue in Jerusalem to countless thousands of his supporters throughout the country. When the Netanyahu government lost its majority in the Knesset, SHAS refused to work for the collapse of the right wing government (Elan, 2000). Then when Deri was indicted in March 1999, Rabbi Yosef and the SHAS movement expressed their lack of confidence in the ruling of the court. Photos of Deri and the slogan, "He is innocent," featured prominently in SHAS's electoral campaign for the fifteenth Knesset. Deri was projected as an innocent Mizrahi oppressed by the elitist and arrogant Ashkenazi establishment.

The SHAS movement attained unprecedented success in the fifteenth Knesset elections (1999). The party doubled its strength to 17 Knesset seats – two less MKs than the Likud – and obtained three Ministers and three Deputy Ministers. The party joined the Labor-led government of Ehud Barak, who preferred SHAS to the secular Shinui party. However, in a dispute over the authority of SHAS's Deputy Minister of Education, the Meretz Education Minister was compelled by Barak to resign in July 2000. Also in July 2000, when Prime Minister Barak went to the Camp David negotiations, the rightist groups, including SHAS, deserted the coalition (Elan, 2000). When the rightist, Ariel Sharon, established his government early in 2001, SHAS joined his coalition and received the Ministries of Health, Labor, Social Welfare and Religion, in addition to two Deputy Ministers (Finance and Education). SHAS also won back the Ministry of the Interior, where Eli Yishai conducted a struggle over what he saw as "the Jewish nature of a state" in light of the many immigrants from the former Soviet Union, most of whom were non-Jews. His Ministry worked against granting citizenship in such cases.

In the 2003 elections, SHAS's strength declined for the first time to only 11 Knesset seats. Security and political issues, including the continuation of the Palestinian Intifada for a third consecutive year, sent many SHAS supporters back to support the Likud. Additionally, the secular liberal Shinui party won 15 seats and became a preferred partner for Prime Minister Sharon. Consequently, SHAS went into opposition.

Reflections about SHAS

A number of interesting questions arise when one looks at SHAS's history. One might ask, for example:

- How deeply rooted in Israeli society were the seeds of the revolution sown by Rabbi Ovadiya Yosef?
- Is the educational apparatus he constructed a lasting one?
- Does distancing SHAS from government benefits and subsidies threaten its ability to mobilize public support? Or does it actually assist in establishing SHAS as an opposition party with a social platform that could enter into coalition agreements with parties on the left?

Research in recent years (Dayan, 1999; Elan, 2000; Tessler, 2003) has concluded that the SHAS movement represented primarily an extremist religious phenomenon, rather than a social phenomenon fighting injustice. Supporting the Mizrahi Jews and the poor would not necessarily revolutionize the structure of the system; it could only change the distribution of resources within the existing system. The radical religious movement was a revolutionary entity that sought systematically to change the secular character of the state. It did not necessarily imply a violent revolution, conducted from outside the conventional political system. Nevertheless, the SHAS strategy of participating in government institutions and exploiting the apparatus of the state does not alter the magnitude of the change the SHAS tried to effect.

The problem of SHAS is manifested in the discrepancy between the orthodox inclinations of its leadership and the traditional – but not necessarily orthodox – approach of its voters. Although dissatisfied with it, SHAS leaders are aware that many of their supporters can be found at soccer matches on Saturdays. SHAS is a religious movement aiming to represent the man in the street and believing in a grassroots, rather than in an extremist, approach to changing the political system.

Political participation among the religious

This section deals with the forms of political participation the religious public in Israel has exhibited. Political involvement by the religious public has been analyzed on two levels: participation in party parliamentarian politics and participation in non-parliamentary politics. Party parliamentarian politics refers, in this instance, to activity directed at acquiring resources through strengthening the group's representation in the Knesset and the ruling institutions. An example of such activity is organization within the party to win voters in the Knesset and local authority elections. Non-parliamentary political participation includes political activities that are not organized by political parties nor directly controlled by them. Public demonstrations, organization within a society and other direct political actions constitute examples of this non-parliamentarian activity.

Parliamentary political participation trends

The political organizations comprised of the religious groups in Israel can clearly be considered as unique. Political parties representing different religious groups exist in various countries; however, the division among the religious groups themselves and the claims for proper representation of different religious concepts and ideologies, are special characteristics of Israeli politics. A historical view of the political behavior expressed by religious Israelis in choosing a political party, must start with a look at the Mizrahi movement – the origin of the National Religious Party (NRP). The Mizrahi movement – a bloc within the Zionist organization – was established in 1902 in reaction to the Zionist demand to make Hebrew education a responsibility of the Zionist movement. Ten years later, the Agudat Yisrael party was established as a reaction to the understanding reached between the Mizrahi movement and the Zionist organization. Some members of the Agudat Yisrael broke away from the Mizrahi and Zionist movements to join the orthodox Haredim sectors that did not participate in the Zionist movement. Thus, the SHAS movement was established in the 1980s, in part to provide solutions to the education problems encountered by Jews of North African origin while studying at the educational institutions of the Agudat Yisrael. SHAS focused its efforts on ending the monopoly of Agudat Yisrael and the NRP over the education institutions, religious councils and government departments that provided religious services.

Comparison of basic political perspectives

The NRP projected itself as a religious Zionist party with a political agenda intent on renewing Zionism and strengthening its religious character, while Agudat Yisrael started as an anti-Zionist movement in competition with other members of the Zionist movement to represent the Jewish people (Fond, 1989; Yuna, 1980). Members of the movement did not accept being identified as members of a secular Zionist nationalist movement; however, the prevailing circumstances forced them to accept Zionist ideology at least as a de facto situation. SHAS is described as a movement with a radical revolutionary Zionist inclination (Tessler, 2003). Its members do not hesitate to use Zionist stereotypes and, in fact, many of its voters describe themselves as Zionists. This portrayal, however, could be viewed as a mask camouflaging an extremist inclination – namely, to change the meaning and structure of Zionism.

Comparison of religious perspectives

Another criterion on which the religious parties may be compared is the degree of religious fanaticism represented by each party. Agudat Yisrael (Yahadut Hatorah) represents the orthodox Haredim community. The term, "Haredim community," describes a community that is afraid of any social or cultural change and is reluctant to accept such change. It is, therefore, an extremist religious party; when compared to other religious parties competing for votes in Israel, about 5 percent of Jews in Israel describe themselves as orthodox Haredim. The SHAS movement represents a different religious concept. Although its founders and leaders were brought up in the Yeshivot of the Lithuanian Haredim, the supporters of the movement portray themselves as traditional, the religious affiliation of approximately 35 percent of the Jews in Israel. The NRP is known as a party with a modern religious vision whose members observe their religious duties, yet, do not socially and culturally cut themselves off from secular society.

The Agudat and the NRP were both parties established in Europe. Both succeeded to some extent in integrating Jews of Mizrahi origin in their institutions. For example the NRP allowed a number of qualified youths of Mizrahi origin to take up leading positions within the party. One of these was Aharon Abu-Hatzeira who was appointed Minister in the first Menahem Begin government. (However, he left the NRP and established the Tami movement.)

The educational institutions of Agudat Yisrael also allowed a large number of qualified youths of Mizrahi origin to take leading positions, yet they never received the chance to win positions of political leadership or general Rabbinical authority. The most prominent among them was Rabbi Ovadiya Yosef who became Chief Sephardi Rabbi for Israel, and decided to establish a party to cater for the needs and interests of the Mizrahi Jews. The SHAS party, which he founded, is considered a success story in establishing the independence of the Mizrahi public from the authority of the Ashkenazi Jews.

Impact of religion on voting trends

Voting in the elections is considered as the major political right of citizens in democratic states, and as an authoritative tool for electing the government. The voting trends of the religious community should be examined in light of religious practices and behavior. Many researchers (e.g. Arian, 1973, 1996) have examined concepts that shape the identity and behavior of the religious. In a study that examined the relationship between religious affiliation, political stands and behavior trends, individuals in the research sample were requested to classify themselves as: (a) *ultra-orthodox*, (b) *religious*, (c) *traditional* or (d) *secular*. About 10 percent of the sample defined themselves as ultra-orthodox; 10 percent defined themselves as religious; 29

percent said they were traditional; and 51 percent described themselves as secular.

Researchers have also found a strong affiliation between individuals' religious affiliation and their beliefs (e.g. belief in an afterlife) or behavior patterns (e.g. attending the Synagogue). When Arian (1973) asked a research sample to describe the degree to which they observe traditions, 10 percent from the religious community indicated that they observe all traditions; 17 percent said they observe most traditions; 51 percent observe part of the traditions; 22 percent said they never observe the traditions. These data correspond with the conclusions drawn by Arian in 1973, indicating that the religious parties have a natural targeted community, 26–27 percent of which considers itself religious.

Nevertheless, the religious parties failed during the period of statehood to use their strength to win an appropriate parliamentary representation. The religious parties have consequently enjoyed 12 to 14 percent of the public votes in the 1950s, 1960s and 1970s. These votes went to the NRP, which enjoyed 10 to 12 seats in the Knesset, and Agudat Yisrael and Poalei Agudat Yisrael which together had between three and five seats. No change was recorded in voting trends for the nationalist-religious community after the 1977 political upheaval and the signing of the peace agreement with Egypt.

The electoral failure of the NRP in the 1981 elections was ironic. Although the NRP had facilitated the shift to a right wing government four years previously, it paid the price for its support of the peace agreements with Egypt and won only six seats in the Knesset. Many of the NRP supporters felt disappointed with the political flexibility of the party and left to support the more rightist Techiyah movement that strongly opposed returning the Sinai Peninsula to Egypt. Another reason for the decline of the NRP was the successful break away Tami movement led by Aharon Abu-Hatzeira. The Agudat Yisrael party was represented by four Knesset members that for the first time joined a government coalition headed by Menahem Begin.

The 1984 elections were a turning point in the voting trends of the religious community in Israel. In these elections the SHAS movement competed for the first time, winning four seats. SHAS candidates were backed by Ashkenazi Lithuanian supporters of Rabbi Schach, who had withdrawn from Agudat Yisrael. They also had the support of voters from the orthodox Mizrahi community, adherents of Rabbi Ovadiya Yosef.

The NRP continued to decline, winning only 3.5 percent of the votes and four seats in the Knesset. The competition between two religious factions, Morashah and Poalei Agudat Yisrael, resulted in Agudat's losing two seats. However, the total ultra-orthodox representation remained, with four seats in the Knesset.

The religious representation in the eleventh Knesset elections resulted in a situation where since non-Zionist religious MKs constituted a majority, the legitimacy of political coalition demands became a basic issue on the agenda of the religious groups. Hence the renewed participation of Agudat Yisrael in the government coalition since 1977 and the SHAS strategy of participating in various government coalitions.

In the twelfth Knesset elections, the SHAS movement became the largest religious party when it won six seats in the Knesset. Seemingly under the leadership of Rabbi Yosef and Arye Deri, the full voting potential of SHAS was realized. The traditional Mizrahi public, which isn't extremely orthodox in its daily life, finally found an attractive address for its votes. On the ultra-orthodox side, Rabbi Schach established the Degel Hatorah party that won two Knesset seats. The efforts of the Lubavitcher Rabbi in support of the Agudat Yisrael electoral campaign succeeded in strengthening the party, which won four seats in the Knesset.

The 13 ultra-orthodox Knesset members were considered a serious threat to Israel's secular Zionist character. Their increased influence and coalition demands were among the basic factors behind the reestablishment of a national unity government headed by Yitzhak Shamir. In 1992 the religious voting trend remained consistent when the Yahadut Hatorah bloc (Agudat Yisrael and Degel Hatorah) lost one seat to the NRP. On the other hand, the SHAS movement remained a natural coalition partner in every government.

The absence of the NRP from the Rabin government allowed the SHAS leaders to deepen their control over different government Ministries and department, in addition to establishing the "Ma'ayan Hachinuch Hatorani" education network, one of the long-standing basic goals of Rabbi Ovadiya Yosef. Throughout these election campaigns voting for all religious parties did not exceed 15 percent. The legitimacy of SHAS among the traditional and religious communities was fruitful in the 1996 elections when the movement received the support of 8.7 percent of valid votes, and won 10 places in the Knesset.

This was the first time that SHAS boosted its power without affecting that of the NRP, which increased its strength to nine Knesset members, or Yahadut Hatorah, which maintained its representation in the Knesset. About 20 percent of the votes went to religious parties. In the next elections of 1999 the SHAS movement continued to increase its strength, winning 17 seats in the Knesset. The NRP declined, yet the total representation of the religious parties in the Knesset rose to 27, an unprecedented number. The increase in SHAS's power is attributed to its attracting the votes of non-religious or non-ultra-orthodox voters.

SHAS's merging of the traditional-ethnic motifs contributed to its success at the expense of the Likud, which continued to decline in these elections to only 19 seats. Yet the Likud reestablished its power in the 2003 elections when Ariel Sharon headed the party. He successfully appealed to voters on the grounds of the security situation. The power of SHAS declined for the first time, and it only won eleven seats in the Knesset.

To sum up, voting for religious parties in the Knesset elections reflected the ideological and cultural divisions within the religious public itself. However, it also reflected the available political opportunities – that is, the competing parties. Thus, changes in voting trends are functions of the dynamics of the Israeli agenda. The NRP suffered electorally following its participation in governments that acted according to a particular political agenda. Throughout the period that Israel was not party to a political process in the Middle East, the NRP enjoyed the representation of the religious community in the Israeli government. As the political process gained more momentum, the party found itself having to evaluate its stance regarding its participation in decisions on regional issues.

The Yahadut Hatorah bloc (Agudat Yisrael) enjoyed a significant electoral consistency throughout the years. This can be attributed to the stable nature of the ultra-orthodox community and the relatively few internal Rabbinical crises which it experienced. Finally, the emergence of SHAS in the political arena pointed to new and different political motives: ethnic identity became an active and prevailing component in religious politics. SHAS targeted the wider community which defined itself as "traditional."

Non-parliamentary political participation trends

A non-parliamentary process that is very common among the ultra-orthodox communities in Israel is organizational meetings held with the participation of Rabbis. The participation of senior spiritual Rabbinical authorities in these meetings or rallies could strip away the political character of the event, given that religious communities consider Rabbis above politics.

On the other hand, the goals of all religious political activity are refrained with phrases that glorify the Torah and the relation between God and His people. Public rallies and meetings that are conducted with the participation of the Rabbis seek to realize general political goals; at the same time, they serve as internal tools in the religious political system. During political crises, thousands of students from religious schools come from all over the country to "listen to the words of Torah." In these cases, the Chief Rabbi utilizes his spiritual authority and charisma to demonstrate political strength. For example, since the 1950s, the Rabbis have conducted mass rallies regarding: (a) military service for women in the Israeli army; (b) education in the transit camps – the temporary housing erected to accommodate immigrants, especially the Mizrahis; and (c) the observance of the Kashrut – dietary laws – in state institutions.

In the Summer of 1952, the ultra-orthodox Rabbis of Agudat Yisrael conducted massive demonstrations to exercise pressure on the representatives of the different religious parties (Horowitz, 2002). These demonstrations established the strength of the ultra-orthodox community. They also affected relations between the Rabbis and ultra-orthodox community on the one hand, and the ultra-orthodox politicians on the other. The Rabbis considered any form of national service for women as a "red line" that must not be violated, or according to the religious expression, "that will not be allowed even at the cost of our lives" (Friedman, 1988). The issue signified the end of Agudat Yisrael's participation in the Ben-Gurion government and also an end to the religious front in the Knesset.

Another famous public rally took place in Tel Aviv's Yad Elyahu stadium in the light of a political crisis in Spring 1990. SHAS had to decide between joining a government headed by the Labor alignment or the Likud. The veteran Rabbi Schach, who was still SHAS's highest authority, gathered about 10,000 supporters to inform them of his decision to separate forever from the left wing government (Dayan, 1999; Rahat, 1998). In what has come to be known as the "rabbits speech," the Rabbi harshly attacked the secular left – especially the Kibbutzim – accusing them, among other things, of non-Jewish behavior (e.g. eating non-Kosher food). The mass rally was both a demonstration of power at the internal level in the SHAS movement and an impressive show of strength for the secular communities.

By the end of the 1990s, the Israeli High Court, which became a symbol for liberal values, enraged many in the ultra-orthodox community. The decisions made by the Court, especially those made by its head, Aharon Barak, resulted in a clash between Israeli law and Torah law. In February 1999, the religious parties organized a rare and massive demonstration before the High Court. According to the ultra-orthodox newspapers, about half a million people participated in the demonstration. Rabbis, whose differences usually stood out, united before the huge crowd to call for the establishment of the "Torah Halacha state." The rally was organized by Menachem Porush, from Yahadut Hatorah (Horowitz, 2001). Those who had organized the 1950 demonstrations remarked that the rally was a continuation of that same activity merely conducted 40 years later.

Demonstrations at friction points

There is another kind of political protest that was clearly expressed in friction points between the ultra-orthodox and the secular community. The cultural-religious differences resulted in clashes over questions like opening cultural institutions on Shabbat, working and traveling on Shabbat in "religious areas," as well as publishing advertisements harming the feelings of the religious community. This friction generated many protest activities, sometimes spontaneous, frequently becoming violent, sometimes without it always being clear who was behind the activities.

One of these friction points was the entrance to ultra-orthodox neighborhoods in Jerusalem. In the 1940s and the 1950s (Friedman, 1988: 63), demonstrations were conducted on the "Saturday avenue" on Geulah Street where these demonstrations became violent more than once. Bar-Ilan Street was also a major point of friction, after the 1967 war and the establishment of new Jewish neighborhoods to the East of the green line. This street is used by the inhabitants of Jewish neighborhoods of North Jerusalem and passes near the ultra-orthodox neighborhoods in West Jerusalem. Ultra-orthodox youths closed the road, physically prohibiting the movement of travel there, and threw rocks at passing cars. In the 1990s, public commissions (the "Shturm commission" and the "Tsameret commission") were established to define regulations for using the street on Shabbat. The commission recommended closing the street during Jewish prayer time on Shabbat and at the same time constructing an alternative road for the secular. An appeal to the High Court resulted in the rejection of the recommendation of the Tsameret commission, and it was ruled that the street remain open to traffic on Saturdays.

The ultra-orthodox community protested other secular Saturday activities as well (e.g. the opening of cinemas, theaters, other cultural institutions and so on). Local authorities flexibly used their power to issue municipal regulations concerning the opening of shops and the use of public transportation on Saturday based on the demographic structure of an area. Owners of shops and entertainment were interested in opening on Saturdays; the secular population wanted to live a normal life, with the free use of leisure activities during their weekend. The orthodox community considered these weekend leisure activities as a threat to the Jewish character of the state and as violations of the status quo in Jerusalem. Consequently, there was constant friction during the 1980s between ultra-orthodox and secular communities.

Direct action

Direct action as a protest activity intended to change a particular reality is viewed by the religious community in Israel as the most effective form of political engagement. Direct activities are not necessarily violent; yet, they challenge the present system, in general and public order, in particular. Direct action has been internationally adopted by the greens, including "Greenpeace," which sometimes conducts activities to sabotage institutions and facilities that pollute the environment.

Settlement activity in the West Bank and Gaza Strip, in spite of the occasional support it receives from Israeli institutions, is considered a direct action conducted by religious movements. As detailed in the section on Gush Emunim above, the motives of the settlers in the West Bank and Gaza Strip, especially during the early days of settlement, cannot be understood outside the context of the Messianic religious urge behind their visions (Oren, 1987; Ravitsky, 1993). The West Bank settlement of Alon Moreh, established in 1975, after a struggle against the first Rabin government, was considered a protest action and a direct clash against the authorities. The settlers considered themselves as opposition even when they joined Likud governments that totally agreed with their goals. The declared goal of the

Gush Emunim concerning the enforcement of Israeli sovereignty over the whole of "Greater Israel" was just one part of this movement's aims; the approach developed in the 1970s and 1980s viewed settlement in the politically disputed areas as merely the first stage in a much more radical, revolutionary goal.

Settlement of new areas in the West Bank is still considered a tool of political protest. Where Israelis fall victim to Palestinian attacks, the settlers speedily establish new settlement outposts to commemorate the memory of the fallen and to protest the policies of the Israeli government, whoever it may be. This form of political action encourages many non-politicized members to participate in the ideological struggle. Thus, settlements in the West Bank and Gaza Strip constitute, on one hand, political action aimed at undermining any possibility of a future political settlement; on the other hand, they promote the concept of religious salvation.

A central religious dimension is clear in the motives of Jewish groups and individuals using violence – an extremist form of political action – against Jews or Palestinians. For example, what was known as the "Jewish terrorist organization" that acted in the occupied Palestinian territories in the late 1970s and early 1980s, committed a number of terrorist aggressions against Palestinian personalities and even planned to blow up and demolish the Dome of the Rock Mosque. Another Jewish terrorist organization, whose activities were revealed in 2002–3, planned to detonate a truck inside a Palestinian school in the Tur neighborhood in occupied Jerusalem. In February 1994, Baruch Goldstein, a settler from the Kiryat Arba'ah settlement, stormed the Abraham Mosque in Hebron and shot to death 39 Palestinians who were praying inside. In 1985, the Israeli prime minister, Yitzhak Rabin, was assassinated by Yigal Amir, a student in the law college in Bar Ilan University. All of the individuals involved in these terrorist aggressions were religious Jews who acted out of a deep religious commitment to changing the political reality.

Achievements during crisis: religion and politics in Israel

The religious parties in Israel have formulated demands regarding politics, security, economy, health, immigration and other items on the political agenda. Yet, their main demands have been religious. The following discussion highlights examples of political issues that developed into crises such as the collapse of a government, early elections, withdrawal of parties from the government coalition, resignation of personalities and legislative amendments.

Education crisis: new immigrants

The 1950s witnessed a deep political crisis revolving around the character of education and the distribution of powers within the educational apparatus.

One of the problematic issues was the education provided to the sons of new immigrants in the transit camps. Immigrants from Islamic countries, most of whom were traditional Jews, were considered by the various parties as easy subjects for political mobilization. Consequently, the source and the control of their education was of great concern. Representatives of the religious front, for example: (a) alleged that Mapai activists were controlling most of the immigrants' educational institutions and preventing their receiving a religious education; (b) accused the non-religious of failing to provide the correct education to immigrants in the transit camps so that they would lose their religious identity; (c) opposed giving Labor responsibility for teaching the sons of the immigrants (Labor subsequently formed a satellite party of "Religious Workers" and Ben-Gurion stressed that it was the state, not a single party, that was responsible for religious education); and (d) maintained that religious students were forced to cut their sidelocks and that Rabbis were not allowed to visit them to organize cultural activities on Saturday nights. When a special commission, headed by judge Gad Brooklyn, investigated these accusations and reported to the Knesset in 1951 that, though the accusations were correct, the mistakes were not deliberate, these findings did not satisfy the representatives of the religious front. Consequently, they resigned from the government.

Education crisis: the struggle for power

The emergence of the SHAS movement in the political arena changed the prevailing balance between government religious education, ultra-orthodox education and general government education. The wish of Rabbi Ovadiya Yosef, the spiritual leader of SHAS, to establish a special education apparatus for Mizrahi Jewish education, had implications for the whole educational system. In 1988, the "Ma'ayan Hachinuch Hatorani" education network was established. This network supports the SHAS movement and the public/sectarian organization of SHAS "El-Hama'ayan." SHAS succeeded in winning for its newly established education apparatus equal status with government and ultra-orthodox education. In 1993, the Ma'ayan Hachinuch Hatorani educational network became an official education apparatus that enjoys government subsidies.

The struggle to control the Ministry of Education became one of the major goals of religious politics in Israel. Although the NRP was in charge and did not allow the education portfolio to go to any ultra-orthodox party, deputy ministers from SHAS and Yahadut Hatorah were appointed to oversee the education apparatus of these two movements. SHAS saw the appointment of Shulamit Aloni as Minister of Education in 1992, as a great danger. Unable to tolerate a Minister of Education who was a woman, a secularist and a liberal, SHAS threatened to withdraw from the fragile government coalition headed by Yitzhak Rabin unless he removed Aloni from the Ministry. In May 1993, Prime Minister Rabin needed SHAS's support in preparation for ratifying the Oslo agreements; consequently, he did remove Shulamit Aloni from her office and appointed her Minister of Science and Culture. Aloni was replaced as Minister of Education by Yossi Sarid, another leader of the Meretz movement. Sarid, however, demanded limits to the autonomous financial administration enjoyed by the SHAS Deputy Minister Meshulam Naharie and received no support for his demand from Prime Minister Ehud Barak, who needed to strengthen his government coalition in preparation for ratifying a possible political agreement with the Palestinians. Thus, Sarid resigned his post in the summer of 2000 and Meretz had to withdraw from the government.

The crisis of the Law of Return

The Law of Return of 1950 did not clearly state who is a Jew. Consequently, clerks at the Ministry of the Interior had make the decision in problematic and sensitive cases, such as children who had one non-Jewish parent or one not fully or properly Judaized (converted) according to the state regulations. This vagueness in the criteria for receiving citizenship caused many procedural delays and problems of registration. In January 1958, the Israeli Minister of the Interior, Bar-Yehuda (from the secular Achdut Avodah party), initiated a law stating that anyone who honestly declared that he was a Jew would be registered as such. Bar-Yehuda interpreted the law in the most liberal way. however, the NRP Minister of Religions, Zerah Warhaftig, said that his party believed Bar-Yehuda's approach violated the status quo.

Thus, in the government coalition, a crisis erupted around defining Jewish religion and nationality.

From a religious viewpoint, the phrase *Jewish nationality* has no meaning; it is not defined as Jewish religion. In effect, members of the Mapai party, most of whom were secular, opposed all compromise suggestions that included abolishing the mention of nationality from the identity card or separating nationality and religion. Government spokespersons and officials, including Prime Minister Ben-Gurion, assured the populace that the government sought only to define who belongs to the Jewish nationality, not to define who is a Jew from a Torah-religious perspective. These assurances did not satisfy the National Religious Party and the subsequent crisis caused the resignation of the NRP ministers in July 1958. Following this crisis, Ben-Gurion sent a questionnaire-like document to Jewish scholars in Israel and the Diaspora, seeking to formulate a clear answer to the question, "Who is a Jew?" Most of the answers tended to accept the strict Torah interpretation. At the end of discussions in the Knesset, Ben-Gurion announced the abolition of all regulations for registering infants who were "sons of mixed marriages" that had been passed since the establishment of the state. He said that a new chapter would be started. Still, the issue of, "Who is a Jew?" remained on the agenda.

The issue of the monk Rufeisen marked the beginning of the interference by the Israeli High Court in the issue of the Law of Return. In early 1960s Rufeisen, who was a Catholic born to Jewish parents and converted to Christianity before his arrival in the country, appealed to the Court against the Ministry of the Interior over his demand to obtain Israeli nationality. He based his case on the separation between Jewish religion and nationality. Though a Christian, he felt that he belonged to the Jewish people. In 1962, the High Court rejected his appeal, as a majority of the judges believed that the phrase Jew as known in our time does not include a person who does not accept the Jewish religion.

Nevertheless, a change occurred in the ruling of the High Court after a few years. In 1968, Binyamin Shalit, a Jew married to a Christian, appealed to the Minister of the Interior demanding that his sons be registered as Jews, without mentioning their religion, in the section of their identity cards devoted to nationality. When the Minister of the Interior rejected his demand, he appealed to the High Court. There, the Judges felt that the decision of the clerk to reject the registration of Shalit's sons as Jews was unjustified. Thus, the High Court accepted, for the first time, the division between Jewish nationality and religion. The sons of Shalit were accepted as having Jewish nationality without being considered as Jews by religion.

This was an intolerable situation for the religious parties and resulted in amending the law, to say that a Jew, "is a person born to a Jewish mother who believes in the Jewish religion as his only religion." For the first time, the law clearly stated who is a Jew.

In the 1980s, the discussion shifted to involve the issue of forms of Judaism. In 1986, Shoshana Miller, who converted to the Jewish religion according to a Reform Judaization process, demanded Israeli nationality; the registration clerk at the Ministry of the Interior added the word "converted" Jew believing that addition of the word "converted" would allow the Rabbis who registered marriages to examine the validity of Miller's conversion when she married.

The High Court decided that this registration constituted discrimination against Miller and ordered removal of the word "converted" from the record. In reaction to that ruling of the court, the Interior Minister Yitzhak Perets, who was the leader of SHAS, tendered his resignation from the government.

Crisis in the Military Service Law

The Military Service Law, first amended in 1949, constituted a major issue of secular–religious controversy. In the early 1950s, the issue of mobilizing women for military service constituted a point of friction. However, with the passing of time, a procedure was adopted that, by law, automatically exempted women from military service. A new issue emerged in the 1980s concerning releasing students from religious colleges, the Yeshivot, from military service.

According to the views of David Ben-Gurion, the Prime Minister and Defense Minister in 1949, the Israeli army had a role beyond its military function. He attributed a pioneering educational role for the army in the areas of immigration, education, settlement and culture. Based on this concept, the demand was made to implement compulsory military service for men and women alike. For security reasons, it was believed that every citizen should become used to handling arms. However, the army was also seen as a social need in the building of a society based on solidarity and equality.

The religious parties rejected the inclusion of women in any military framework, arguing that it "totally contradicts the spirit of Israel" and that "the dignity of Jewish women is in her home." Agudat Yisrael thought that conscripting women "violates the teaching of the Torah."

Those calling for passing the law agreed that married women, pregnant women, mothers or those whose religious situation prevents them should be exempted from army service. Nevertheless, this draft did not satisfy representatives of the religious front who warned against harming the religious character of the state with this law.

Differences erupted around this issue within the religious front. While the Mizrahi members, especially Hapoel Hamizrahi, sought to come up with a compromise solution, Agudat Yisrael totally opposed such a move. The highest spiritual authority for the Agudat "Hazon-Esh" not only opposed this law but described it as an issue of life or death. The tenth conference for the Hapoel Hamizrahi party in October 1949, proposed requesting the government to act for amending the law.

In the end, a temporary agreement within the front was reached to support the law, but amidst clear reservations against the article that permits mobilizing women for military service. The opposition of senior Rabbis within religious Zionism to the law disappointed Hapoel Hamizrahi and Mizrahi members, and was considered as accepting the dictates of Agudat Yisrael. In the summer of 1952 the ultra-orthodox Rabbis organized massive rallies aiming at exerting pressure on the representatives of the religious parties. In the wake of the Hebrew New Year, the Minister for Social Affairs Isaac Meir Levine from Agudat Yisrael tended his resignation. This resignation not only speeded the collapse of the government but also reflected new trends of relations both between the ultra-orthodox parties and the government, and between the different religious parties. Since then the Agudat never returned to join the Israeli governments until the Likud government was established in 1977, when the Mizrahi and Hapoel Hamizrahi parties decided to participate in the government.

In 1986 the Israeli Knesset discussed a proposal calling for the abolishment of the system of exempting Yeshiva students from military service. Minister of Defense Yitzhak Rabin agreed to discuss the suggestion within a special parliamentarian commission. This body concluded that the system of postponing military service for the students of religious schools was aimed at allowing them to complete their studies before enlisting them in the military service in a later age, and that this was not being practiced. Postponing military service was in effect being transformed into totally exempting them from that service, which created discrimination in favor of the ultra-orthodox. Moreover, this was when the secular are forced to serve as reservists for many days throughout the year. The commission recommended the reevaluation of the criteria passed in 1986, which had defined the number of those acquitted of military service to 3 percent of the total annual number of those called for military service.

The government, however, did nothing to implement the report of the commission, for members of the national unity government were wary of changing the status quo. In the 1980s the issue was discussed before the High Court, which ruled in 1988 that while it did not legally reject the agreement for exempting citizens from military service, the present situation was unsatisfactory, and if the number of exemptions was drastically increased, it would be justified to review this issue once again. In the 1990s secular pressure for abolishing the agreement increased. As Israel moved toward a more liberal economy with a shrinking state expenditure, economic pressure was exerted against subsidies for students of Yeshivot. Secular pressure was exerted against those "evading military service."

On the other hand, the ultra-orthodox realized that without military service, graduates of religious schools could not get work and could become "social problems." After the engagement of the High Court in the issue of military service during the 1980s and 1990s, an official commission headed by a retired judge, the "Tal commission," was established to discuss the issue. According to its compromise suggestion, every student of a religious institute who receives a postponement of military service (or exemption) must leave the "Torah community" at the age of 23 and spend a year in the job market. After that he could choose between two options: a compulsory military service for a short time before joining the reserves, or doing "national service" (various forms of social work) for one year. The law sought to solve social problems caused by postponing military service, yet it actually boosted inequality as it provided a legal coverage for postponing or avoiding military service.

The controversy over the differences around the "Tal law" (army service for the religious) is yet another example of a crisis: one created by secular–religious relations. In 1999, the Shinui party became the first to define itself as a secular party. In 2000, the party opposed the Tal law, considering it a dangerous precedent to acquit a complete community from military service.

The Tal law was passed in its first reading in the Knesset despite opposition by the secular Shinui movement. The Israeli government that was established in 2003 and included the NRP and the Shinui parties – with no ultra-orthodox party – stressed, in its policies, that it would abolish the Tal law.

Crisis over the status quo

Israeli political history is replete with crises erupting over the issue of observing the sanctity of the Shabbat. In the first Knesset the religious front sought to ratify the "Shabbat law" at a national level, as part of the Israeli judicial system. These efforts did not succeed. The Shabbat crisis involved violation of the day of rest both by government institutions and by secular individuals pursuing their own way of life.

The religious Israeli public has always had deep concerns regarding the observation by the state of the holiness of the Shabbat. One of the crises on this issue finally resulted in the collapse of the first Rabin government, 1974–77 (see below for details). Another example of these crises broke out in the Summer of 1999 when the Israeli National Electricity Company had to transport a massive electric generator throughout country roads. So as not to disturb the traffic, the police asked the company to do the work on a Saturday evening. This process required employing a large number of police personnel, transport and electrical workers on Friday evening. The Yahadut Hatorah bloc that was a member of the government coalition objected, newly elected Prime Minister Ehud Barak was adamant, and the crisis resulted in the withdrawal of Yahadut Hatorah from the government coalition.

On a different matter, the NRP protested against the decision of Defense Minister Binyamin Ben-Eliezer to dismantle unlicensed settlement outposts in October 2002, calling reserve soldiers to do the work on Shabbat. The state's respecting and observing the holiness of the Shabbat constitutes the essence of the concept of the "Jewish state" in the eyes of the religious parties. Crises are also very common at the municipal level. The municipal councils control rules and regulations concerning opening shops and operating public transportation on Shabbat. In most of the Jewish cities public transportation does not operate on Saturdays yet in a city like Haifa buses operate seven days a week.

One of the most sensitive friction points throughout the years has been traffic on Shabbat in Bar-Elan Street near the Meah Sha'arim neighborhood in Western Jerusalem. This street, which has been called the Saturday Street, is the focus of violent struggles between ultra-orthodox demonstrators and the police, who want it to remain open. The road is important for the secular inhabitants of the Ramot neighborhood and is near to ultra-orthodox communities. This made the traffic movement issue a very difficult one for the government.

Opening the cinemas and theaters, as well as shops and other businesses, on Shabbat has always been a friction point. Secular leisure and cultural activities on Saturdays are seen in religious circles as a threat to the Jewish character of the state and a challenge to the status quo. During the last decade a new friction point emerged with the establishment of large major shopping malls for the enjoyment of secular citizens also on Saturdays.

The Law of "Labor and rest hours" of 1953 allowed the Minister of Labor and Social Welfare to impose fines on shops and business offices who make their staff work on Saturdays. The Ministry sends inspections from the Druze community to report shops that operate on Saturdays. However, up to now these penalties have not deterred businessmen and malls from operating on Saturdays.

Soon after the establishment the second Sharon government in 2003, the NRP caused the first government crisis when the Minister of Labor, Ehud Olmert, decided in consultation with the Minister of Justice, Yosef Lapid, to stop the work of the Saturday inspectors. The two NRP ministers protested but remained in the government with an assurance that the stoppage was temporary.

The December 1976 crisis

The crisis ending the first Rabin government term (1974–77) provides a model for a political crisis caused by religious demands. The special feature of the crisis, concerned with the arrival of the F15 US made jet fighters, can be attributed to two reasons.

The active engagement of the NRP in creating the crisis was very significant. During the ten years since the 1967 war, and until the 1977 political coup led by Menahem Begin, the NRP underwent a substantial change of policy. The party ceased functioning as a natural ally for the Israeli left and adopted the ideology of "Greater Israel" and settlement in the occupied territories. The Rabin government was established in early 1974 following the resignation of Prime Minister Golda Meir. In the 1973 elections, the Labor party, in spite of criticism following the October 1973 war, succeeded in winning 51 seats, allowing the party to establish a coalition with the NRP and ensure the support of the left wing parties.

In this period, the NRP suffered from internal problems. There were differences between the veteran and youth factions and between extremist and pragmatic wings. The youth factions, including members of Gush Emunim, demanded enforcement of Israeli sovereignty over the territories occupied in 1967, with the full support of the party's leading Rabbis: Rabbi Tsvi Yehuda Kook, Moshe Tsvi Neria and Chief Rabbi Shlomo Goren. The debate resulted in the breakaway of Gush Emunim from the party. The Council of Rabbis expressed dissatisfaction over the 1970 political agreement on the Law of Return and demanded amending the law of " Who is a Jew?" in the spirit of the Halacha.

As the party took the portfolio of the Ministry of the Interior, Minister Yosef Burg sought to keep from registering as Jews, converts who did not undergo traditional orthodox Jewish conversion.

The NRP placed itself on the right of the Israeli political map. Gush Emunim's withdrawal from the NRP in 1974 and its conversion to a non-parliamentarian movement, constituted a turning point in the party's activity. The views of the Gush Emunim members were not based primarily on political or security extremism, but on concepts of religious salvation. Following the shock of the October 1973 war, members of Gush Emunim attempted to establish new settlements in the West Bank. The youth section of the NRP maintained good relations with the Gush Emunim; members of the section participated in settlement activities conducted by the Gush Emunim in 1975 in Kadum, near Nablus in the West Bank. The youth section also succeeded in convincing the older leadership of the NRP to adopt their views, even though the party was partner to the Rabin government coalition which was seeking a peace agreement.

The internal struggle within the NRP was not only centered on ideological views. The internal structure of the party was characterized by the existence of many blocs divided along demographic and other lines: Moshavim and Kibbutzim, ethnic "Mizrahi communities" and so on, youth and older members, not to speak of the influence and hegemony of leaders from different backgrounds and generations. This bloc structure defined the composition of the party conference, of the Knesset faction and of government officials. These blocs within the NRP struggled against each other, with the youth bloc, which agreed with the strong body of those supporting Gush Emunim, demanding larger representation and changes in the platform of the party.

In early December of 1976 the Israeli Air Force received a first delivery of US made F15 jet fighters, a very important military step signifying the rebuilding of the Israeli army after the 1973 war, and the strong military alliance between Israel and the United States. The first three planes were planned to arrive on Saturday evening and Prime Minister Yitzhak Rabin was to receive them in an official ceremony. This show of power was also to demonstrate Rabin's leadership of his party.

The representative of Poalei Agudat Yisrael asked the Minister of Religions, Yitzhak Raphael of the NRP, to cancel the official ceremonies or reschedule them. It was decided that the planes would land at the Israeli airport on Friday at 3pm, one hour before the Shabbat, though it was known that any delay in the ceremonies would prevent the return of the spectators from returning home before the start of the Shabbat. Minister Raphael, who was invited to the ceremony, promised to speak about this with Prime Minister Rabin. Raphael was promised that the religious Ministers would be returned home by helicopter but this was not considered a satisfactory answer.

Under pressure from the Minister of Religions, Prime Minister Rabin was persuaded to cancel the official ceremonies and to be satisfied with only an internal military ceremony. However, the invitations that were sent to a large number of citizens, and the nature of the ceremony, were not changed. About 3000 people would attend a ceremony ending one hour before the start of the Shabbat. It was clear that the large number of invitees would not be able to return to their homes by the start of the Shabbat. The Minister of

Religions demanded that Rabin clearly apologize for the event and the Prime Minister published an apology that was accepted by the religious Ministers.

A crisis was developing among the religious Knesset members. The Poalei Agudat Yisrael party, that was not in the government coalition, presented a no-confidence move against the government in order to pressure the NRP. The latter found itself in a tough situation and had to choose between supporting the government and adhering to its commitment to promote the status of religion in the state.

The Minister of Religions Yitzhak Raphael wrote that the NRP would be satisfied with an apology from Prime Minister Rabin and a commitment by him to not repeat the incident. Yet the pressures exerted by the religious public and parties forced the NRP to act in a different way. In the internal discussion within the party, Minister of the Interior Yosef Burg opposed working for the collapse of the government, arguing that the no-confidence move did not serve the goals of the NRP at that time. During the no-confidence vote in the Knesset, NRP ministers Raphael and Zvulun Hammer abstained from voting, while Burg voted in support of the government. The government survived the no-confidence vote but Prime Minister Rabin accused the NRP Ministers of violating the concept of "collective responsibility" and considered their abstention as a vote of no-confidence in the government. He therefore dismissed them.

It seems that Prime Minister Rabin had his own considerations for favoring early Knesset elections, that were scheduled for early in 1978. One of these considerations was the establishment of a new centrist party, the "Democratic Movement for Change" ("Dash") which was gaining increasing public support. The party included a large number of elite military and political leaders, as well as scholars and businessmen, mainly from the middle class. Dash demanded reform in Israel's political behavior and sought to express the public's feelings against corruption in the Labor alignment. Consequently, Rabin wanted to limit any further increase in Dash's strength by going for early elections, and he tendered his resignation. He thought this would also prevent Shimon Peres from competing against him for the leadership of the Labor party, and that he would benefit from his strong stand against the NRP.

Ironically, Rabin's plan turned out to be a total failure. Shimon Peres won the party leadership after Rabin and his family were found to hold an American bank account – contrary to foreign currency regulations. Dash, however, gained strength, winning 15 seats in the Knesset elections in 1977, including former Labor supporters.

The National Religious Party ran in the elections under the new leadership of Zevulun Hammer, who was head of the youth bloc and held extremist views. Aharon Abu-Hatzeira, who was Mayor of Ramleh and representative of the North African immigrants in the party list, also joined the party's leadership, attracting many traditional Mizrahi voters (see the section on Tami above). During the elections, the party was able to increase its representation to 12 Knesset seats instead of 10. After the elections the NRP was for the first time considered a natural ally for the Likud party (Gahal) which, until then, had formed the right wing opposition to the government.

The Likud leader Menahem Begin formed the government that was mainly based on a coalition between the Likud and NRP. The support of Agudat Yisrael from outside the coalition (the first time since its withdrawal from the Ben-Gurion government of 1952) contributed to ensuring the needed majority of the government in the Knesset. After a few months the Dash party also joined the government, ensuring a stable majority for Begin's policies.

To sum up, creating any crisis based on the holiness of the Shabbat is considered as an important electoral issue for the religious parties, in order to enable them to prove to their voters that as members of the Knesset and the government they remain faithful to the basics of the Jewish religion. Not every crisis over a religious issue brings resignation from the government. Nevertheless, crises based on religious issues can be considered a central feature of Israeli politics since the ideological essence of these crises is rooted in the basic prevailing difference between the religious and the secular in their vision for the state. The increasing engagement of the High Court in political decisions continued to constitute a subject of deep controversy. According to the religious parties, the Court is used as a tool for liberal secularism. The religious parties consider the strict judicial line adopted by the Israeli High Court during the last decade as a threat to the character of the state. The secular reaction to the political achievements of the religious parties was manifest in the 15 seats won by Shinui in its peak days, a success carrying sweeping implications for religion–state relations in the country.

Conclusion

The religious–secular fissure has always existed in Israeli/Jewish society. Already in the pre-state period there was a conflict between secular Zionist currents, on the one hand, and religious Zionists and anti-Zionists on the other. Today the Israeli political system displays a number of foci that continue this fissure. The religious bloc, which advocates subordinating social and political life in Israel to Halacha, Jewish religious law, has three main streams. The religious Zionist stream is represented in the Israeli political system by the National Religious Party. This party first contested the Knesset elections in 1956. From then until the 1980s it remained the dominant representative of the religious sector and generally won 10 to 12 Knesset seats. Its stability was the outcome of a stable and active organization that maintained a network of party activists on the one hand and avoided schisms on the other, while its Jewish-religious-Zionist ideology maintained the movement's unique character (Don-Yihya 1997: 17–18).

During the 1980s the National Religious Party underwent a series of schisms and secession of members in various directions, both rightward and leftward. The most prominent splits involved the secession by Aharon Abu Hatzeira, who established his Tami movement as a Mizrahi religious party, the establishment of Morasha and Meimad, and the defection of some of its supporters to the Likud, Tehiya and SHAS. These fissures and splits, which dominated the NRP during the 1980s, were associated with the sharpening of the debate, inside and outside the party, about the future of the West Bank and Gaza Strip, as well as with Ashkenazi ethnic hegemony and control of the party, even though a majority of its supporters were Mizrahim (ibid.: 22–23).

The second stream in the religious bloc is Haredi and anti-Zionist; its current representative in the Knesset is Yahadut Hatorah. This stream rejects Zionism and is opposed to the establishment of a political entity as a form of Jewish self-determination. It is steadfastly in favor of the application of Halacha both internally (following Halacha in practice) and externally (dress, beards, etc.) and committed to the study and dissemination of the Torah (Friedman, 1988). For many years the Haredi anti-Zionist stream was represented by two rival factions, which gnawed at each other's power: Agudat Yisrael and Degel Hatorah. They had different sources of support. Degel Hatora was supported by Ashkenazi Haredim, while Agudat Yisrael had broad support from Mizrahim as well as Ashkenazi Haredim (Friedman, 1988).

The third stream is the religious-traditional one, which has no clear positions with regard to Zionism (even though most scholars treat it as a non-Zionist stream). It is represented by SHAS. The Mizrahi Jews who immigrated to Israel in the 1950s developed in three main directions. Some experienced processes of modernization and rapid secularization and settlement in the big cities and became part of the secular Zionist-Jewish milieu in Israel. Others retained their traditional and Mizrahi customs; they settled chiefly in the development towns and came to constitute a significant share of the working class. The third group, under the influence of Ashkenazi Haredi society, became Haredim; these constitute the hard core of SHAS activists and supporters.

Against the background of intercommunal power struggles within Agudat Yisrael, Rabbi Ovadiya Yosef decided to give his patronage to a number of lists that ran in the local elections in Jerusalem and Bene Beraq in 1983 and turn them into a countrywide movement. SHAS was established in advance of the elections for the tenth Knesset in 1984. It presented itself as reshaping the unique identity of Mizrahi Jews in Israel and as aspiring to work a change in the Israeli system, challenging the Ashkenazi-secular hegemony and aspiring for a power structure balanced between Ashkenazim and Mizrahim (Dayan, 1999; Peled, 1998).

The religious bloc is opposed by the secular bloc, which places the crusade against "religious coercion" at the top of its priorities and presents this issue as part of its political propaganda. During the last two decades this bloc contained three main sub-divisions. The Zionist left is represented by Meretz, which was established in 1988 as a coalition of the Citizens' Rights Movement, Mapam and Shinui. Meretz emphasizes its unique political program, which supports Israeli withdrawal from the West Bank and Gaza Strip, and its identity as a secular party that is opposed to "religious coercion" and in favor of freedom of religion, expression and movement in Israel. Meretz draws its support from Kibbutz members, secularists in the larger cities and a few Israeli Palestinians.

The second sub-division is represented by the center-right Shinui, which seceded from Meretz before the 1999 elections and invited the journalist Tommy Lapid to head its ticket. This party takes a center-right position on the Israeli political map, but its chief calling card is its unbridled anti-religious stance (see Pedahzur and Canetti-Nisim, 2001).

The third is the Russian stream, represented by Yisrael Ba'aliyah, headed by Natan Sharansky, and Yisrael Beitenu, headed by Avigdor Liberman. Since the start of the 1990s, the immigration of about a million Russian speakers from the former Soviet Union has created a large community with unique characteristics that distinguish it from other segments of Israeli society (Al-Haj and Leshem, 2000). The Russian-speaking community has a secular orientation that was nurtured over the years by the Communist regime in the Soviet Union.

5 Russian immigrants
Imposing multi-culturalism in the public sphere in Israel

Russians comprise the second largest group of immigrants discussed in this book. Mizrahi (Orientals) and Russians tried to enforce their collective interests through ethnic policies, without changing the socio-ethnic structure of Israel. However, unlike in the case of the Mizrahi, the Israeli concept of power did not reject the Russian culture. Instead, Israel accepted the legitimacy of political organization by the Russians, thus easing their situation. The legitimacy of Russian political organization enabled the Russians to act both within parliament and outside it. This legitimacy also enabled the Russians to give strong support to Russian political parties. District analysis of the election results in the late 1990s indicates that the Russian political parties were enjoying 60 percent of the Russian immigrant votes.

Jewish immigration from the former Soviet Union to Israel took place as an outgrowth of the globalization process; the reasons behind the immigration were basically economic and were not limited to ideological reasons having to do with Zionist-Jewish nationality (Al-Haj, 2004a; Della-Pergola, 2001; Leshem and Lesak, 2000). The immigration cannot be attributed to possible danger that Jews faced in these countries; their Jewishness posed no danger in the Asian republics, nor in the European republics. The dangers they faced were mainly because they settled as Russians in republics outside Russia itself during the Soviet period. Nevertheless, the collapse of the Soviet Union resulted in a series of wars that created real security problems and a deterioration in the economic situation of citizens of the former Soviet Union. These conditions contributed to Jewish immigration from the former Soviet Union countries.

The number of immigrants coming to Israel from the former Soviet Union countries in the years 1989 to 2002 was 886,000. As with previous immigration waves, most came to Israel for pragmatic reasons (e.g. security or better living conditions), rather than for ideological reasons related to Zionism. They wanted a better future for their children. Many saw Israel as a chance to go to the West. If they had gotten the chance to go to the United States of America or Canada, half of them would have chosen to do so (Al-Haj and Leshem, 2000). In addition, Israeli state institutions and mayors of local councils exerted tremendous effort to attract immigrants into Israel;

this, too, encouraged Jews from the former Soviet Union to come to Israel and resulted in Israel's largest ever immigration wave from a single country. The immigration waves in 1990 amounted to 35,000 immigrants a month and there was talk of the arrival of not less than two million by the end of the decade. However, the first Gulf War and the relative stability in Russia reduced the number to 5000 immigrants a month in 1992 (data of the Ministry of Immigrant Absorption, 2002). In early 2001, another decline was recorded in the number of immigrants coming to Israel from former Soviet Union countries. This drop was attributed to: (a) the security threat created in Israel by the Al-aqsa Intifada; and (b) indications of stability in the former Soviet Union countries.

The immigrants from the former Soviet Union countries were not a homogeneous group; differences existed between those coming from the various European countries (80 percent of the immigrants) and those coming from Asian republics (20 percent) in terms of age, origin or family status. The character of these immigrants – especially their cultural character – made them a desired group in Israel. We must remember that the origins of Israel's founders were deeply rooted in Russia. Even the hundred years that separated the immigration of Israel's founders from the modern Russian immigration did not eliminate the longing for Russian classical culture as a common factor between the groups. Other common cultural factors between the two immigrant groups were their sense of superiority and a kind of hostility towards the Mizrahi (Oriental) Jews and the Arabs. In addition to their cultural advantage, the Russians immigrants were known to have high professional abilities. Sixty percent have academic professions compared to 29 percent of Israelis. The percentage of engineers among these Russians is very high. For example, 11 percent of the total number of workers in Israel are Russian engineers (Central Bureau of Statistics, 2000). In spite of these traits, most of these immigrants were not well to do. It seems that Israel did its best to convince them to come to Israel and agreed with the USA that they should be prevented from going to America. This process was referred to as the "Lautenberg Amendment" (November 22, 1989) (Kimmerling, 1998). From a cultural point of view, the ruling group used the arrival of these immigrants as part of its demographic war against the Palestinians, the Haredim (Jewish fundamentalists) and the Mizrahi Jews (Kimmerling, 1998).

Russian immigrants in Israel: integration or segregation?

The first wave of immigrants – 200,000 – arrived in Israel in 1966. This initial wave included Jews from the Baltic countries, Moldavia, Ukraine and Georgia. Religious and national factors were strong motives for the immigrants of the 1960s and 1970s. As of 1972, immigrants started to arrive from the central areas, especially from Moscow and Leningrad. Most of the immigrants from Russia arrived in North America and settled there as refugees;

only a very few arrived in Israel. The first wave continued through the late 1970s and knew what it wanted: this wave also had ideological motives. Some charismatic leaders were included in this immigrant wave. One could argue that Israel welcomed these immigrants for cultural and economic reasons, yet they were qualitatively incapable of establishing a viable Russian population within Israeli society. Moreover, this wave (unlike that in the 1990s) was expected to melt into the society. For these reasons, the Russian immigrants who came in the 1970s were warmly welcomed by the Israeli establishment. This wave of immigrants provided hope for future waves from the Soviet Union (Vise, 1997). It also served as a mechanism for building the Israeli settler nation in the occupied Palestinian territories, further raising hopes for the wave that arrived in the 1990s.

The early Russian immigrants, especially the elite among them, established the political and cultural institutional basis into which the second wave of immigrants was absorbed. The establishment of the "Zionist Forum," as well as the institutionalization of the Russian media by early immigrant leaders, were the means for absorbing immigrants of the second wave. Russian-speaking cultural institutions, such as the Gresher Theater, and dozens of bookstores with imported books from Russia (books written by authors in Israel) and Hebrew literature translated into Russian were established in the early 1920s. Furthermore, Russian-speaking newspapers became prolific, with one million copies per week distributed during the 1990s. *Vistee*, established by the "Yediot Tikshorit," was the most widely distributed newspaper among these. It was renowned for its high cultural standard and for its extremist right wing viewpoints. Yet, it also reflected various political and social views. Other important Russian newspapers were *Verma*, established by Anatoli Sheransky and *Novosti Nadlie*. According to statistics for the year 2000, four daily Russian-speaking newspapers, nine local newspapers and 12 local weekly magazines were published. All dealt with important issues and translated English and Hebrew articles into Russian. There were also five weekly cultural and art magazines for children.

The Russian newspapers took extremist right wing stands and were hostile towards the Palestinians. These views reflected the hostility toward anything related to Communism or Socialism that arises from the immigrants' bitter experience in the former Soviet Union (Kimmerling, 1998). Animosity toward the Palestinians can be explained as stemming (a) from a feeling, by Russian Jews, of belonging to the Jewish nationality; and (b) from a hostile stand against Islam. To these factors one might also add Russian feelings of cultural superiority and of competition with Palestinian labor power in Israel. The Russian media adopted a similar stand toward the Mizrahi Jews though it was somewhat restrained in accordance with the Jewish solidarity process. Above all, the Russian media adopted a critical stance toward the Mizrahi culture in Israel and established a new media reality, quite different from the Hebrew media in Israel. Some researchers have established a connection between the Russian reluctance to integrate as part of the Israeli culture and the absence of nationalistic reasons for their immigration. Researchers also opine that some Russian immigrants viewed Israeli culture as too Oriental (Al-Haj and Leshem, 2000).

Discussion of Russian political behavior in Israel must address the establishment of the Zionist Forum when analyzing voting trends among the Russians in the fourteenth Knesset elections (May 29, 1996). Establishment of the Forum and preservation of the Russian language via Russian-speaking newspapers and Russian cultural institutions all reflected the concept of Russian seclusion and indicate a reluctance to integrate into Israeli society. This tendency toward seclusion was the main cause of the emergence of groups calling themselves Russian in Israel. Despite the differing origins of the immigrants – some Asian, others European – most preferred to be classified as Russian (which is also how they were classified by the Israeli society).

The Russian example raised questions that have generated a number of discussions and debates among Israeli sociologists: Do Russians in Israel represent a new ethnicity capable of preserving its cultural and geographical identity and, as a result, its political identity? If so, will this level of cultural preservation present a new ethnic rift in the Israeli Jewish society? Or alternatively, will this group cease to exist and integrate within the Israeli Ashkenazi group? Kimmerling (1998) considers the Russian seclusion and the emergence of a new Russian cultural ethnicity as criticism of the Israeli identity with all its cultural and national concepts and as a contradiction of the Zionist vision of absorbing immigrants (i.e. "merging of the Exiles," in Zionist terminology). This critical vision was considered as non-affiliation to Zionism and a contribution to fostering a pluralist character within Israeli society.

Other researchers reject the idea of Russian seclusion and do not even agree that Russians will remain existent as an ethnic group with a distinct character. Politically, this would mean that Russians would adopt voting trends similar to those among the Israeli Jewish population and that Russian politics would disappear (Al-Haj, 2004a). Research supports two major schools of thought regarding these questions. First, the Al-Haj research concluded that Russian political organization does not embody any social or cultural motive of preserving Russian culture; rather, Russian political organization and activity support a goal of merging with Israeli society from a perspective of strength (Al-Haj, 2004b) that is best realized by the accumulation of power and by influential politics. This school of thought suggested that the ethno-political Russian organization will remain a strong, stable part of Israeli politics for some time. The aim, however, would be to merge with the social system rather than remaining as a separate ethnic group. The second school of thought, arising from studies conducted by Tschomsky (2001), concluded that the Russians want to merge with Israeli Jewish society, but that they face criticism for their weak national Zionist

Jewish identity and their excessively moderate dealings with the Palestinians. This has led them to organize separate political instruments and – reflecting the political-cultural programs of the former Soviet Union – has led them to emphasize a relationship with the most radical majority within the Jewish identity.

Tschomsky (2001) used the sociological concepts of *ethnos* and *ethnicos* to shed further light on questions regarding the influence of Russian immigrants on the Israeli political scene. Specifically, Tschomsky pointed out the creation of two identities within the former Soviet Union: (a) the *ethnos* (in this case, the Jewish nation); and (b) the *ethnicos*. The "ethnos" represents an eternal biological body present on a certain land for a long period of time. The "ethnicos" has an ethnic identity that does not share ownership of ethnic land; it constitutes a form of national minority, whose presence has created much tension with the ethnos. The ethnos–ethnicos dichotomy has practical implications for political stability in a multi-ethnic milieu (as reflected by legitimizing the geographic expansion of the ethnos into territories inhabited by the ethnicos. The concept also explains feelings of hostility in the Soviet Union toward Islamic and Oriental Jews from the Asian republics (ethnicos) that were formerly part of the Soviet Union.

In describing the similarity between Russian political organization and the geopolitical situation in Israel, Tschomsky interpreted the Russian political organization as very similar to Israeli nationalist right wing stands, particularly with regard to its hostility toward the Palestinians – a feeling that cannot be attributed solely to Jewish nationalism. He felt that this hostility is connected to the identity-building process that was established within the Soviet Union: when immigrants from the Soviet Union arrived in Israel these identities were "rearranged" to reflect a feeling of belonging to the ethnos, while they dealt with Palestinians as a national ethnicos minority. In other words, immigration from the Soviet Union to Israel was accompanied by an elevation in national status and transformation from a minority ethnicos group into a Jewish ethnos group. This process led to a new vision of Russian immigrants coming to Israel as part of the Zionist battle against the Palestinians. The new vision was reflected in the statement:

> Any action taken by the minority aiming at the changing of the prevailing situation is understood as a threat to the Jewish majority; accordingly, the majority can take every necessary defensive measure, including the denial of the minorities' right to stay in the country.
> (Tschomsky, 2001: 35)

The demands of Russians in Israel

Russian ethnic politics gained momentum during the 1990s, resulting in the acceptance of a number of demands made by Russian immigrants. According to the Central Bureau of Statistics, during the period between

1990 and 2000, more than one million immigrants arrived in Israel – most from the former Soviet Union countries. Such a huge immigration (around 20 percent of the population) created a new population sector and engendered many difficulties and problems. The resulting economic burden on the absorbing country, the cultural clash and social problems all imposed innumerable demands on the political system and culture. Many studies conducted in the 1990s on the political culture of the majority of the Russian immigrants found that this culture was one that considered the citizen as a dependent, rather than a full partner in duties and rights. This understanding of citizenship, no doubt a remnant of the former totalitarian Soviet Union system, was bound to make way for a culture of demands.

As of the mid-1990s, signs of change began to surface in the political culture of the Russian immigrants (Horowitz, 1996). The establishment of Russian immigrant parties and their new understanding of their ability to affect politics as individuals resulted in alienation between these immigrants and the political system. Numerous civil society organizations were established to serve the immigrants and in 1996, for the first time, an independent Russian immigrant political party won representation in the Knesset. The Russian immigrant parties played the role of mediator in implementing a political absorption process that aspires to meet the needs of this particular sector through political means.

The Russian immigrants arriving in Israel since 1989 were not a heterogeneous group, exhibiting differences and contradictions that resulted in different demands. Nevertheless, there were basic priorities for all of the immigrants coming from the Republics of the Soviet Union. These issues included: (a) material privileges, (b) the right to citizenship, and (c) preserving the cultural identity of the Russian immigrants in Israel.

Material privileges for Russian immigrants

Any discussion of the absorption of immigrants in Israel must take into account the legal framework relating to all Jews who show an interest in settling in the country. The right to citizenship is not the only right provided. There is also an "absorption package" that includes various material privileges aimed at making Israel an attractive destination for Jewish immigration. These privileges include a study period at a Hebrew language institute (Ulpan); encouragement of technological projects for Russian immigrant scientists; facilitation of the purchase of apartments; reduction of car sales taxes and so on. The immigration wave of the 1990s was of high quality in terms of its high percentage of educated and skilled people. Nevertheless, as was the case with previous waves of immigrants, many had to accept a lower social status than that to which they were accustomed. The fact that many Russian engineers and scientists could not work in their area of expertise created a gap between expectations and reality and often resulted in feelings of disappointment (Horowitz, 1996). Many polls have indicated that 30 percent of Russian immigrants believed that their professional status was much below their expectations.

The 1990s wave of immigrants also had a high percentage of older people. Data of the Ministry of Absorption indicate that 13 percent of the Russian immigrants arriving in the 1990s were above the age of 65 and that 35 percent were above 45 years of age. Those who immigrated at or around the age of retirement did not believe in their ability to merge into Israeli society and economy, yet, they had numerous needs that were translated into demands made of the Israeli political system. The victims of the Chernobyl nuclear reactor and World War II veterans were sectors in need of assistance who also carried considerable electoral weight. Those of approximate retirement age were the most politically active among the Russian immigrants; they had free time and more political freedom than they had enjoyed in the Soviet Union. Consequently, these immigrants became an important sector in Israeli society.

Promised material privileges did not always come to pass for Russian immigrants. For instance, the demands of the Russian immigrants were represented in the pressure exerted by their party (Yisrael Ba'aliyah) to control the Ministry of Absorption and Immigration in 1996. Although this Ministry did not enjoy many privileges, Minister Edelstein used it to increase his influence and woo voters. A project called *Housing Groups* was intended to resolve the housing problems of old and poor citizens living alone. The goal of the project was to redesign existing buildings to create smaller flats that could then be rented to older citizens. State assistance would help pay the rent for these elders. However, in practice, these flats went to the friends and supporters of the Yisrael Ba'aliyah party, sometimes without any compensation provided for the housing facilities. The Russian immigrants in need of social welfare faced other difficult problems. For example, the Israeli social welfare institutions were not based on sensitivity towards social issues, but rather, on the importance of absorbing immigrants into Israel according to the Zionists' model. However, the long socialist rule in the former Soviet Union had resulted in a deep feeling of dissatisfaction among the Russian immigrants towards all kinds of socialism; anything smacking of socialism was mentioned only in a negative manner in the Russian media.

The programs adopted by the Russian immigrant parties clearly called for: (a) limiting state intervention in the economy and accelerating the privatization process; (b) increasing competition in the financial markets; and (c) removing bureaucratic obstacles to economic development. Parties such as these cannot support poor citizens on a national basis. The assistance provided to Russian immigrants indicated that their parties were sectoral ones, working, not to promote a vision, but to ensure specific privileges for their voters. Still, some researchers (Horowitz, 1996) found that a considerable percentage of Russian immigrants described themselves as having democratic social beliefs. About 61 percent supported government intervention in the economy; 45 percent supported worker's participation in the administration boards of the different companies; 65 percent expressed the belief that the social gaps in Israeli society must be bridged and reduced. This contradiction between the official posture of the parties and their voters indicated the marginal role and status economic factors played, compared to other aspects of the protest movement.

The right to citizenship

Unlike former waves of immigrants, the wave that arrived in Israel from the former Soviet Union republics was also characterized by its high percentage of non-Jews. Between 1990 and 1995, Russian immigrants classified as Christians constituted 38 percent of the total increase in population.[1] In 1996, the Ministry of the Interior started to register these immigrants as having "no religion." By the year 2000, around 116,000 new Russian immigrants – or 83 percent of the population increase resulting from immigration – had been classified in this way. The Law of Return, that ensures the right to citizenship for every Jewish immigrant and his family, serves as the basis for Israel's conceptualization as a state of the Jewish people. This law provides the right of "secondary return" to Jewish relatives and family members of those who have the right to return by virtue of their Jewish religion. The right of "secondary return" includes the sons and spouses of a Jewish father and the grandchildren of a Jewish grandfather.

Israel was the only country that not only allowed immigrants to arrive, but also received them warmly and pledged to ensure them full citizenship the moment they arrived in the country. However, there were difficulties in interpreting the right to citizenship provided by the Law of Return. The basic legislation did not provide solutions for cases that pertained to fathers and mothers of Jews, relatives of Christians who converted to Judaism in Israel or relatives of non-Jews who received citizenship by virtue of secondary rights.

The secular character of the society in the former Soviet Union legitimized intermarriage between members of different religions; consequently, there were many Jews married to non-Jews. In many families, this intermarriage led to a Christian way of life, even though a spouse might have been of Jewish origin for at least one or two generations. When immigration started from the Soviet Union, many families benefited from their Jewish origin – they received citizenship in Israel (which they usually perceived to be a Western country). The law, in allowing for the return and Israeli citizenship of every Jew or relative of a Jew, contributed to preservation of the Jewish majority in Israel; however, it also weakened Jewish ethnic identity.

A legal religious monopoly exists in Israel, with regulations dictating that Jews may only marry and divorce according to the Halacha. These rules do not allow Jews to marry non-Jews, just as they prevent the burying of non-Jews in a Jewish cemetery. The law, as implemented in Israel, does not afford any official status to secular marriage, divorce or burial rituals. Until the 1990s, Israel did not allow any large-scale, secular marriage rituals; ethnic separation between the Jewish and Palestinian societies automatically precluded the possibility of integration between these two societies. Hence, the arrival of tens of thousands of non-Jewish immigrants created real problems for the state. For example, in many cases, burial of the dead might be delayed for days because the authorities were unsure whether the deceased was a Jew (Cohen and Susser, 2000). Individuals who wished to marry often had to conduct civil marriage rituals abroad because the religious authorities forbade them in Israel.

The human and financial suffering of non-Jewish Russian immigrants were caused by Jewish religious interests and by Israeli economic interests. The Jewish establishment saw limiting the right to citizenship as a tool to control any affinity between the Jewish and non-Jewish sectors. Limiting the immigration of non-Jews could, for example, prevent imposing a burden on the state economy. The official solution suggested for this problem was seen in intensified Judaization efforts. Converting non-Jews and half Jews to Judaism would solve the Jewish religious problem; absorbing the largest number of non-Jewish immigrants and providing them with the right to Israeli citizenship would preserve the existence of the state.

In 1997, the "Neeman commission," headed by Professor Yaakov Neeman, was established to find a solution for the overall Judaization problem – not merely the problem of immigrants coming from the former Soviet Union republics. The commission recommended the establishment of a Judaization Institute with representatives of different Jewish streams. It also recommended that special Judaization Courts should be appointed by the Chief Rabbinate and should ratify the Judaization.[2] Though perhaps expected to mollify the Russian immigrants, this solution was not compatible with the immigrants' interests and wishes. Cohen and Susser (2000) have pointed out that enforcing the requirement to join the Jewish religion had negative results among Christians, who manifested a growing animosity towards the religious establishment and towards the Jewish religion, in general. The existence of a large Christian minority among the Russian immigrants – 200,000 according to estimates in the year 2000 – created feelings of solidarity among those immigrants who sought to preserve their Christian identity.

Against this backdrop, Russian immigrant political parties focused on facilitating the right to citizenship. Control over the Ministry of the Interior, responsible for issuing citizenship documents, became a major goal for these parties. Party leaders believed that authority over citizenship resided in the hands of the Interior Ministry staff and that the relevant legislation was implemented in these offices. During the 1990s, SHAS Interior Ministers used their powers to withhold citizenship rights to many Russian immigrants. Consequently, in the 1999 electoral program of the Yisrael Beitenu (Israel Our Home) party, a clear demand was made to hammer out new regulations for the Ministry of the Interior pertaining to Israeli citizenship and passports. The 1999 campaign of the Russian party, Yisrael Ba'aliyah, also focused on this issue and promised its voters that it would take control of the Ministry. Research has documented mutual animosity between SHAS and Yisrael Ba'aliyah – both parties whose ethnic character helped to boost their influence.

Natan Sharansky was appointed Minister of the Interior during the Barak government; he remained in office until resigning in July 2000. During his term, a tangible change was implemented in the Ministry's dealings with applications from Russian immigrants. After a period in the first Sharon government, during which SHAS leader, Eli Yishaa, was Interior Minister, Avraham Poraz, from the Shinui party was appointed Minister of the Interior (2003). He adopted a liberal line, continued the Sharansky policies in the Ministry and generally avoided withholding the right of citizenship and residency from the relatives of Jews.

Preserving cultural identity

Perhaps the major and most problematic demand of the Russian immigrants was their insistence on preserving their cultural identity. Immigrants from the former Soviet Union republics usually considered themselves as having a European culture superior to the Middle Eastern culture in Israel. Studies indicate that Russian immigrants saw themselves as a distinct group with the right to preserve their culture and enjoy various privileges as a group (Al-Haj, 2004a; Ben-Rafael *et al.*, 1998).

The demands of the Russian immigrants presaged a change in the Israeli attitude toward immigrants in recent years. Israeli society is now divided between (a) considering itself a melting pot for different cultures – a basic concept in Israeli Jewish nation-building from its inception until the 1980s; and (b) reacting to internal social factors (e.g. the awakening of sectarian Oriental feelings) and external factors (e.g. the decline of the security threat) that have weakened the melting pot model and even portrayed it as a model of oppression. For example, previously, Russian immigrants had to change their names so that they appeared "more Israeli"; today, it is legitimate and socially accepted to retain the old names, even if they have non-Israeli cultural significance. The cultural approach of the Russian 1990s immigration wave troubled veteran Israelis of Mizrahi origin, who saw in the Russian immigrants a new European ethnic entity that could easily join the elite Ashkenazi sectors. They feared that this would adversely impact the efforts of the Mizrahi Jews to merge into Israeli society. The SHAS movement that had been established a few years previously served as an incentive to the Mizrahi religious movement. Traditional religious Israelis also perceived the Russian immigration wave of the 1990s as a threat: they felt that the non-Jewish character of the immigrants threatened the Jewish character of the state and that mixed marriage and integration between Jews and Christians threatened the whole Jewish people.

The Israeli authorities and their institutions did not remain passive in the face of this "danger," but reacted against all the Russian immigrants, branding them with humiliating descriptions. The statements of the Israeli Minister of Labor, Ora Namir, on the high percentage of needy Jews among the Russian immigrants and the statements of the Israeli Minister of Police, Moshe Shahal, on the infiltration of the Russian Mafia reflected real social problems created by the Russian immigration to Israel. As might be expected, neither the Israeli officials nor Israeli society understood the degree of humiliation these factors caused the Russians; nor did they understand the level of misunderstanding and alienation growing between the two parties. On the other hand, the Russians' sense of belonging to a culture that did not need Israeli legitimacy, prevented the possibility of a cultural dialogue between the groups. Consequently, there were sectarian or ethnic-based clashes and sometimes violence in some of the underdeveloped towns when these new Russian immigrants encountered veteran immigrants who had come to Israel in the 1950s from North Africa. There were, for example, cases of arson, where shops that sold ham – very popular among the Russians – were set on fire. There were conflicts on the streets between gangs with different ethnic affiliations; there were even cases of ethnic-based stabbings in different parts of the country.

The demands of the Russian immigrants for acknowledgment of their cultural identity were reflected in the platforms and programs of their political parties. Yisrael Ba'aliyah stated in 1999 that:

> We don't accept the social structure of formulas that existed before the Russian immigration to Israel. Rather, we consider this immigration as enriching all walks of life through the qualifications and abilities of the newcomers. We consider this enrichment process, and the mutual spiritual exchanges between the parties, is the prevailing culture in the country.

Tackling the issue of negative sectarian attitudes toward the immigrants, the platform demanded punishment of every journalist or editor who published a news item that was hostile or threatening to the identity of the Russian immigrants.

The Yisrael Beitenu further stressed in its platform the significance of Israel's foreign relations with the former Soviet Union republics, pointing out that these strategic relations should be manifested in the fields of trade, science, technology, culture and sport. The party considered that such Israeli relations strategically constituted a point of sufficient strength to replace the United States. At the same time, these relations constituted a channel for impacting the Russian culture. According to the vision of the Yisrael Beitenu, such a relationship between Israel and the former Soviet Union republics would facilitate the legitimization of Russian culture, just as the Israeli–American alliance of the early 1960s had generated a cultural change in Israel towards the liberal West. The party also pointed out that Russian culture was the basis upon which Jewish settlement society in the country was based prior to the establishment of the state.

In the civil arena, many Russian ethnic-cultural societies and volunteer organizations that focused on the cultural development of immigrants coming from the former Soviet Union republics were established throughout Israel (see the website for Tel Aviv Institute for Political Researches www.psr.org). The large number of these organizations reflected the cultural separatism between these immigrants and others and reflected their striving to constitute a distinct Russian cultural group. In many Israeli cities, bookstores were opened that sold only Russian books. A huge media network was established that included radio and television stations, websites, newspapers and periodicals – all for Russian-speakers only. Concerts and cultural events performed by artists from Russia were very popular among the immigrants coming from the former Soviet Union.

Numerous educational institutions and organizations were established for Russian youths, based on educational methodologies imported from the former Soviet Union republics. For example, a school network (Mofit network), founded on the educational methods of scientific institutes in Russia, teaches mathematics and physics to Russian youths. The Shobor school network provides religious education to Russian-speakers with funds provided by the followers of Rabbi Leibovits. In many schools in different cities and towns where there is a majority of Russian immigrants, students and teachers are Russian-speakers.

Political organization of the Russians

Over the last decade-and-a-half, the Israeli political arena has witnessed the establishment of a large number of political organizations of immigrants coming from the former Soviet Union. It must be noted here that problems exist in gathering information, and coordinating and classifying data concerning this large number of Russian political organizations.

The Zionist Forum

The Soviet Union Jewish Zionist Forum was an organization for Russian immigrants established in 1988 by former Zionist Jewish prisoners in the former Soviet Union. The Forum was headed by Natan Sharansky, who himself was, for many years, a political prisoner in the former Soviet Union (Horowitz, 1996). Sharansky was born in 1948 in the Ukraine. Following the Soviet invasion of Prague in August 1968, he joined the struggle for human rights in the Soviet Union. In 1973, he applied for a visa to emigrate to Israel, but was arrested by Soviet intelligence (KGB). On March 15, 1977, he was accused of treason and espionage, as well as incitement and anti-Soviet propaganda, and was imprisoned for nine years under difficult detention conditions. After a stubborn struggle, mainly conducted by his wife, Sharansky and five German spies were released on February 11, 1986, as part of a spy swap.

During the long campaign to secure his release, Sharansky became a well known personality among the Russians, in Israeli society and even at the international level. Following his release and emigration to Israel, Sharansky established the Zionist Forum in June 1988, in expectation of a new wave of immigration from the Soviet Union.

The Forum was established to support the absorption and integration of former prisoners into Israeli society and to represent the interests of the Russian immigrants in Israel, with the assistance of the Jewish agency. However, the beginning of the 1989 immigration wave of Russian Jews to Israel transformed the Forum from a volunteer organization into an important lobby that included the majority of Russian organizations and bodies in Israel and was active on the regional and national levels. In 1993, the Zionist Forum formed branches in different parts of the country and accumulated significant political power through public rallies and social-cultural projects for the Russian immigrants (Horowitz, 1996). By 1995, the organization had 42 branches with 66,000 members, and was to serve as a basis upon which the Yisrael Ba'aliyah party was later established.

The Zionist Forum was only one of a network of many organizations among the Russian immigrants. Many were based on the origin of the members in the former Soviet Union or on professional affiliation. The first type of organization represented those of Caucasian, Ukrainian, Belorussian, Bukharian and other origins, reflecting the ethnic and cultural diversity prevailing among the Jews from the former Soviet Union. Other associations included World War II veterans, engineers, scientists, teachers and other similar unions. These organizations signified a high level of political engagement among these immigrants and a comprehensive civil society catering to the needs of the Russian community.

In a more recent (2003) poll conducted by the Tel Aviv Social Institute which specializes in studies on the immigrant communities (www.isbr.org), around 80 percent of the immigrant respondents said that they knew about the Zionist Forum; however, 90 percent of them said that they had never participated in any of its activities or used its services and 50 percent thought it had become irrelevant.

Immigrant blocs in existing political parties

The veteran Israeli parties, especially the Likud and Labor parties, fully understood the electoral potential of the Russian immigrants in the 1990s (Frankel, 1996). However, they failed to understand the real demands of these immigrants. This gap led to the emergence of the Yisrael Ba'aliyah party and its sudden success in the 1996 and 1999 elections, although the Russians also supported other parties (e.g. Shinui), as well.

The Labor party

Ever since the 1992 elections, the electoral potential of the Russian immigrants was clearly felt. About 65 percent of these immigrants voted for the Labor party; in fact, the party's success was largely attributed to these voters. Some interpreted this trend as a vote against the ruling authority (Gitelman and Goldstein, 2001). Others attributed it to the social problems encountered by the Russian immigrants and to their financial problems at a time when the Likud government was investing so much in the settlements (Horowitz, 1996).

Following the elections, the different parties established special institutions to win the support of the immigrants. In 1993, the Labor party established, for this purpose, a special "Russian team." In early 1995, Prime Minister Yitzhak Rabin inaugurated the first conference of the "Russian action." The number of registered members in 34 branches was 20,000 – most of them young Ashkenazim with an academic background. Although the party looked after these members, it could not maintain the support of Russian voters in the subsequent election campaigns. According to the polls following the 1996 elections, only 21 percent of the Russian immigrants voted for the Labor party, while only 34 percent voted for Shimon Peres as Prime Minister (Vise, 1997). The reasons for this "protest vote" (Gitelman and Goldstein, 2001) were explained by political scientist Professor Shevah Vise, a former Speaker of the Knesset (1992–96) as:

1) the lack of a possibility for promotion by the immigrants within the party leadership;
2) a negative stereotypic image of the Russian immigrants (e.g. a statement by Labor party Minister of Police Moshe Shahal about "Mafia Immigration," or by Minister of Labor and Social Welfare, Ora Namir, that one-third of the new immigrants worked in prostitution, another third were social cases, and the other third were single parent families);
3) the tendency of the Russian immigrants to accept an extreme nationalist ideology contrary to the peaceful tendencies of the Peres–Rabin government.

The election results of 1996 were disappointing for the Labor party. By 1999, only 6000 members remained in the Russian team, a large number having left and joined the Center party or the Yisrael Ba'aliyah party.

The Likud party

Within the Likud party, too, special organizations worked on mobilizing support from Russian immigrants. Twenty-seven thousand of them, divided into two major groups, joined the party in the mid-1990s. One group was comprised of people with right wing ideologies from the early waves of immigration; the other was an organization named "Immigration for the sake of the Land of Israel." Unlike the Labor party, the Likud party had no official immigrant organization. Rather, a communication officer was in charge of coordinating with the activists within the Russian community. The Likud did appoint active personalities from among the immigrants to important political positions within the party; these individuals served as a source of strength in election campaigns. One of these was Avigdor Lieberman, who was appointed by Binyamin Netanyahu as Director-General of the Likud party. (Actually, a large number of Russian Likud activists received government positions, thus weakening their affiliation with the party.) Lieberman later moved over to direct the Prime Minister's Bureau. When Lieberman left the Likud party in 1998 and established the Yisrael Beitenu bloc, it was an unexpected blow, because he took with him, to the new, extreme right wing party, a large number of Likud members.

Major Russian political parties

Yisrael Ba'aliyah party

Established in 1996 in order to serve Russian immigrants and in preparation for the 1996 elections, the Yisrael Ba'aliyah party was the first such with an adequate apparatus and resources. At the founding conference in Jerusalem, attended by 1500 representatives from all over the country, the Prime Ministerial candidates, Binyamin Netanyahu and Shimon Peres, congratulated the party on its establishment. Natan Sharansky, who was elected to head the party, was known locally and internationally as a Zionist activist in the former Soviet Union.

Having been President of the important Zionist Forum, Sharansky was able to enlist many supporters (and also opponents) into the new Yisrael Ba'aliyah party. The party included strong supporters of both the right and the left and party structure reflected a political balance between the right and left wings. The party took a neutral stand on the election for Prime Minister, despite the rightist inclinations of Sharansky.

Yisrael Ba'aliyah designed its platform carefully, as a representative of the Soviet immigrants, on the one hand, and as a legitimate party within the Israeli political system, on the other. Its goal was integration of the immigrant community into Israeli society, rather than alienation and segregation. The first article of the party platform dealt with economic issues. Unlike the Likud and Labor parties, which afforded priority to political, rather than social issues, the right wing Yisrael Ba'aliyah party projected a socio-economic vision. The vision, however, was neither clear nor systematic. The party stated its commitment to develop a competitive market economy, to end monopolies, and to support the policy of privatization; nevertheless, it did not neglect its voters, most of whom were dependent on Israeli welfare services. It pledged to help old-age pensioners and single-parent families.

Also, it demanded that immigrants be assured of the ownership of houses and flats.

Education and culture were important issues for the party; it criticized the educational system on two points. First, it criticized the poor standard of Israeli schools, especially in scientific education; second, it was critical of the Israeli culture, which it considered inferior to the European culture imported by the immigrants. In its education platform, Yisrael Ba'aliyah proposed: (a) extending the school day from kindergarten through high school; (b) improving educational standards; (c) developing a network of schools specialized in mathematics, sciences and foreign languages; (d) deepening education in Jewish values; and (e) focusing on the diversity of Jewish culture.

The interaction between religion and the state was also a primary focus of the party, particularly in light of the fact that many of the new immigrants were non-Jews who had acquired Israeli nationality via family relationships with Jews. Given the monopoly of the orthodox Rabbinate over marriage and family laws, issues of marriage, divorce, burial and the conversion of non-Jews to Judaism, and given the resultant problems for the non-Jews among the immigrants, Yisrael Ba'aliyah pledged to tackle the Judaization issue and to find a legal framework for civil marriage.

The party achieved a significant victory in the 1996 elections. Of the Russians who participated in the polling, almost half were voting for the first time (Horowitz, 2003). The party got 175,000 votes, accounting for 43 percent of the Russian immigrant votes; it won seven seats in the Knesset. As a result of 1996 election, Yisrael Ba'aliyah joined the Netanyahu government as a major partner; Natan Sharansky was appointed Minister of Trade and Industry; and Edelstein became Minister of Absorption. In the wake of the 1996 elections, the party adopted a centrist-rightist political stance. It acknowledged the agreements signed between Israel and the Palestinian Authority, but required Palestinian respect of their commitments and a Palestinian system committed to democracy and human rights as conditions for implementing these agreements. The party stressed the right of the Jewish people to " the whole of the land of Israel" and saw Jerusalem as "the eternal united capital of Israel."

In 1997, the party ratified a charter that defined the organizational and election rules within the party. A democratic organizational structure was defined that addressed the role of the party's 70 branches and the role of the highest representative body – which had 1500 members.

The party used its influence to win over new members and other registered voters who in 1996 numbered only a few thousand, but who by the Fall 1998 municipal elections, numbered 20,000 (Khanin, 2000). In the local elections held in November 1998, the party won 100 seats in 60 local councils; its representatives assumed the post of Deputy Mayor in 17 local authorities (Khanin, 2000). The party also succeeded in fund-raising activities, particularly through Sharansky's skills in this area.

In its campaign for the 1999 elections, Yisrael Ba'aliyah stressed its commitment to solving the problem of immigrants' citizenship and housing rights. The campaign focused on acquiring the Ministry of the Interior, especially since SHAS people, who ran the Ministry during the 1990s, had used it to place obstacles before many Russian immigrants seeking citizenship.

In spite of its internal problems, Yisrael Ba'aliyah maintained its strength in the fifteenth Knesset elections. About 172,000 individuals voted for the party, which – although it had not officially supported Ehud Barak for Prime Minister – joined Barak's government with six Knesset members and Sharansky as Minister of the Interior. The immigrant community clearly supported Ehud Barak, who won approximately 55 percent of their vote, compared to 35 percent for Netanyahu. Once again, the Russian vote was an important factor in the Israeli elections.

With the end of its first term in the government coalition, Yisrael Ba'aliyah faced an ideological crisis. Various interest groups were dissatisfied with the performance of Yisrael Ba'aliyah in general and with Sharansky, in particular. The party encountered criticism of: (a) Sharansky's centralized approach to running party affairs and (b) the lack of internal democracy in the party.

Critics included the Russian bloc which had been successful in municipal elections, veteran Zionist activists such as Yosef Begun, and people who had become famous in the struggle against the Soviet authorities. The "Wye River" agreement and the law of religious conversion were particularly problematic decisions for the party and its leaders. Two of these leaders, Stern and Nudelman, left the party in the wake of the 1999 elections, in protest against the political leniency of Sharansky and the disputes occurring among the party leadership. Stern and Nudelman joined Avigdor Lieberman's party, Yisrael Beitenu.

Sharansky, himself, left the government before Barak's journey to Camp David in July 2000 to take part in the negotiations held under the patronage of US President, Bill Clinton. Sharansky's departure, however, did not become a major public issue, since the government faced collapse in any case.

The sixteenth Knesset elections, held in 2003, marked the beginning of the end of the Yisrael Ba'aliyah: security and political issues dominated the agenda; the party joined the right wing forces following the general trend in Israeli public opinion during the conflict with the Palestinians (the second Intifada); and the party expressed reservations about the Palestinian Authority. Social issues of the Russian immigrants (e.g. housing and labor) were not top priorities, although the party supported the Neeman Commission recommendations regarding conversion. In the election, the party suffered a strong defeat, winning only two seats. Sharansky responded with the observation that, "The role of the Yisrael Ba'aliyah has, in practice, ended with these elections."[3] Sharansky and Edelstein joined the Likud party, where Sharansky was appointed Minister for Jerusalem and Diaspora Affairs in the first and second governments of Ariel Sharon.

Yisrael Beitenu (Israel Our Home)

The Yisrael Beitenu movement was established by the end of March 1999, in the wake of the fifteenth Knesset elections. Initially the party included members who had broken away from the Likud and Yisrael Ba'aliyah. The first three places in the party leadership were occupied by former members of these parties: Lieberman – who had withdrawn from the Likud party following the signing of the Wye River Agreement; and Stern and Nudelman – who had left the Yisrael Ba'aliyah party.

Yisrael Beitenu was distinguished from Yisrael Ba'aliyah by its clear right wing political line. The platform published by the Yisrael Beitenu contained the statement, "Ensuring Israeli strategic military and economic superiority in our region, constitutes an existential need."[4] The movement announced, in 1999, that it respected the Palestinian autonomous areas, but that any future political settlement would not include the evacuation of any Jewish settlement in the West Bank or Gaza Strip. With respect to other areas, the party platform:

1) demanded far-reaching reforms in the free market economy (much like Yisrael Ba'aliyah);
2) stressed the need for government intervention to solve the problems of housing, new immigrant absorption and assistance to single-parent families;
3) proposed laws to improve the situation of Zionist activists who had been imprisoned in the former Soviet Union, World War II veterans and the victims of the Chernobyl nuclear reactor catastrophe;
4) demanded the drafting of a constitution for Israel, the introduction of a presidential system and the establishment of a constitutional court and a council for national security;
5) urged the liberalization of procedures for acquiring Israeli citizenship, passports and entry visas to Israel – demands constantly raised by the Russian immigrant community.

Before the fifteenth Knesset elections, the party had won 40 representatives in the municipal elections. In the Knesset elections themselves, Yisrael Beitenu won four seats. This admirable achievement paled, however, in light of the victory achieved by Ehud Barak in the Prime Ministerial elections and the success of SHAS, which won 17 seats. Naturally, Yisrael Beitenu did not join the Barak government coalition; it became part of the right wing opposition. Subsequently, in conjunction with the Moledet and T'kumah movements, Yisrael Beitenu established a right wing parliamentary bloc called the "National Union."

The National Union

In the 2003 elections, the National Union fought as a united bloc. The assassination of Tourist Minister Zeevi and the withdrawal of Benny Begin from the political stage for personal reasons, made Avigdor Lieberman the leader of the new coalition party. The National Union bloc won seven seats in the Knesset, three of them going to Yisrael Beitenu. The conflict with the Palestinians prompted the National Union to adopt a more extreme line, calling for the use of maximum military force in the West Bank and Gaza Strip. The party even called upon the Palestinian citizens in Israel proper to declare their loyalty to the Jewish character of the state. It seems that Yisrael Beitenu had become an Israeli party whose ethnic character reflected the ideological stands popular among the immigrants from the former Soviet Union.

In the 2006 elections, Yisrael Beitenu ran by its own list and won 11 seats. Most votes in the 2006 elections came from the Russian voters. Although Lieberman did his best to change or downplay the image of the party as a "Russian" one (including having non-Russian candidates on the Yisrael Beitenu list), he was unsuccessful. Even in the 2009 elections, survey results indicate that most Yisrael Beitenu votes come from the Russians.[5]

Other Russian political parties

In recent election campaigns, many blocs that previously had been unable to gain representation in the Knesset competed. Their existence reflected the divisions and conflicts present within the Israeli Russian community. Several of these parties are described below.

The DA party

The DA party ("yes," in Russian), ran in the thirteenth Knesset elections in 1992. The party depended on the immigration wave of the 1990s and attempted unsuccessfully to include the head of the Zionist Forum – Natan Sharansky, at the time – in its list. The DA bloc won approximately 12,000 votes – a number far short of the minimum needed for a place in the Knesset.

Unity and immigration

In the 1996 elections, Avraham Gur, a former Knesset member of the Labor party and then of the Likud, headed an independent immigrant bloc. Gur, who was of Georgian origin, had parliamentary experience and expressed an interest in joining the Yisrael Ba'aliyah party. He failed, however, and subsequently established a bloc to which many immigrants of the Asian and Caucasian republics were attracted (Khanin, 2000). Gur directed his campaign toward immigrants from the Bukharan and Caucasian territories and emphasized the ethnic factor to win over the immigrants. He won 22,000 votes, far below the minimum required to enter the Knesset.

Immigrants' Heart for Israel

A basic problem facing Israeli society has been the alienation of some ethnic groups. They have not held strong positions in the Knesset, the state apparatus or the business sector. Furthermore, these alienated groups have been also almost non-existent even in the local authorities.[6] In 1999, the Immigrants' Heart for Israel saw Israel as a multi-ethnic state joined by a common affiliation to Jewish values and saw itself as the representative of Middle Eastern immigrants. The party pledged to represent the smaller ethnic groups and devised a detailed plan for improving the situations of immigrants coming from central Asian countries – specifically for sustaining their traditions, raising their economic status and engaging them in local and national political life. Nonetheless, the Immigrants' Heart party, despite its detailed platform and high aspirations, achieved only 6,300 votes in the Knesset elections. Many of the Bukharan immigrants voted for SHAS, which included a representative of these immigrants in its list.

Tikvah

The Tikvah party ran in the fifteenth Knesset elections, headed by Alex Tentsir, a veteran observer for the Russian Immigration Institution (Khanin, 2000). Tentsir had, in the early 1990s, headed a "general commission for following up electoral promises." Tikvah supported the struggle of mixed immigrant families to institute civil marriage. It won only 7000 votes.

A Citizen and a State

This party was formed by Knesset member, Tsinker, in preparation for the sixteenth Knesset elections. Tsinker had been elected to the fifteenth Knesset as a representative of Yisrael Ba'aliyah. However, he had broken away, accompanied by Roman Bronfman, to establish a bloc called the Democratic Choice (sixteenth Knesset elections). They supported civil law in Israel on issues of marriage, divorce and burial but only won a few hundred votes.

Leader

Leader is a Russian Christian ethnic party whose leader, Alexander Redco, boasted of his relations with the extremist Russian nationalist leader, Vladimir Gerenovisky. (Gerenovisky visited Israel during his electoral campaign to assist his friend.) The Leader party did not call on Russians to merge into Israeli society; the party focused primarily on the affairs of the Russian community in Israel and particularly on internal Russian politics.

Political participation of the Russian immigrants

Three years after the beginning of the new wave of Russian immigration to Israel until the thirteenth Knesset elections on June 23, 1992, the Russian immigrant population in Israel grew to 375,000 (Ministry of Immigrant Absorption, 2002). Of these immigrants, 240,000 were eligible to vote in the 1992 general elections (Horowitz, 2003). Many politicians among the Russian community noted this electoral potential and established two Russian political blocs shortly before the elections. The reaction of the official establishment to these new political groupings was substantially different from its reaction to the Mizrahi parties in the 1950s. In practice, the establishment of these parties did not challenge the basic values of society (Anderson, 2000). Thus, because they posed no threat to the power balance within Israeli society, the official reaction to these Russian political blocs was far more tolerant at all levels (Kimmerling, 2001). Despite the electoral potential and legitimacy afforded to the Taly and DA blocs, neither could secure the minimum number of votes needed to cross the electoral threshold. Gitelman (1995) maintains that they failed in the elections because their leaders were not well known among the Russian community and therefore, could not win the confidence of the public.

Voting trends in the thirteenth Knesset elections

The Labor and Likud parties received most Russians votes in the 1992 thirteenth Knesset elections; the majority of Russian immigrants voted for the Labor party. Their level of support was 8 to 10 percent higher than the support the party received from the veteran Israel public (Fien, 1995). This trend in Russian voting, in the first election in which they participated, was interpreted in different ways. One interpretation by Horowitz (1994) maintained that the vote was a protest against the Shamir government, given that the Russian immigrants suffered, during this period, from high unemployment rates and poor housing conditions. The second interpretation (also provided by Horowitz), suggested that the voting of Russian immigrants for the Labor party was ideological. According to this interpretation, people brought up in a Communist regime considered the Labor party's social-democratic agenda as a responsible social and economic policy.

The third interpretation (most simply presented) maintained that the Russian immigrants voted for the Labor party because of their concern about Israel's settlement intentions toward them. Specifically, as a result of pressure exerted on the Israeli government by Americans, Russians and Palestinians that Israel desist from settlement activities and expansion in the occupied Palestinian territories, Israel and the United States had made an agreement. According to the agreement, the USA would guarantee 10 billion dollars in loans to Israel for settling and absorbing immigrants from the former Soviet Union republics. In return – as a precondition for receiving the American guarantees – Israel would not settle the immigrants in the occupied Palestinian territories (Fien, 1995; Gitelman, 1995). Israel's pledge not to settle Russian immigrants in these territories was also influenced by the threat of Russian authorities to cease issuing visas and permits allowing Jews to leave the Soviet Union. However, according top American media reports, Israel – despite its promise – settled about 30,000 new Russian immigrants in the occupied Palestinian territories in 1990. This figure includes those Russian immigrants settled in the neighborhoods established around Eastern Jerusalem on the Eastern side of the green line (Aronson, 1996).

As the 1992 election approached, the Russian community in Israel, recognizing the importance of American loans to improve its living conditions, was concerned that Shamir would not adhere to his commitments and would, thus, negate his chance to receive financial assistance for absorbing Russian immigrants. At the same time, Labor party propaganda stressed that voting for the right wing would divert finances away from absorbing Russian immigrants and toward financing Jewish settlements in the occupied territories. As a result, the Russian community directed its electoral support to the Labor party.

Voting trends in the fourteenth Knesset elections and the establishment of the Yisrael Ba'aliyah party

Natan Sharansky, a prominent leader among the Russian public in Israel, established the Yisrael Ba'aliyah party. Yisrael Ba'aliyah was officially registered as a political party on February 11, 1996. The party claimed that it was neither leftist nor rightist, but only catered to the needs of Russian immigrants in Israel (Horowitz, 2003; Katz, 2000). The Yisrael Ba'aliyah party, in the fourteenth Knesset elections of June 29, 1996, put an end to the similarity in voting trends between the Russian community and the veteran Jewish public.

Russian immigrants' ability to seek political power through the establishment of Yisrael Ba'aliyah was seen as a major achievement. The leadership of the new party consisted of immigrants from the 1970s whose political activism led to institutionalizing the demands of the Russian immigrants in terms of their cultural identity (referred to as *identity politics*). These activists received public support from the *Veste* newspaper, the largest in the Russian language (Horowitz, 2003). The party adopted the slogan, "Dignity and Security," and supported the institutionalization of Russian ethnicity. Like other cultural and ethical groups in the history of Israeli immigration, this one strove to merge into Israeli society without posing any threat to its power base. It saw this strategy as the way to maximize its acquisition of budgets and resources to meet the needs of the Russian immigrants (Kimmerling, 2001).

The fourteenth Knesset elections (1996) were the first for Russian immigrants from the 1990s wave; approximately 40,000 Russian voters participated. These elections occurred at a time and in a milieu of significant disturbance. For example: (a) a large Israeli offense was launched in Lebanon; (b) Prime Minister Yitzhak Rabin was assassinated; and (c) Ministers Ora Namir and Moshe Shahal had made public disparaging remarks about Russian immigrants (e.g. old people were being sent to Israel to get pensions and social assistance; Russian immigrants had imported criminal gangs with them into Israel). Nevertheless, many of the Russian voters believed that they could play a decisive role in changing the government – a feeling that was bolstered by the entry of Yisrael Ba'aliyah into the political arena.

In the fourteenth Knesset elections, Yisrael Ba'aliyah won the support of 157,000 voters, more than 40 percent of the Russian votes. A similar percentage of support was revealed by analyzing a poll conducted before the elections (Horowitz, 2003) and analyzing the voting trends in polling centers where Russians constituted at least 95 percent of the voters (Vise, 1997). Katz (2000) estimated that 50 percent of Russian voters voted in these elections for Yisrael Ba'aliyah while the rest were split as follows: 12 percent for the Labor party and Meretz; 13 percent for religious parties; and 20 percent for the Likud and Moledet parties. In the elections for Prime Minister (according to election results at the polling centers where Russians constituted at least 95 percent of voters), 30 percent of the Russian immigrants voted for Peres, while 70 percent voted for Netanyahu (Vise, 1997).

Why did Yisrael Ba'aliyah win such Russian support? Researchers have concluded that this party helped the Russian immigrants preserve their cultural identity and language and their contacts with the Motherland – Russia (Kimmerling, 1999). And so Yisrael Ba'aliyah, as a result of the fourteenth Knesset election, joined the Netanyahu government and received the Ministry of Absorption. Ironically, Yisrael Ba'aliyah was to become one of the first factions to oppose Netanyahu in making peace with the Palestinians.

It is my belief that Yisrael Ba'aliyah's presentation of itself as a national party created by the Zionist Forum was the reason behind the sweeping support the party received from Russian immigrants. Sharansky's charismatic personality among the Russia community, in addition to his image as a former Prisoner of Zion, gave legitimacy to his policies for the Russian immigrants. As in the thirteenth Knesset elections, the Russian immigrants understood in the fourteenth Knesset elections how to use the mechanism of power to influence the institutions in Israeli society. Once again, the party did not define a clear platform concerning the conflict with the Palestinians.

Voting trends in the fifteenth Knesset Elections

In the fifteenth Knesset elections, both Yisrael Ba'aliyah and Yisrael Beitenu competed for the Russian vote. Yisrael Beitenu's animosity towards the Palestinians and Yisrael Ba'aliyah's call for material benefits for the Russian public brought a wave of Russian votes for both parties. A large percentage of the 750,000 Russian immigrant population participated in the 1999 fifteenth Knesset elections. Horowitz (2003) maintains that the percentage of Russian immigrant voters in the fifteenth Knesset elections was higher than in the fourteenth Knesset elections. Although Horowitz did not present the documentation or data upon which she based her opinion, that opinion does suggest that the influence of Russian immigrant parties was increasing. Furthermore, the Russian response in the fifteenth Knesset election refutes the contention expressed by Kimmerling in an analysis of the fourteenth Knesset elections (1999), that the influence of Russian parties would gradually diminish as time passed.

YISRAEL BA'ALIYAH

A major achievement of Yisrael Ba'aliyah during the fourteenth Knesset elections was encouraging the party to prepare, in advance, for the fifteenth Knesset elections – especially in those cities and towns where the party could compete for the post of mayor or deputy mayor (*Tel Aviv Newspaper*, October 16, 1997). The party established organizational infrastructure in many local authorities to assist it in the elections. A few months before the fifteenth Knesset elections (June 17, 1999), local council elections were held (November 1998). The party's advance preparation paid off: of the 1049 members elected to local councils in the 1998 elections, 162 were representatives of Russian parties. Of these, 93 were members of the Yisrael Ba'aliyah; 40 assumed the post of deputy mayor; one became mayor of a local council (Horowitz, 2003). The Russian immigrants also made important electoral achievements in the development towns, where there was conflict in the election campaign between Russian and Mizrahi Jews (Tzefadia, 2000; Tzefadia and Yiftachel, 2001).

Although the Yisrael Ba'aliyah party did not take a clear political line (unlike Yisrael Beitenu), it pledged to its voters to do its best to ensure efficient running of the Ministry of the Interior under the slogan, "Nash Control." The SHAS movement's control of that Ministry was portrayed as inimical to the Russian public. The Ministry was accused of causing problems for mixed families (Jews and non-Jews) and for immigrants who wanted to bring their non-Jewish family members and relatives to Israel. The party's aspiration to manage the Ministry of the Interior was one factor that accounted for the support Yisrael Ba'aliyah obtained. Another factor was the hatred many secular Jews, from all sectors of Israeli society, felt for SHAS. The slogan, "only without SHAS," expressed the reaction of a silent secular majority that was fed up with the speeches of Rabbi Ovadiya Yosef and the SHAS leaders. Hatred and animosity for SHAS were the common denominators uniting this large clan. (See Neri Livneh in *Haaretz*, August 24, 2000.)

In the fifteenth Knesset elections, Yisrael Ba'aliyah achieved 3000 fewer votes than in the fourteenth Knesset election. Nevertheless, the party achieved 172,000 votes or 5.1 percent of the voters and won six seats.

YISRAEL BEITENU

During the fifteenth Knesset elections, two important phenomena emerged pertaining to Russian ethnicity. First, the Yisrael Beitenu political bloc appeared on the political scene. Unlike the Yisrael Ba'aliyah party, Yisrael Beitenu suggested a more strict line in dealing with the Israeli–Palestinian conflict and a stronger commitment to privatization in the economy. Avigdor Lieberman was a strong and credible leader whose personality and previous experience (e.g. Director of the Prime Minister's bureau) contributed to the results of the party. Second, Yisrael Beitenu did not abandon basic radical Zionist concepts, as expressed in its platform: "The essence of Zionism is manifested in the immigration movement that is pivotal for the existence and strength of Israel. The State of Israel is the heart of the Jewish nation." To preserve the Jewish character of the state there is a need to invest additional effort and resources in Jewish education for "potential immigrants in Russia." Naturally the platform also included the promise of privileges for the Russian voters: for example expansion of conversion frameworks; solution to the housing problem of the 1990s immigrants who occupied a lower economic status; increased efficiency of rehabilitation and professional empowerment systems; employment of immigrants in jobs where those from the former Soviet Union have experience and qualifications; increased assistance with locating job opportunities; allocation of additional resources for Hebrew studies; support and assistance for Russian media and cultural activities. Yisrael Beitenu won roughly 86,000 votes, or 2.6 percent of the total voters (four seats).

Polls conducted by Al-Haj and Leshem (2000) indicated that the majority of supporters for Russian parties were either veteran immigrants or those who had not been in Israel for more than a few years – the majority of first wave Russian immigrants did not vote in these elections for the Russian parties. Sixty-one percent of the Russian voters supported Ehud Barak for Prime Minister, compared to 39 percent for Netanyahu (Horowitz, 2003).

Another important phenomenon is worth noting about Russian voting in the fifteenth Knesset elections: 80,000 Russian immigrants did vote for SHAS. These voters, represented by Amnon Cohen, who occupied the sixth place on SHAS nomination list, were mainly immigrants from Asian republics of the former Soviet Union (Katz, 2000).

RUSSIAN INVOLVEMENT IN THE BARAK GOVERNMENT (1999-2001)

A number of factors prevented Yisrael Beitenu from joining the government coalition that was established by Barak, the new Prime Minister, following the 1999 elections. These factors included the extremist political stands adopted by Yisrael Beitenu, the party's public support for the nomination of Binyamin Netanyahu as Prime Minister, and the existence of a personal commitment between the party's leader, Avigdor Lieberman, and Netanyahu. On the other hand, the neutral political stand adopted by the Yisrael Ba'aliyah party during the election campaign enabled that party to join the Ehud Barak government.

In the coalition agreement, Yisrael Ba'aliyah insisted on taking the Minister of the Interior portfolio in order to implement its commitment to its voters (Nash Control); Sharansky, party leader, became Minister of the Interior. In addition, the government pledged not to make any decision that contradicted the interests of the Russian immigrants and to give a larger role to the Yisrael Ba'aliyah party on all subjects pertaining to the Russian immigrants' absorption in Israel. The coalition agreement with the Barak government also stipulated that there would be no governmental reform without the agreement of the party and that it would appoint a deputy minister of absorption and immigration.

In addition to Sharansky becoming Minister of the Interior in the Barak government, he also played a role in the peace process. Specifically, Sharansky sometimes solved crises during negotiations with the Palestinian Authority, though he was opposed to what he saw as concessions and unacceptable bargains. Sharansky's involvement in the Barak coalition guided Knesset members Bronfmann and Tsinker to withdraw from Yisrael Ba'aliyah and to establish the leftist Russian party, "The Democratic Choice" (See *Maariv*, December 8, 2000). Their departure constituted the first step in the collapse of the Barak government and the announcement of early elections for Prime Minister.

In the early elections for Prime Minister that took place in January 2001, Ariel Sharon won a sweeping victory. It was estimated that he was supported by a high percentage of Russian immigrant votes (70 percent). Esther Stern, mother of Knesset member, Uri Stern (from the Yisrael Beitenu bloc), explained her support of Sharon as follows: "I don't know much about Sharon, but he is strong and knows what to do with the Palestinians. Barak doesn't understand anything" (*Haaretz*, February 7, 2001).

This time, both Yisrael Ba'aliyah and Yisrael Beitenu (which was united with the National Union) joined the government. In the coalition agreement signed between Yisrael Beitenu and Prime Minister Sharon, the National Union got two ministerial posts: one for Rechavam Ze'evi and one for Avigdor Lieberman. Rather than referring to the financial needs of the Russian immigrants, the coalition agreement included paragraphs regarding: (a) the peace process and settlements on the Palestinian territory; (b) privatization of the economy; and (c) preservation of the religious status quo. Another subject addressed by the agreement was the appointment of a Knesset member from the bloc to head the committee for immigration and absorption in the Knesset. From his ministerial post, Lieberman called for a constitutional amendment, pointing out that Israel was "a police state" and that the "court enjoys powers that are stronger than that of the Prime Minister." Lieberman suggested, instead, establishing a strong centralized governmental system. He was determined to address issues that went beyond the interests of the Russian immigrants. He hoped to establish a coalition comprised of different sectors to struggle against what he described as the ruling elite in Israel. He anticipated that this coalition would include Russian immigrants and the rest of what he called "oppressed Jews" in the state.

The Yisrael Ba'aliyah party also signed a coalition agreement with the Sharon government. However, unlike the Yisrael Beitenu party, the Yisrael Ba'aliyah party insisted on including items regarding the absorption of Russian immigrants. One such item dealt with the appointment of a representative of the party as Deputy Prime Minister with assurances that he would be a full partner in drafting official politics towards the republics of the former Soviet Union and the Jewish minorities there. The Yisrael Beitenu agreement also required that the Deputy Prime Minister should head a ministerial committee for the Diaspora, immigration and absorption and that the Yisrael Ba'aliyah party should have a Deputy Minister for absorption and immigration.

The fifteenth Knesset elections signified the peak of Russian immigrant's support for the Russian political blocs. These blocs understood their inability to continue as Russian parties in the government and maintain neutral stands on political issues. Yisrael Beitenu was the first to take a clear political stand; Yisrael Ba'aliyah followed. Both of these Russian political parties turned to the right and were countered by the establishment of a leftist Russian party, the Democratic Choice. It is worth pointing out that, until the end of the fifteenth Knesset government term, no conflict erupted between Yisrael Ba'aliyah and Yisrael Beitenu.

Voting trends in the sixteenth Knesset elections

In the year 2001, at the peak of the Al-aqsa Intifada and of the economic crisis in Israel, the immigration wave from the former Soviet Union to Israel was declining. Russian immigrants that year numbered only 34,000, compared to 185,000 in 1990 (Central Bureau of Statistics, 2002). Data prepared by the Human Resources Department of the IDF General Staff noted that one-quarter of the soldiers in the Israeli army were Russian immigrants. Their percentage in field units drastically increased during the ongoing conflict and became similar to the percentage of Israeli veterans in these units. The same data revealed that 83 percent of Russian immigrants tended to enrol in the Israeli army – a higher percentage than the enrolment of veteran citizens (*Haaretz*, November 28, 2002).

Furthermore, the Russian immigrants suffered great losses as a result of military attacks by Palestinian commandos during the Intifada; this created a feeling of joint fate with the veteran Israelis. Moreover, during this period, the image of Natan Sharansky, the Yisrael Ba'aliyah leader, deteriorated among the Russian public. Sharansky, who had enjoyed total support from the Russian media in Israel, became the target of harsh criticism for his neglect of the Russian immigrants and his poor administration of the Yisrael Ba'aliyah party and the Zionist Forum. He was depicted as an oppressive person who cared only for his own interests, rather than those of the people whom he represented. In *Sharansky without a Mask* (1999), written in Russian by Michael Nudelman, a member of Yisrael Beitenu, this Russian politician attacked Sharansky's integrity and questioned his heroic past, describing him as a coward and a liar who had sold his comrades to the Soviet KGB when he was in Soviet prison. Sharansky successfully filed a lawsuit against Nudelman accusing him of defamation; but the coverage of the Russian-speaking media on the issue was not in Sharansky's favor. This media attributed the sudden withdrawal of a number of Yisrael Ba'aliyah Knesset members, before and after the 1999 elections, to Sharansky's negative qualities.

These issues weakened the Russian parties in the sixteenth Knesset elections. Yisrael Ba'aliyah won only 67,719 votes – 2.2 percent of eligible votes. This outcome secured only two Knesset seats for the party, which subsequently merged with the Likud and ceased to exist as independent political entity. Yisrael Beitenu joined a coalition with the National Union, Moledet and T'kumah to form the most extreme rightist political bloc in the Knesset. This coalition won 173,973 votes, or 5.5 percent of eligible votes, entitling it to seven seats in the Knesset.

The Tsemah election polls for the sixteenth Knesset elections revealed two noteworthy phenomena:

1) A great decline in Russian support for Russian parties occurred in the sixteenth Knesset elections.
2) Support for Yisrael Beitenu was much greater (28 percent of Russian voters) than support for Yisrael Ba'aliyah (17 percent of Russian voters); while the remaining votes went to the Likud (26 percent), Shinui (19 percent), Meretz and Labor (4 percent for both parties combined).

Back to the academic debate regarding the status of Russian immigrants in Israeli society, we find voting trends indicating that the Russian immigrants joined the radical rightist Jewish nationalist forces and considered themselves a supportive element against the Palestinian-Arab ethnic minority. In the early years, this was manifested in the rightist stance adopted by the two Russian parties, Yisrael Ba'aliyah and Yisrael Beitenu, who considered the issue of the Jewish–Palestinian conflict their topmost priority and consequently, increasingly neglected the daily interests of the Russian immigrants. Now, after more than a decade of life within Israeli society, the pure Russian ethnic parties, joining the extremist Israeli political parties, point to a self-image of the Russian immigrants as the "saviors" of extremist Jewish nationalism (Al-Haj, 2004a, 2004b).

Conclusion

The weakening of the Soviet Union in the late 1980s as a result of the policies of Mikhail Gorbachev, its last President, opened the gates of the Soviet Union, its successor states and its European satellites to significant immigration to Western Europe, the United States and Canada. Israel invested major effort in steering these Jews to its shores. Between 1989 and 2000, almost one million "Russian" immigrants came to Israel; a large percentage of them (up to a third) were not Jewish (Lustick, 1999). In addition to Zionist considerations of "aliya" and the ingathering of the exiles, Israel exerted international pressure to guarantee the arrival of these people, out of concern for demographic balance with the Palestinians in Israel proper and in the West Bank and Gaza Strip, as well. The question of the immigrants' *Jewishness* was pushed aside so as not to interfere with their arrival. It was only some years after the start of the Russian immigration that Jewish politicians and intellectuals began a public discussion of the compatibility between the Russian immigrants and the terms of the Law of Return (Lustick, 1999).

The Russian immigrants of the 1990s, unlike their predecessors of the 1970s and 1980s, did not quickly assimilate into Israeli society. They constituted a distinct group and imposed a multi-cultural situation on the Israeli localities where they live (Al-Haj, 1996). Russians in Israel have maintained the unique attributes and customs that distinguish them from other Jews. In general, they have held onto their mother tongue, (Russian or some other Eastern European language); continue to spend their leisure time and behave in key areas as they did in the old country; live in their own neighborhoods; and watch Russian television channels. They have established a broad network of newspapers, as well as voluntary organizations and Russian political parties, to promote their own special interests.

A quantitative study conducted among Russian immigrants in 1999 – about 10 years after the start of the wave of immigration – discerned a number of basic characteristics that corroborate the assertion that the Russians constitute a distinct group in Israeli society, with their own unique social, cultural and political orientation (Al-Haj and Leshem, 2000). First, Al-Haj and Leshem found that:

1) Most of the Russians support cultural continuity: the maintenance of

ethnic institutions and organizations, preservation of the Russian language and Russian culture, and support for organizations and institutions that promote this continuity.
2) Years after the start of the wave of immigration, the Russians still constitute a distinct and relatively close-knit social group with regard to their intra-group relationships, their relations with the outside world and with regard to their sources of information.
3) A large percentage of the Russians affirm that their ethnic identity is "Russian Jew." They thereby distinguish themselves from other groups in Israeli society and express a special affiliation that they consider makes them superior to other groups.
4) Russian attitudes and behavior reflect a pronounced secular identity that rejects the preservation of religious or traditional customs.

Second, Russian political organization gained new momentum in 1996 when Natan Sharansky founded the Yisrael Ba'aliyah party and again, in 1999, when Avigdor Lieberman founded Yisrael Beitenu. This political action was stimulated by the Russians' basic living conditions and by their status in Israeli politics, including their basic educational and occupational parameters (e.g. more than two-thirds have a higher education and aspire to find work in high-tech industry or institutions of higher education and research). In practice, the Russians understood the significance of political organization for promoting their particular interests. For example, after the 1992 elections and the replacement of the Likud government – led by Yitzhak Shamir, with a Labor government – headed by Yitzhak Rabin, it was widely believed that the Russian vote had been responsible for the change of government. This significantly enhanced the Russians' awareness of the weight of their votes and of their importance in future political processes in Israel. It produced a significant improvement in: (a) their self-image; (b) their perception of their ability to exert influence; and (c) their thoughts about effective organization.

Third, as soon as they arrived in Israel, the Russians began to organize in voluntary organizations, non-profit associations and non-partisan political bodies such as the Zionist Forum, meant to represent them and speak for them on both domestic and foreign issues. This organization provided the infrastructure for political advancement. Fourth, the Russians continued the tradition, well developed in the former Soviet Union, of publicizing and promoting political views through journalistic writing. They set up dozens of competing newspapers and periodicals that provided a forum for various opinions on "internal" Russian questions, Israeli questions and issues associated with the Palestinian conflict and its resolution. These media were available to the overwhelming majority of the Russian immigrants. This journalistic activity and exchange of opinions helped consolidate the positions and cultivate the unique concerns that pushed Russian activists to establish Russian political parties. Fifth, the Russians remained committed to preservation of their language, culture and traditions. The establishment of political parties was meant, in part, to defend the Russian community and its unique culture, so as to preserve the unique identity of the Russians in Israel. Sixth, the paltry representation of Russians in the veteran Israeli parties accelerated the search for new frameworks that would increase the percentage of Russians in the Knesset and in the decision-making echelons of Israeli governments. This strengthened the trend of establishing Russian ethnic parties that would garner Russian votes and work to promote the special interests of the group (Horowitz, 2003).

The literature offers a number of explanations for the Russians' political behavior (Fien, 1995; Gitelman and Goldstein, 2001; Horowitz, 2003; Reich, Dropkin and Wurmser, 1993). The most important and distinguishing are the following:

1) Frustration: The Russians' electoral behavior stems from their ongoing frustration with the nature of their absorption and their treatment by the Israeli establishment and general public. They believe that the establishment did not make a sufficient effort to facilitate their integration and find them appropriate employment or help them attain a decent standard of living relative to other Israelis. As a result, sentiments of frustration and revenge accumulated. The basic assertion is that the Russians developed voting patterns that are essentially different from those of other Israelis, with a proclivity to vote against the ruling party and replace it with the opposition.

2) Ideology: The Russians carry a right wing ideology that was originally developed in their country of origin, where they fostered anti-Palestinian and anti-Islamic sentiments as a result of the assistance extended by the Soviet Union to the Palestinian world in its clashes with Israel or as a result of confrontations with local Palestinian and Muslim communities in the Soviet Union. After their arrival in Israel, the Russians continue to hold anti-Palestinian and anti-Muslim political positions that take a hawkish line on a resolution of the conflict.

3) Internal agenda: The Russians tend to vote for or against domestic policies adopted by governments that stand to improve or worsen their living conditions. Thus, for example, it may be argued that part of the Russians' proclivities in their electoral preferences are associated with the degree to which they are satisfied by their absorption as against government support for other sectors of Israeli society, with the degree of liberalism or religiosity in Interior Ministry decisions to grant or deny citizenship to some of them and so on.

4) Unique identity: The Russians have developed a unique identity in Israel, which is distinct from all others. When they go to the polls they prefer their own ethnic parties or the political bloc whose ethnic leaders tend toward it. The argument is that this identity sought an outlet, through its electoral behavior, for the self-expression and empowerment

of their group. This explanation is associated with another, namely, that the Russians as a group tend to hold on to their position as the swing vote. Hence, their political behavior derives from exerting pressure on the political blocs in order to get them to adopt policies that are beneficial to the Russians.

6 Group divisions, the external conflict and political instability in Israel since Oslo

The February 2009 elections were the seventh held in Israel since 1992. The 1992 elections brought victory to the left wing, which attained a one-seat majority in the Knesset. This allowed Yitzhak Rabin to set up a government consisting of Labor and Meretz, with outside support from the Democratic Front for Peace and Equality (DFPE) and the Democratic Arab Party (DAP). Three-and-a-half years later, after Rabin's assassination, and because of Shimon Peres' desire for a mandate of his own, the 1996 elections for the fourteenth Knesset were held. This time the right wing challenger, Netanyahu, eked out a narrow victory and became the tenth Prime Minister of Israel. Netanyahu's tenure was marked by many power struggles and failures on both the external and domestic fronts. These forced him to advance the elections and face the Labor candidate, Barak, in a race for the fifteenth Knesset and the office of Prime Minister in May 1999. This time, Netanyahu lost to Barak, who took 56 percent of the vote. Netanyahu resigned from the Knesset after publication of the first results. Barak, in turn, called for a special election for Prime Minister in February 2001, after only a year-and-a-half in office. In this election, Barak lost to Sharon who became Israeli Prime Minister until December 2005. Then, on the eve of preparation for the March 2006 election, Sharon suffered a stroke. He was succeeded as the leader of the newly formed party, "Kadima," by MK Ehut Olmert. After the 2006 general election, Olmert become Prime Minister following his success in establishing a coalition between Kadima, Labor and the religious parties. In 2008, Olmert resigned, his successor in leading the Kadima party, Tzipi Livni, failed in her efforts to create a new coalition, due to huge financial and political demands raised by the SHAS party on one side and Livni's refusal to negotiate with the Arab-Palestinian parties on the other side. Israel then called for new elections in February 2009.

Each election during the period from 1992 until 2001 saw the incumbent lose and the victory of a candidate whom the electorate viewed as representing a policy and personality that contrasted with those of the incumbent.[1] For example:

- In 1992, Rabin replaced the incumbent Likud Prime Minister, Yitzhak

Shamir. Rabin stressed his position and the fact that he offered the voters a change in national priorities and an end to the conflict with the Palestinian world.
- In 1996, Netanyahu upset Shimon Peres, again on the basis of his promise to change the national priorities and do a better job resolving the conflict with the Palestinians.
- In 1999, Barak rode to victory on his promise to put an end to the conflict (including the withdrawal of the Israeli army from Lebanon) and to modify the national priorities.
- In 2001, Sharon promised to deal with the second Palestinian Intifada and set up a coalition of parties and groups opposed to Barak's foreign and domestic policy.
- In 2006, Kadima and the Labor party took over the election. They succeeded in establishing an alternative government to the one created after the 2003 election. This result occurred, in part, due to the split of the Likud party and the establishment of Kadima as a center party.
- In the 2009 election, Netanyahu and the extreme right won the election; again they promised to defeat the Palestinian challenge.

Most scholars, politicians and followers of Israeli politics viewed the change of the administration in 1992 and Rabin's accession to the premiership as the start of a new era in Israel. The signing of the Oslo accords reinforced this view. There were expectations that the region was moving toward resolving its conflicts and that Israel would enjoy diplomatic and economic relations with Arab countries. Scholars, politicians and others believed that Israel had completed its probationary period; successfully consolidated itself militarily, politically and economically; and produced a stable system. At the start of the decade, it seemed that Zionism had realized one of the main motives for the establishment of the state – the ingathering of the exiles – and had brought most of the Jews from places where they were in danger (e.g. the Arab world, Asia, Africa and the former Soviet Union) to the Jewish state; here, despite their differences, the various groups had emerged from the crucible of Israeli society to share a unified identity (Israeli) superimposed on their distinct sub-identities (Kimmerling, 1999). The willingness of the PLO and Arab states to negotiate with Israel was viewed as a reaction to their assessment that the Israeli system was stable and that Israel was a strong country, militarily, economically and politically superior to the Arab countries. The latter were coming to terms with this reality, on condition that Israel help resolve the Palestinian problem and return the land occupied in 1967.

One of the manifestations of Israel's stability and success has to do with voting patterns in Israeli general elections and the motives and considerations that guide Israelis when they go to the polls. The literature on elections offers two complementary explanations for the behavior of the Israeli voter. The prevailing explanation – "political-security" – asserts that when

Israelis vote they can be categorized according to their position on the resolution of the Israeli–Arab and Israeli-Palestinian conflict. (After 1993, this meant support for or opposition to the Oslo accords.) In the context of this explanation, supporters of the left wing parties (Labor, Meretz, the Palestinian parties) are viewed as supporting: (a) an end to the conflict; (b) diplomatic relations with Palestinian countries, including open borders between Israel and its neighbors; and (c) recognition of the PLO and the right of the Palestinian people to establish a state. Those who vote for the right (for example the Likud, Yisrael Ba'aliyah and the religious parties) are viewed as being opposed to the Oslo accords and the establishment of a Palestinian state, although at times they supported Oslo as an unpleasant fact (Arian, 1990, 1996; Arian and Shamir, 1999; Shamir and Arian, 1999).

The second explanation, which is less widespread but, I believe, more profound and comprehensive, could be termed "civil-primordial." This explanation holds that Israelis can be divided into two camps according to their fundamental principles. Supporters of the left tend to have a civil, secular and democratic orientation and a willingness to make a historic compromise with the Palestinian people, as an expression of their civil and liberal outlook. Supporters of the right, on the other hand, tend to have a "primordial" identity that is a mixture of religious and nationalist orientations (Kimmerling, 1999). The idea that the Israeli political map and Israeli voting patterns are drawn by political logic embodies the assumption that Israel has a bipartisan political system that rests on relevant considerations of war and peace, on one hand, and of civil and national identity, on the other. In practice, these two dimensions merge into two camps, one "civil and liberal"; the other "nationalist and conservative." Thus, the hypothesis of the research literature is that the Israeli melting pot has succeeded and that the Israeli public behaves rather like the electorates in Western democracies, who are divided along lines associated with liberalism, on one hand, or with advocacy of conservative or nationalist positions, on the other.

In this book, I argue that the main factor behind Israeli political system stability or instability is related to the politics of identity that has come to constitute the primary political strategy of Israeli citizens. This strategy was reinforced by the legitimacy the identities of marginal groups were granted as a reflection of the hegemonic ethnic state system created by the Ashkenazi group and used by that group to ensure its superiority and domination over other groups. Each group was unique and distinctive with regard to the level at which it used identity as a means of political mobilization and as a catalyst for political action among sectarian movements and parties. However, the action and the level of protest or accommodation of all these groups – besides indicating the level of identity consolidation – also reflected the external threats or opportunities that have confronted Israel since its independence, in general, and since the signing of the Oslo agreement, in particular. Thus, the level of confrontation with the Palestinians and the Arab world has been one of the main factors behind the rise or fall of identity as a political tool.

This argument is developed, in the current chapter, by analyzing the politics of identity in Israel during the past two decades. I have used the second Palestinian Intifada (since 2000) as a defining moment in the politics of unrest among various groups in Israel after Oslo. I maintain, first, that the politics of identity played a role in creating the unstable situation in Israel during the 1990s and that this role reflected the circulation of a misleading concept: that Israel, following the implementation of the Oslo agreement, would soon enjoy peaceful relations with the Palestinians and the Arab world. Second, I analyze and explain the stability experienced since 2001, under the Sharon and Olmert governments, as reflecting the *intensification* of conflict with the Palestinians, following the second Intifada and the growing level of external threats to Israel and the Israelis.

The role of group identity in the creation of political instability in Israel during the 1990s

The repeated defeats of incumbents in Israel during the first decade following the signing of the Oslo agreements reflected sharp oscillations in the political habits of the groups that defined the fissures that beset Israeli society. These oscillations contributed to the instability of the political system. In order to provide an empirical illustration of this chapter's main thesis regarding the causes of Israeli political instability, this section provides a summary of the primary changes in voting patterns for the groups enumerated above.

The electoral behavior of the Palestinians in Israel during the first decade after Oslo was an expression of the intensity of their alienation: it reflected the opposition between them and other (Jewish) citizens of the state and the opposition between them and the Jewish-Zionist establishment, including differences regarding the implementation of peace agreements with the PLO.

Since 1949, Palestinians in Israel, who now account for 14 percent of the electorate, have served as a reservoir of votes to help the Jewish left maintain its grip on the reins of political power. At first, the Palestinians voted directly for Mapai and its successors; not until the 1970s and 1980s did their voting habits begin to shift significantly toward Palestinian or mixed Jewish–Palestinian parties (the DFPE). This process was accelerated by changes in the electoral system and the institution of direct elections for Prime Minister, separate from the Knesset ballot (Ghanem and Ozacky-Lazar, 2001). Even after the change in voting patterns, however, Palestinian Knesset members continued to be hostages of the Jewish-Zionist left; their votes on major questions were based on the assumption that their conduct in the Knesset must not detract from the prospects of the left to govern Israel and promote Israeli–Palestinian peace. Azmi Bishara's withdrawal from the prime ministerial race in 1999, two days before the elections, and his call upon his supporters to vote for Ehud Barak, clearly exemplified the double-bind into which the Palestinian leadership had gotten itself and its constituency (Ghanem and Ozacky-Lazar, 2001).

In this arena, the essence of the distress among Palestinians in Israel was the dilemma of whether to work as an extra-parliamentary force and be accused of denying the legitimacy of the state, or whether to remain at the political mercies of the Jewish left, which had created and built the system of institutional discrimination positioned against the Palestinian citizens of Israel. By excluding the Palestinians from participation in government coalitions, the system also rendered Palestinian votes illegitimate and contributed to a disregard for Palestinian lives that ripened into the killing of 12 Israeli Palestinians by security forces in October 2000 (Ghanem and Ozacky-Lazar, 2003).

Toward the end of the twentieth century, it was clear that one way out of the "Jewish left trap" was for a Palestinian to run for Prime Minister, win virtually the entire Palestinian vote, and make preparations to negotiate, in advance of a runoff, the advancement of Palestinian interests. Following Barak's resignation and the passage of the so-called Netanyahu law, it was clear that the Palestinians in Israel supported this option and anticipated its realization. However, the Palestinian members of the Knesset, beset by fierce internal struggles, failed in their mission and threw away their chance to advance the interests and positions of their constituency.

After the Palestinian leadership rejected the option of a Palestinian candidate for Prime Minister, the only remaining choice for Israeli Palestinians in the 2001 elections for Prime Minister, was to stay away from the polls. The public at large took the reins into its own hands to escape the double-bind of Palestinian politics in Israel. Understanding that it could not stem the flood, the Palestinian leadership retroactively adopted the public's stance. Some leaders called for staying home on election day; others favored casting a blank ballot; while the majority sat on their hands until the storm had passed. This time the street had its say and the leadership played virtually no role in steering the course of events. The situation created by this mass abstention of Israeli Palestinians (only about 20 percent did vote) was, without doubt, the most important development in Israeli Palestinian politics since 1949, when the Communist Party – as an expression of its "two states for two peoples" program and the implementation of the partition plan – called on the Palestinians to turn out and vote.

Two possible explanations exist for the Palestinians' political behavior in the 2001 elections. First, they may have sought revenge on Ehud Barak and the Labor party for the killing of young Palestinians and the continuing war against the Palestinian national movement in the West Bank and Gaza Strip. Second, they may have come to the conclusion that it was difficult, perhaps even impossible, to realize their group aspirations and desires through parliamentary struggle. Turning their collective back on the parliamentary arena represented a vote of no confidence in the Israeli political system and a slap in the face to Palestinian Knesset members who continued to advocate a parliamentary struggle, though this approach had been unproductive.

The role of the religious–secular fissure in the creation of political instability

The intensity of the antagonism towards the Ashkenazi-secular group has been of crucial importance for political fluctuations in Israel. The religious side of the fissure consists chiefly of the National Religious Party, Yahadut Hatorah, and SHAS. In the 1990s, there were significant fluctuations in support for the NRP and in the size of its Knesset faction. The NRP, viewed as an integral part of the right wing bloc, suffered from a radical right wing image and the party's support reflected the public mood about the future of the West Bank and Gaza Strip, after the Oslo accords. In the elections to the thirteenth Knesset, in 1992, the NRP won only six seats, continuing its decline. In the elections for the fourteenth Knesset, in 1996, the NRP won nine seats (Arian and Shamir, 1999), and asserted that it was on the road back to its glory days. This rebound can be attributed to the change in the electoral system that allowed supporters to vote both for the party and directly for a candidate for Prime Minister. In addition, right wing support for the NRP increased – at the expense of the Likud and other parties that did not present a strong platform against Oslo – because of the public climate, division about implementation of the Oslo accords and a sharpening of the struggle between supporters and opponents of compromise following the assassination of Prime Minister Rabin. In 1999, the NRP again declined, winning only six seats (Arian and Shamir, 2001). This time the decline reflected a schism in the party that occurred as a result of Meimad joining the Labor party's One-Israel list and as a result of some NRP voters seeking escape from the Israeli–Palestinian quagmire through the promises of Ehud Barak, Labor's candidate for Prime Minister.

The religious anti-Zionist stream (Agudat Yisrael–Yahadut Hatorah) has always been represented in the Knesset. In the 1990s, it maintained a stable faction of four to five seats, even after the change in the electoral system. The stability of this stream attests to the high solidarity among its voters and to party loyalty that precluded seeking alternatives outside the Ashkenazi Haredi community.

The religious and traditional stream represented by SHAS won four seats in the 1984 elections for the tenth Knesset. Since then the party steadily expanded its power, winning 17 seats in 1999 under the leadership of Arye Deri. Various factors explain SHAS's success: (a) the party's appeal to and cultivation of the Mizrahim's feelings of having faced discrimination by the Ashkenazi establishment since their arrival in Israel; (b) the party's broad appeal to various groups in Israeli society, including those that were not religiously observant; (c) the provision of basic support services for underprivileged groups, including an educational system that was an alternative to the state system; and (d) a pragmatic and general platform that was neither radically right wing, nor identifiable with the positions of the Israeli left.

On the secular side of the divide, the Meretz, Shinui, and Russian parties benefited from their voters' intense antipathy toward religion, in general and toward the religious parties, in particular. For example, in 1988, after it was formed, Meretz won 10 Knesset seats; subsequently, it won 12 seats in 1992, nine in 1996 and 10 in 1999 (Arian and Shamir, 1999, 2001). Before the 1999 Knesset elections, the Shinui party, headed by Tommy Lapid, gained broad support from various anti-religious sectors and won six Knesset seats by conducting a campaign that hurled abuse at the ultra-orthodox and SHAS groups. Likewise, the Russian parties fought against religious demands and insisted that Russian immigrants be allowed to live according to their values and positions. One major Russian party, Yisrael Ba'aliyah, established before the 1996 elections, won seven Knesset seats in the 1996 elections and six in the 1999 elections. While a second major Russian party, Yisrael Beitenu, established before the 1999 elections, won four seats in that election (Gitelman and Goldstein, 2001).

These election results indicate that the religious–secular fissure played a decisive role in the preferences of Israeli voters and the sharp fluctuations that took place on the Israeli political map during the 1990s. The fissure, also, was associated with how voters saw the role of religion in Israeli society. During the 1990s, the impact of the religious–secular fissure on Israeli voting preferences was reflected in the rise in the support for the NRP and ultra-orthodox parties on one hand and for anti-religious parties such as Meretz and Shinui on the other. No reliable data are available for the elections for Prime Minister held on February 6, 2001, but one may infer from newspaper reports that an overwhelming majority (almost 98 percent of those who went to the polls) of the national religious and ultra-orthodox voted for the right wing candidate, Ariel Sharon – approximately the same support they gave his predecessor, Binyamin Netanyahu, in 1999.

The role of the Mizrahi–Ashkenazi fissure in the creation of political instability

Mizrahi awareness and an increasing ethnic orientation created a broad foundation for particularistic political behavior among Mizrahim, on one hand, and Ashkenazim, on the other. Research data indicate that Mizrahim with an ethnic awareness and developed sense of discrimination tend to support political activity to change their situation and are inclined to vote for parties that are seen as defending Mizrahi interests.

Over the years, the two major parties, Labor and the Likud, and their satellites (Meretz and its components on one side and the radical right wing parties on the other) have been Ashkenazi dominated. Both parties were born and have continued to function as Ashkenazi parties, even though electoral patterns have correlated with ethnic affiliation (e.g. since the 1960s most Mizrahim have voted for the Likud and most Ashkenazim have voted for Labor). On the other hand, most attempts over the years to set up parties to represent the Mizrahim and their interests have met with little success. For example, in the first 10 Knesset campaigns (through 1984), 31 Mizrahi-identified lists ran for the Knesset, but only five crossed the threshold and won seats in the Knesset.

In 1992, SHAS, the religious Mizrahi party, won six seats, raising its total to 10 seats in 1996 and 17 in 1999. Gesher, headed by David Levy and also viewed as a Mizrahi movement, ran in the 1996 elections on a joint list with the Likud and won six seats; in 1999 it ran on a joint list with Labor and Meimad and won four seats. Ever since the 1960s, the Mizrahim have tended to vote for the right wing bloc and then for SHAS (particularly in 1996 and 1999 – see Peled, 2001). Even though there are no reliable data on the 2001 elections for Prime Minister, one may infer from newspaper reports that most Mizrahim and residents of development towns (70 percent) voted for Ariel Sharon, while fewer than one-third of the Mizrahim supported Ehud Barak.

The role of the Israeli–Russian fissure in the creation of political instability

The Israeli–Russian divide was the latest to appear; however, its political significance has been no less than that of the other fissures. The Russians' electoral behavior during the last decade has shifted back and forth, reinforcing the argument about their decisive role in the political fluctuations in Israel during this decade. In the 1992 elections, when Rabin replaced Shamir as Prime Minister, there were about 250,000 Russians eligible to vote, or some 8 percent of the electorate. Most – approximately two-thirds – voted for Labor and Meretz; in essence, it was they who gave Rabin and the Labor bloc the bare majority of 61 Knesset seats that ousted the Likud government and brought Rabin's Labor government to power (Gitelman and Goldstein, 2001). In the 1996 Knesset and prime ministerial elections, there were 400,000 Russian voters, or 13 percent of the electorate. Approximately 43 percent of them voted for Yisrael Ba'aliyah, which was making its electoral debut and won seven seats. Another Russian party, Unity and Aliya, ran but failed to cross the threshold, while the rest of the Russian vote was split among the veteran parties, mainly the Likud and Labor. In the voting for Prime Minister, Binyamin Netanyahu took about 70 percent of the Russian vote, while Shimon Peres won only 30 percent. The Russian vote was one of the important factors that gave Netanyahu his razor-thin margin (50.49 percent of the vote) and kept Peres from being elected Prime Minister (Horowitz, 1994).

In the 1999 elections, the Russians constituted about one-sixth of the electorate. They were a major target of both prime ministerial candidates (Netanyahu and Barak), who assumed that other sectors (e.g. the Palestinians, the ultra-orthodox and the settlers) were already guaranteed to support one or other candidate. Thus, the Russians were viewed as: (a) a group that had not yet coalesced ideologically; and (b) a group that could determine the election results. In the Knesset race most of the Russians voted for ethnic parties – 34 percent for Yisrael Ba'aliyah and 17 percent for Yisrael Beitenu (Gitelman and Goldstein, 2001). At the same time, a majority of the Russians voted for Ehud Barak (about 57 percent), chiefly because of his promise to give the immigrants control of the Ministry of the Interior; but also because of Yisrael Ba'aliyah's covert support for Barak's candidacy – which was itself revenge for Netanyahu's support of the establishment of Yisrael Beitenu (Horowitz, 1999).

In the 2001 prime ministerial race, the Russian parties mobilized on behalf of Ariel Sharon. Though there are no precise figures available, newspaper analyses support the assumption that most of the Russians (about 70 percent) preferred Sharon over Barak and helped contribute to Sharon's landslide victory (63 percent) over Barak (37 percent). The Russians' electoral behavior in the most recent elections can be clarified by a combination of the explanations previously posited: frustration, ideology, holding the balance and social agenda. Primarily, however, it stemmed from the resentment that had accumulated among the Russians against Prime Minister Barak, who did not bother to woo the Russian parties and give them ministerial and financial rewards commensurate with their support for him in 1999.

The impact of the post-Oslo era and the Palestinian second Intifada on identity politics in Israel

During the last decade of the twentieth century, relations between the main groups composing Israeli society underwent a transformation. The peace process with the Palestinians created the illusion of progress towards a resolution of the Palestinian problem and paved the way for an intensification of internal conflicts once peace was achieved. Elections were held every three years – each time the opposition parties managed to form a new government. Palestinians within Israel took up their Palestinian nationalist identity with greater passion, now that it had been legitimized by the peace agreement with the PLO and the emergence of a new generation of political leaders among them. Russian immigrants gained demographic and cultural momentum following the massive immigration from countries of the former Communist bloc and proceeded to set up two new political parties, Yisrael Ba'aliyah and Yisrael Beitenu. The religious continued to press their demands for enhanced status, while SHAS, the religious Mizrahi party, enjoyed unprecedented support. Feeling threatened, the secular faction set up the Shinui party, led by journalist Tommy Lapid. Some of the Israeli elites began to realize that the success of the peace process would intensify internal conflicts by exacerbating social divides.

Ariel Sharon's ascent to power in 2001 signified Israel's abandonment of the Oslo peace process with the Palestinians (Ghanem, 2003). The escalation of the external threat to Israel posed by the Palestinians and by the Arabs, in general, fostered a certain stability in Israel, at least among Jewish groups. Israel's transition under Sharon – from attempting to find a solution to the Palestinian problem, to a new approach of managing the conflict, rather than resolving it – was a calculated step. A key motive behind this step was the fear that success of the peace process with the Palestinians would further polarize and divide Israeli society.

Following the outbreak of the second Intifada in 2000, the Israeli leadership and Israeli elites drew a sharp distinction between Jewish groups "on the inside" and Palestinian citizens of Israel on the "outside." Different and even opposing goals, approaches and policies were applied to the two groups. Exclusionary policies that removed the Palestinians from the *in-group* gathered steam. At the same time, efforts were made to reduce tensions and strengthen solidarity among Jewish groups as part of coping with the external threat – the second Intifada and Palestinian resistance to the Israeli occupation.

The contour lines on a political map showing the relations between the major groups in Israeli society, indicate a complex reality of diverse groups seeking to maintain their differences. During the last decade, the Palestinians in Israel have become more isolated, more threatening and more threatened than they were in the past. The profile sketched by Rouhana and Ghanem in 1998 remains valid, despite the intensification of the crisis in relations between the Jewish majority and the Palestinian minority (Rouhana and Ghanem, 1998). A rupture in relations between the two groups may eventually be caused by the Jewish refusal to compromise on the Jewish character of the state, on the one hand, and the unyielding insistence of Palestinian citizens of Israel that there be a change in this Jewish character, on the other.

Relations between the secular Ashkenazim and the various religious streams are becoming a complex combination of segregation and integration in the various spheres of life. The Mizrahim seem to have accepted their marginal position; they demand equality while displaying a willingness to come to terms with the Ashkenazi system as it is. Russian immigrants, who have achieved optimal recognition, status and impact, are beginning to reach for political power, mostly on the right, while preserving their culture and their separate status. What follows analyzes these trends and offers possible ways of managing the tensions that are part and parcel of the divided reality.

Palestinians in Israel in the last decade

The Palestinians in Israel continue to be marginalized, as a group that is excluded from the project of the Jewish state and Judaization. Their marginalization has been exacerbated by political activity that gives expression to this marginal status. A number of significant developments since the beginning of the current decade clearly attest to the evolution of the Palestinians and the exacerbation of their status as a marginal group seeking to change its status and situation in the direction of greater equality.

The relations, during the first five decades of Israel's existence, between the Palestinian minority and the Jewish majority and state have been portrayed as in perpetual crisis (Rouhana and Ghanem, 1998). The crises intensified following the failure of the peace process between Israel and the Palestinian national movement, and the outbreak of the Al-aqsa Intifada in 2000. The latter deepened the estrangement of the minority from the majority by amplifying the nationalist discourse among Jews and the sense of marginalization and alienation among the Arabs.

The failure of the peace process at the end of the 1990s undermined the political discourse that had drawn a connection between resolution of the Palestinian problem and civil equality for Israeli Palestinians; it became clear that a successful or unsuccessful resolution of the national problem would not affect the civil status of Palestinians in Israel proper. This generated a new political discourse and awareness that perceived a link between the status of Palestinians in Israel and the character of the Jewish state. New scholarly theories expounded on the dual and undemocratic nature of the Israeli political regime (Yiftachel and Ghanem, 2004a). These scholarly analyses also identified the obstacles posed to Arabs' individual and collective equality by the two-faced regime (Ghanem, 2001b). This political insight helped shape Palestinian political discourse that focused on patriotism and its latent power with regard to the Jewish identity of the state.

The Israeli Palestinians' cultivation of a defiant public discourse and entrenchment of the positions of the Jewish government and the public highlight the crisis situation in which Palestinians live in Israel. Part of this crisis is due to the Jewish character of the state and its historical and symbolic hegemony, which excludes Arabs in every domain. Government and public resolve have spawned continual efforts – including legislation – to strengthen the Jewish character of the state. These efforts have culminated in a constitution, proposed by the Israel Democracy Institute, that would emphasize the Jewish character of the state through its symbols and its historical narrative (Shamgar, 2006). This issue of the Jewishness of the state has been the crux of the conflict and debate between the Palestinians and the Jews over the last decade. The Palestinians have linked the Jewish character with their own status as a national minority, while the Jews understand it as connected to their legitimate right to self-determination in the state. In the light of this debate, Palestinian nationalism has become a codeword for the status of the Palestinian minority. Indeed, some individuals have begun to link these two topics (i.e. altering the Jewish character of the state and Palestinian nationalism), and have proposed the establishment of a bi-national state in historical Palestine (Ghanem, 1999, 2005a).

Many maintain that Israeli democracy is locked in a permanent conflict with the Jewish character of the state (Smooha, 2005). As the Palestinians see it, the Jewishness of the state contradicts its democratic nature and results in something like apartheid or an anti-democratic ethnocracy (Gavison, 1999; Gavison and Hacker, 2002; Ghanem and Mustafa, 2009; Smooha, 2005). On the other hand, there is a Zionist current which holds that the "enemy within" is exploiting Israeli democracy to undermine the Jewish character of the state. They see a perpetual need to contract the scope of democracy while simultaneously expanding the Jewish character of the state and conditioning citizenship on the fulfillment of certain obligations.

Within the maelstrom of the debate over the Jewish character of the state, the Jewish elite feels the need to stress this character by creating a wall-to-wall Jewish-Zionist consensus on this issue. These efforts culminated in the "Tiberias document," which reflects the national Jewish consensus regarding the Jewishness of the state, while stressing the deplorable condition of Arabs in Israel. Deliberations about the "Tiberias document" were conducted exclusively within the Jewish elite, with no attempt to include others – the Arabs who live in Israel – in the discussion. Thus, a document that claims to faithfully represent the situation of the country excludes Arabs and Arab elites a priori, for Jewish-nationalist reasons.

In addition to the "Tiberias document," several inclusive joint initiatives by Jews and Arabs have formulated theoretical academic alternatives regarding the status of Palestinians in Israel (see Ozacky-Lazar, Ghanem and Pappe, 1999). Continuing these initiatives, a group of Arabs and Jews, primarily from academia, came together at the Van Leer Jerusalem Institute to draw up a joint document. The group of 20 Arab and Jewish academics met 17 times during 1999–2001 to discuss the matter. The participants reached agreement on civil equality, but steadfastly differed about the question of the Jewish character of the state. Neither side was willing to even discuss the matter; consequently, the Arab members rejected the proposed document, the aim of which had been to confer joint legitimacy on a "constitution by consensus." Journalist Uzi Benziman edited the group's discussions into a book entitled *Whose Land Is It? A Quest for Jewish-Arab Compact in Israel* (Benziman, 2006).

The Israel Democracy Institute also drafted and circulated a document for a "constitution by consensus," that underscored the Jewishness of the state from a symbolic, legal and practical standpoint. The Knesset Constitution, Law and Justice Committee is basing its deliberations regarding a national constitution on this document. Intensive legislative efforts and sensitive legal activity have been and still are being conducted to confer internal legal content on the Jewishness of the state and the fact that the state is the "state of the Jewish people." This process has culminated in the effort to formulate an Israeli constitution (Ghanem and Mustafa, 2009). The proposed constitution proclaims that Israel is a "democratic Jewish state" and emphasizes this character from a legal standpoint. The first article of the first section of the constitution, entitled "Fundamentals," states that the name of the country is "Israel." The second article begins, "Israel is a Jewish and democratic state" (Shamgar, 2006: 91). The various articles of the constitution stress and clearly explicate the Jewish character of the state with regard to the Right of Return, citizenship and state symbols (Shamgar, 2006). A series of Israeli laws guarantee the official privileges enjoyed by the Jewish majority in a number of areas. According to polls by the Israel Democracy Institute, a majority of Arabs support this version of the constitution and the Jewish identity of the state; however, other surveys contradict this claim.[2]

Along with efforts to enact a constitution that stresses the Jewish character of the state, vigorous efforts have been made to pass other laws that do the same. The amended Citizenship Law of 2003 is an obvious example. Although security considerations are the stated official reason for the law, the actual reason is demographic – as a number of Knesset members have declared in public. For instance, Likud member, Yuval Steinitz, has stated, "I'm not interested in talking about the security dimensions that were added to the law.... The state is fully entitled to defend itself from a demographic standpoint" (Sultany, 2004: 57).

In light of these developments indicating the position of the state and the Jewish majority regarding the status of the Palestinians in Israel, the minority citizenry took a number of steps. A new proactive approach signified increased confidence on the part of the Arabs, who were ready to take action to achieve equality and terminate the Jewish character of Israel. Arab willingness to take action to change their status was illustrated during the Al-aqsa Intifada, in late September and early October 2000, when hundreds of Palestinian citizens of Israel took to the streets to protest Israel's policies towards their Palestinian brothers in the occupied territories and to express their demand for equality. The killing of 13 Arab citizens by Israeli security forces in clashes with the demonstrators sparked an unprecedented deterioration in relations between the Arab minority and the state and intensified the estrangement between Arabs and Jews in Israel.

The Israeli government's decision to set up a state commission of inquiry (the Or Commission) to investigate the killings calmed the waters, to some extent. The Commission wrestled with the issue for about three years and then wrote a wide-ranging report that included individual recommendations concerning those responsible for the events of October 2000. The report elaborated on the need for a fundamental change in the government's policy toward minorities. However, the Commission was unable to ensure that those among the police and other security forces responsible for the killings, or those responsible at the political level, paid the price for their actions.

Nor did the report succeed in effecting change in the state's approach to minorities (see the Sikkuy reports on the issue: www.Sikkuy.org).

In September 2005, following publication of the Or Commission recommendations and one week before the annual memorial for the events of October 2000, the Police Investigations Unit of the Justice Ministry published its investigative report. The Unit did not file a single indictment against any of the policemen who participated in the events. Palestinian citizens viewed the report as legitimizing the killing of Arab citizens and as an expression of the state's lack of concern for a large proportion of its centers. Over time, Palestinian citizens' trust in state institutions declined as a result of these institutions' ethnic approach and exclusion of Arabs (Arian et al., 2004, 2005).

The most striking expression of the Arabs' loss of confidence in the Israeli system is the significant increase in the number of Arabs who boycott national elections. Political scientists stress the connection between the form and substance of a democratic regime and the rate of political participation (Almond and Verba, 1963). People's desire to participate in elections increases when they feel they have an impact on political decision-making. The less people feel that they influence decision-making, the less interested they are in voting in elections (Nie et al., 1974). More recent studies hold that a marginalized minority that organizes politically looks for a way out of this situation (Gurr, 1993). However, the case of Palestinians in Israel also indicates that political mobilization is liable to provoke disagreements with the majority over goals and strategy, that soon become entrenched (Kaufman and Israeli, 1999).

Over the last decade, a crisis has been created in Arab politics. The trend in Arab political behavior has been to stay away from the polls; the participation of Palestinians in Knesset elections is declining. In the elections for the seventeenth (2006) Knesset, the boycott rate reached a high of 44 percent, compared with 38 percent in the 2003 sixteenth Knesset election (Mustafa and Ghanem, 2007).[3] The low turnout of Israeli Palestinians for the seventeenth and eighteenth Knessets indicates a continuing trend of boycotting elections. It suggests that the Arab minority has no expectations of success in the parliamentary arena and that most Palestinians in Israel have despaired of achieving their political goals through the Knesset. The structural obstacles erected by the Israeli ethnocracy fuel the Arabs' sense of impotence with regard to collective rights and daily life (Ghanem, 2001b; Ghanem and Rouhana, 2001). Because of the barriers erected against them, the Arab Knesset factions are unable to improve the condition of Palestinian citizens; nor are they able to influence political decisions that affect either the status of the Arab minority or the Palestinian national issue (Ben-Eliezer, 1993; Ghanem, 1997).

Consequently, some Palestinian citizens of Israel are organizing extra-parliamentary political activity, which Arab society has found to be more effective than parliamentary activity. Examples of extra-parliamentary entities include the Islamic Movement, the Sons of the Village, and various civil-society organizations (Mustafa and Ghanem, 2007; Payes, 2005; Rekhess, 1993).

The "future vision" of the Palestinians in Israel

In December 2006, a group of politicians and intellectuals, led by Shawki Khatib, the head of the Supreme Follow-up Committee – the highest and most authoritative representative body of the Palestinians in Israel – and Leader of the National Committee of Arab Local Council Heads, published the "Future vision of the Palestinian Arabs in Israel." The document, an expression of Arab processes of internal empowerment and of their increased frustration with official policy, attracted national and international interest and elicited a wide variety of responses across the political spectrum. The document was an historic event in the annals of the Palestinians in Israel and of their relationship with the Jewish majority and establishment. It marked the first time a representative national body of Palestinians in Israel had prepared and published a basic paper that described both the existing situation and the changes needed across a broad spectrum of Palestinian life: relations with the Jewish majority; the legal situation; land, social and economic issues; the status of civil and political institutions; and so on. The document, written by activists from all political tendencies among the Palestinians in Israel, delineated the achievements necessary for defining the future relationship between the majority and the minority in the State of Israel.

The document is based on three theoretical principles that have constituted the foundations of human social, political and cultural development for at least the past two centuries. The first principle addressed is human rights; the document addresses and demands the realization of fundamental human rights for the Palestinians in Israel: the right to economic and social development; rights for women and children; the right to live without violence and so on. The second principle invokes civil equality – the basic democratic right to equality before the law – and demands the annulment of laws, structures and symbols that alienate the Palestinian citizens of Israel and ensure Jewish superiority. Finally, the third principle addresses the right of communities to self-determination, including the autonomous right to manage specific areas of life, such as their own education and cultural and religious affairs. In order to realize these foundations, the document's writers demanded that a consociational system/bi-national state be implemented in Israel to replace the existing liberal system that: (a) is exploited automatically by the Jewish majority; and (b) constitutes a "tyranny of the majority" in which, in the name of liberal democracy, the majority takes draconian steps against the Palestinian minority and its fundamental rights.

Identity and politics within the Jewish community in the past decade

Within the Jewish sector, the Oslo agreement reshaped identity patterns while structuring a political discourse marked by numerous elements of conflict. The chimera of peace relocated the spheres of conflict and identity politics within Jewish society. This new set of identities was a function of the reduction of the perceived threat posed by the Palestinians. In other words, the Oslo process reshaped the Palestinians in Jewish eyes, greatly reducing their function as an "external threat." This restructuring provided an opening for identity politics and for attempts by various cultural groups within Jewish society to redefine their demands in the internal Jewish arena. Most of my focus in this context will be on the three biggest divides in Israeli society: the rifts between the Mizrahim and the Ashkenazim, between the religious and the secular communities, and between veteran Israelis and Russians (immigrants from the former Soviet Union).

The 1990s were a time of "conflict-oriented nationalism," or multi-cultural competition among sectors of Israeli society, primarily within the Jewish majority. The recasting and manipulation of the "external threat" – from an Israel surrounded by a sea of Arab hatred whose aim is to "drive all the Jews into the ocean," to an almost messianic vision of peace between Israel and its neighbors – was accompanied by a meteoric rise in demands for cultural recognition of the constituent groups within the Jewish majority. SHAS, for instance, which highlighted the ethnic divide between the Ashkenazi elite and the Mizrahim, was on an electoral upsurge. The party was a member of every coalition during the 1990s, doubling its strength in the 1996 elections and tripling it in 1999, to an astonishing 17 mandates (the third-largest faction in the Knesset).

Grinberg provides the following description of the changing of the guard, from the illusory threat posed by the Palestinian-Arab world to the domestic kulturkampf in Israel, with regard to SHAS, the crisis of the Zionist ethos and its former methods of mobilization:

> In the past the "external" threat forged the boundaries of the national community while also legitimizing a social hierarchy in which modern and Western secular Ashkenazim had the upper hand. This was a "conflict-oriented nationalism," which legitimized a dominant group through its military service in elite units and as high-ranking officers, thereby marginalizing all the rest.... With the appearance of sectoral politics in the 1990s, the post-conflict agenda reflected the dismantling of the "conflict-oriented nationalist" identity and the absence of an alternative collective identity that would legitimize the hierarchical structure and the superiority of the secular Ashkenazi group.
>
> (Grinberg, 2007: 346)

Despite challenges and crises, such as the criminal indictments of SHAS Knesset members and the conviction of its charismatic leader, Arye Deri, Mizrahi identity seemed to be on the ascent. At the height of the movement's power, after the 1999 elections, it was impossible to form a coalition without SHAS. The coalition negotiations that followed Ehud Barak's election as Prime Minister were marked by a broad-based public campaign to exclude SHAS, featuring the slogan, "Just Not SHAS." This campaign may have been an attempt by the Ashkenazi elite to stuff the "ethnic genie" back into the bottle by resurrecting the call for "unity" (i.e. the reassertion of Ashkenazi hegemony in culture and society) in the Jewish–Israeli discourse. However, SHAS's power as the third-largest party, together with other coalition constraints, made this impossible. The "threat of the Orient and Orientalism" found expression in academic research as well. Sociologist Baruch Kimmerling's *Ketz Shilton ha-Ohselim* [The end of Ashkenazi hegemony] (2001) is worthy of note in this context. "Ohselim" is an acronym for "socialist/nationalist veteran-Israeli secular Ashkenazim." Kimmerling analyzes this group's loss of its hegemony in Israeli society over the course of the 1990s.

A number of other events reflected the crisis and schism-ridden politics of the 1990s. "The Mizrahi Democratic Rainbow," which advocated a multicultural society, equal allocation of resources and the promotion of previously suppressed Mizrahi discourse and culture, was founded in 1996. Sami Shalom Chetrit founded the "Kedma" school network in 1994 to provide egalitarian education for residents of the Israeli periphery, while shaping the content of "Israeliness" according to multi-cultural rather than hegemonic codes. A State Commission of Inquiry to investigate the disappearance of Yemenite children during the 1940s and 1950s was set up in 1998. David Levy's Gesher party, while not stressing the Mizrahi ethnic affiliation the way SHAS did, was surely identified as such by voters and was considered an electoral asset by candidates for Prime Minister, because of its presumed appeal to Mizrahim.[4] Finally, Ehud Barak, the "One Israel" candidate for Prime Minister in 1999, issued a public apology for the injustices the state had perpetrated against the Mizrahim.

All this activity rapidly disappeared with the outbreak of the second Intifada in September 2000 and particularly after the snap election for Prime Minister in 2001. The "return" of the "external threat" effectively silenced internal Jewish demands. What is interesting is that the reinsertion of an external threat into the Israeli discourse was common to all the Jewish Zionist political parties. Public opinion was unanimous in condemning the cycle of violence as exclusively of Palestinian origin and in blaming it on Yasser Arafat. The argument that it was the visit by Ariel Sharon, then leader of the opposition, to the Temple Mount that sparked the violence was repeatedly stifled in the Israeli discourse. During the 2001 election campaign, even Ehud Barak explicitly rejected any notion of Sharon's responsibility and held the Palestinians alone responsible for the cycle of violence.[5]

Given the sense of crisis among the Ashkenazi elite, constructing such a narrative and nurturing an external enemy were needs of the highest order. The Ashkenazi longed to restore their lost hegemony and to retrieve their decisive influence by resuming their battle cry of "unity." Grinberg sums up the process as follows:

> The "outbreak of peace" posed a problem for the dominant groups – the absence of an alternative to conflict-oriented nationalism and to the myth of security – an alternative that would justify their superior status and subordinate the other sectors composing Israeli society to them.
> (Grinberg, 2007: 364)

In these conditions, the Mediterranean culture began to pose a threat to the Ashkenazi cultural hegemony. The cultural anxiety concerning the East, which supposedly threatened to spread and wipe out the achievements of the European culture that had been constructed in Israel, "reflected a fear that the national project to build a 'modern' people that was neither exilic nor religious, was liable to collapse in conditions of peace and of borders open to economic and cultural exchanges" (Grinberg, 2007).

SHAS's electoral strength has declined in every election since 2001, reversing the trend that had characterized it since its founding in 1984. To this we can add the disappearance of the Gesher party before the 2003 elections and the resurrection of the unity discourse that had been part and parcel of the Israeli Zionist narrative in times of crisis. This discourse was a convenient tool for silencing threatening rival voices, such as the Mizrahi. A similar phenomenon, but with a completely different outcome, can be seen in the split between "Israeli" and "Russian" during these years.

The crisis-oriented discourse of the 1990s strengthened the voices of the immigrants who arrived during that decade from the former Soviet Union. In this case the autonomous cultural pattern was far clearer and more dominant. The Yisrael Ba'aliyah party, founded before the 1996 elections, won seven Knesset seats. Al-Haj (2004a) has studied the immigrants' efforts to preserve their culture by promoting their mother tongue, setting up alternative schools to maintain their children's fluency in Russian, following different consumer trends and establishing their own media outlets. Politically speaking, the immigrants veered towards the extreme right with the establishment of the Yisrael Beitenu party. They adhered to this cultural segregation even after the unity discourse returned with the outbreak of the second Intifada. Moreover, it was precisely in 2002, when the internal Jewish unity discourse was gathering strength, that "Israel Plus," a commercial Russophone television station, took to the airwaves. This was an unprecedented phenomenon among the cultural groups that make up secular Jewish society, which were previously part of the "melting pot."

What distinguishes the Russian–Israeli divide from the Ashkenazi–Mizrahi split? Why did the unity discourse fail to contain or suppress

Russian cultural self-segregation? The answer seems to lie in the ethical and cultural dimensions of these divides in relation to the Ashkenazi elite. Mizrahi culture was the preeminent threat to the Western cultural character of the Zionist state. It represented the cultural alternative to the establishment of genuine multi-culturalism, rather than the ersatz variety of the "melting pot." Due to the dominance of "Eastern Europeanism" both during the pre-state period and after the founding of the State of Israel, immigrants from the former Soviet Union did not pose a similar threat to the Ashkenazi elite; Ashkenazim could identify with them or view them as much like themselves. The preference for Eastern Europeanism was highlighted in a remark made by Moshe Sharett, the Israeli Foreign Minister who subsequently became Prime Minister, to Soviet Foreign Minister Andrey Vyshinsky in December 1948, not long after the establishment of the Jewish state. Sharett was attempting to persuade Vyshinsky that, unlike the case of the North African Jews, the immigration of Soviet Jews was a Zionist imperative:

> There are countries, and here I am referring to the countries of North Africa, whose Jews should not immigrate [to Israel]. It's not a question of how many of them there are, but of their caliber. Our concern in this country is that we be pioneers, and we need people who are adaptable. . . . We cannot rely on the Jews of Morocco to build the state by themselves, as they are not equipped to do so. . . . We need people who can withstand difficulties and suffering. You know that when it comes to building the state in the present, the Eastern European Jews are the salt of the earth.
>
> (Segev, 2008: 183)

In addition to the external threat – a decisive factor in silencing sectoral demands, made on the basis of ethnic identity – and in addition to the intensifying consolidation of a collective Jewish identity that began with the eruption of a new cycle of confrontation in October 2000, other factors and variables helped moderate the sectoral demands generated by the ultra-orthodox–secular, Mizrahi–Ashkenazi, and "Russian"–Israeli divides. These factors and variables are addressed below.

The change in the electoral system

The electoral reform adopted in 1992 was implemented for the first time in the 1996 elections. Israel thereby made the transition to a unique system of government that was more or less a cross between the presidential and parliamentary systems. The main element of the reform enabled citizens to cast two ballots: once for a party and once for a candidate for Prime Minister.

Even before the votes were counted in the 1996 elections, many speculated that the double-ballot system would strengthen the sectoral parties, effectively vitiating the intention of the reform initiators, who had aspired to reduce the sectoral trend. Research conducted after the reform was repealed and the country returned to the single-ballot system in 2003, conclusively confirmed that the double-ballot system had strengthened the sectoral parties (Kenig, Rahat and Hazan, 2005). According to this research, the sectoral parties won 48 Knesset seats in 1999, compared with 34 in 1996. The change was even more striking when compared with the stagnation of the non-sectoral parties, which received the same number of seats as in the two elections that preceded the reform (1988 and 1992).

The decline of sectoral identity

In the 2003 elections, the sectoral trend weakened and changed direction. Sectoral parties received 41 mandates, seven fewer than in 1999; polls revealed a similar result in 2006. The most conspicuous change was experienced by parties such as SHAS, that lost almost a third of their 1999 vote in 2003. This was another sign of the weakening of the sectoral Mizrahi identity. Furthermore, the Gesher party, which had been considered a magnet for Mizrahi votes during the 1990s, disappeared. Further evidence of change lay in the performance of Yisrael Ba'aliyah, composed mainly of immigrants from the former Soviet Union; it won seven seats in the 1996 elections and six in 1999, but collapsed almost completely in 2003, winning only two seats and then folding itself into the Likud. Some might argue, however, that Yisrael Beitenu, headed by Avigdor Lieberman, was a political home for voters from the former Soviet Union, although it presents itself as non-sectoral. The attempt to brand Yisrael Beitenu as a mainstream party might be one explanation for the increase in its electoral strength.

The repeal of the direct-election reform did not affect the Ashkenazi ultra-orthodox parties, which maintained their strength. However, it did influence the rapid rise and decline of the secular Shinui party. The meteoric rise of Shinui began in the 1999 elections and reached its zenith in 2003, when the party won 15 mandates and created a new internal-Jewish political order. Shinui was perceived, correctly to a large extent, as a party with an anti-ultra-orthodox agenda that strove to fight against "religious coercion, the exploitation of government funds for religious purposes, and the attempt to turn the State of Israel into a halakhic state." Shinui's growing strength and the fact that it was one of the first parties to be included in the coalition after the 2003 elections created a certain "balance of terror" vis-à-vis the ultra-orthodox parties. Sharp exchanges between the ultra-orthodox parties and Shinui became a frequent event during the fifteenth and sixteenth Knessets (1999 and 2003, respectively). These verbal clashes notwithstanding, the demands of the ultra-orthodox parties and the budgetary resources allocated to them changed significantly. When they had constituted the balance of power, the ultra-orthodox enjoyed considerable budgetary and legislative resources, especially in the interface between state and religion. However, thanks to Shinui's aggressive campaign, which carried the day with Likud leader Ariel Sharon, for the first time in 20 years, a coalition was formed that excluded the ultra-orthodox parties, whether Ashkenazi or Mizrahi.

The effect was sharp and immediate, and brought with it far-reaching changes among the ultra-orthodox sector in Israel. The changes were registered in a number of ways. For one thing, the number of Yeshiva students dropped considerably. Between 1983 and 1999 the number of Yeshiva students who received an exemption from military service tripled, reaching a peak of 186,313. In 2004, the trend reversed itself, and for the first time in Israeli history there was no increase in the number of those granted exemptions.[6] In addition, the Ministry of Religious Affairs closed and its authority was dispersed among various government ministries. As a result, financial support for religious institutions and religious services declined by 6.3 percent in 2004.[7] Shinui did not stay in the coalition, however; after its vote against the 2005 State Budget bill, which included supplementary budgets for Ultraorthodox education, Shinui ministers were dismissed. This paved the way for the Ultraorthodox parties to reenter the government.

Nevertheless, Shinui, with its anti-ultra-orthodox agenda, swept up over a quarter of a million Israelis and left a lasting imprint on the conduct of the ultra-orthodox sector, in general, and of its political parties, in particular. In his explanation of why the ultra-orthodox parties must moderate their demands, ultra-orthodox journalist Moshe Grylak gives an interesting example of how Shinui helped curb ultra-orthodox demands through the creation of a "balance of terror":

> When Tommy Lapid succeeded in turning his anti-Ultraorthodox sentiment into success at the ballot box, all of the lay leaders in the Ultraorthodox community, particularly the Knesset members, admitted that 'We are also to blame.' Our lay leaders [learned to] lower their profiles in their public utterances. In practice, this lower profile helped us a great deal. Shinui disappeared, and now there is a risk that the cumulative effect will evoke a new Shinui, Heaven forfend!
> (Grylak, 2007)

After Sharon: the revival of the peace process with the Palestinians and possible repercussions on intergroup relations

Ariel Sharon's ascent to power marked an important stage in the evolution of the conflict with the Palestinians. It signaled the end of a fascinating period in the history of Israel and the Palestinians, in which the two sides had sought to reach an agreement on separation and the end of the conflict. This attempt climaxed at the Camp David summit in 2000, which brought together Israeli Prime Minister Barak and Palestinian leader Arafat, with

US President Clinton acting as the go-between. Arafat's refusal to accept the parameters of the agreement that the Israeli Prime Minister urged him to accept led to a deep crisis in the peace talks and to the eruption of the second Palestinian Intifada shortly thereafter.

Sharon, who was elected Prime Minister of Israel in 2001, led the transition from attempting to reach an agreement with the Palestinians to simply trying to manage the conflict (Ghanem, 2004). This effectively put efforts to end the conflict into deep freeze, thereby boosting Sharon's popularity to unprecedented heights. It also helped pacify the tense intergroup relations among the Jewish public. Sharon's illness during the campaign for the seventeenth Knesset, held in January 2006, brought Ehud Olmert to power. Olmert served as Prime Minister of Israel for about three years, until the elections for the eighteenth Knesset, which were held in February 2009. During the first few months after the elections, Olmert and his coalition benefited from the calm that Sharon had achieved in inter-Jewish relations. SHAS and the ultra-orthodox Ashkenazi parties were smaller and, together with Yisrael Beitenu, which was dominated by Russian immigrants under the leadership of Avigdor Lieberman, were central components in Olmert's coalition. The stability of his government led Olmert to try to reach a new agreement with the Palestinians under the leadership of Arafat's successor, Mahmoud Abbas (Abu Mazen). This attempt deviated from the model Sharon himself had constructed. Towards the end of 2008, Olmert, under investigation for corruption, was forced to resign. His successor as head of the Kadima party, Tzipi Livni, failed in her attempts to form a coalition and the Knesset voted in favor of new elections, which were held in February 2009.

Livni's failure was intimately linked to the weakening, during Olmert's tenure, of the intergroup relations Sharon had forged. Intergroup quarrels erupted between representatives of different groups, primarily regarding the inclusion of SHAS in the government Livni hoped to set up. Renewed efforts by Olmert's government and by his Foreign Minister, Tzipi Livni, to reach a peace agreement based on separation from the Palestinians led to the reemergence of the internal Jewish ethnic discourse (in addition to the reemergence of the dialogue with Palestinian citizens of Israel, as discussed above). This reemergence was clearly evident at the height of Livni's efforts to set up an alternative to Olmert's government.

Livni announced her failure to set up a government in October 2008 after trying unsuccessfully to persuade SHAS to join her coalition and in light of her unwillingness to negotiate with the Arab parties for nationalist reasons. Preparations were begun at once for elections to the eighteenth Knesset, which were fixed for February 10, 2009. Immediately after the decision to call new elections, Industry and Trade Minister, Eli Yishai, gave the signal for what would happen during the months of the campaign. He attacked Livni vigorously, accusing her of racism because, in his eyes, she was both anti-religious and anti-Mizrahi. He maintained that:

when they portrayed us as extortionists, it was racism – unequivocal racism. After the negotiations with us broke down on Friday, Livni continued to negotiate with United Torah Judaism. Their demands were similar to ours, but no one called them extortionists. It was Kadima that released the ethnic genie when it claimed that we were extortionists.[8]

The clash ended abruptly due to the war in Gaza, which broke out at the end of December 2008 and continued until mid-January 2009. Israel claimed that the purpose of the war was to stop Hamas from firing missiles into southern Israel. During the course of the war Israel bombarded the Gaza Strip from the air and killed and injured thousands of Palestinians. The war had the effect of calming intergroup relations among the Jewish majority during the election campaign.

In summary, due to the Gaza war and the election campaign, Palestinians in Israel were once again excluded and ignored in Livni's refusal to conduct coalition negotiations with Knesset members from the Arab parties. Livni was willing to sacrifice her only opportunity to form a government so as not to rely on Arab votes in her coalition. This state of affairs was exacerbated by the war in Gaza, when the Arab leadership accused Israel of war crimes. In tandem, the Arabs in Israel showed an unprecedented willingness to protest against the war itself and Israel's conduct of it. Many Arabs participated in spontaneous demonstrations; some were arrested and charged with disturbing the peace. On January 3, 2009, the Supreme Arab Monitoring Committee organized some 150,000 Arabs and a few Jews for an anti-war protest in the Arab town of Sakhnin. The size of the demonstration was unprecedented in the history of Palestinians in Israel. It expressed their frustration, disappointment and opposition to Israeli policy on the Arab–Israeli conflict, in general, and on the war in Gaza, in particular.

Among Jewish groups, the situation was entirely different. On the one hand, the elections reignited intergroup tensions; on the other hand, the war in Gaza served to alleviate these tensions, as Jews united in solidarity against the "threat" from Gaza. This situation changed with the approach of election day. The main parties (Likud, Kadima and Labor) continued to argue that they had the public interest at heart and represented all Israelis. The Arab parties (along with Hadash, a mixed Arab and Jewish party), by contrast, continued to champion an Arab nationalist ideology, while emphasizing their national and political differences from the other parties. SHAS mobilized on behalf of religious and Mizrahi Jews in light of the increasing strength of Avigdor Lieberman's Yisrael Beiteinu, which was considered a secular Russian party.[9] The old divides within Israeli society deepened in all the ways mentioned above.

The elections to the eighteenth Knesset, on February 10, 2009, exacerbated the polarization of Israeli society. The percentage of Arabs who stayed away from the polls held steady, at some 45 percent of registered

Arab voters. However, the Arab parties increased their strength to an unprecedented 11 mandates, because of the sharp decline in the number of Arabs voting for Jewish parties. Yisrael Beitenu increased its strength significantly, receiving most of its support from Russians. The party spouted anti-Arab slogans during the campaign, such as, "No citizenship without loyalty," while also running on a secular, anti-religious platform that generated friction with the religious parties, especially SHAS. The religious parties maintained their strength; SHAS won 11 mandates, United Torah Judaism, the Ashkenazi religious party, won five seats, and the religious Zionist Habayit Hayehudi (formerly the National Religious Party) took three seats.

Conclusion

In view of the cumulative experience of the last decade, and particularly since the outbreak of the second Intifada in 2000, one can sum up intergroup relations in Israeli society as oscillating between the stability conferred by the external danger of the Israeli–Palestinian conflict and the sharp contrasts and extreme instability issuing from the internal fissures within Israeli society. The latter are fraught with ideological, political, cultural and class tensions. Relations among the groups are structured around the principle of group mobilization in opposition to other groups. The five groups of Ashkenazim, Palestinians, Mizrahim, religious Jews and Russians are the axes of the Israeli political scene, especially the Ashkenazi subgroups.

Now, as in the past, the divide between the Jewish majority and the Palestinian-Arab minority is very stark and the cause of the inability to attain political stability in Israel. On the one hand, Palestinians in Israel oppose the official policy towards the Israeli–Palestinian conflict, Zionist ideology and the state's policies towards the Arab minority. On the other hand, we have seen an intensification of the ethnocentric discourse; racist attitudes within the Jewish public and the Jewish elite, along with policies denying the Arabs' right to equality; and entrenchment of Israeli policy vis-à-vis the conflict. These serve to intensify the contrast between the two groups and to exacerbate relations to extremes not seen in the past. The fundamental change that would be required within the Jewish majority or at least in the center-left bloc in order to forge a coalition with the Arab parties and confront the right is not achievable; the consequence is a protracted crisis between the two blocs. This situation can only be aggravated by the passage of time.

The religious–secular divide seems likely to become stuck in a protracted conflict that finds political expression in the form of religious Jewish political parties, whether Ashkenazi like United Torah Judaism or Sephardi like SHAS. The divide has been exacerbated by the demands that the religious parties make to secular-Ashkenazi establishment and by the combination of the religious and Sephardi/Mizrahi groups in SHAS. The divide is organized around two ostensibly conflicting principles: separation in the areas of culture, society and lifestyle, on the one hand, and significant cooperation in economics and politics, on the other. It has thus become impossible to form a coalition in Israel without the participation of the religious component in its assorted hues. These two principles of separation and cooperation can coexist because they occupy parallel planes and never come into open conflict or total concord with the secular Ashkenazi side.

The story of secular Mizrahim is very different from that of Mizrahi SHAS supporters. They have become a subordinate element in an Israeli political, cultural and economic milieu controlled by Ashkenazim. The geographical segregation of the secular Mizrahim, due to their concentration in development towns, has not spawned a secular Mizrahi political party. The closest attempt was Gesher, founded by David Levy in 1996. Gesher evaporated following its merger, first with the Likud, and later with Labor (as One Israel). The secular Mizrahi–Ashkenazi divide finds some expression in the form of NPOs such as the "Mizrahi Rainbow" and other local initiatives, but there seems to be no significant political expression for it on the horizon.

The case of the Russians differs substantially from that of the Mizrahim. The massive influx of Russians to Israel following the collapse of the Soviet Union at the beginning of the 1990s coincided with a new openness in Israeli society. This openness was due to the peace process initiated by Rabin's left wing government that fostered a new ethos of pluralism and multi-culturalism and made it possible for the Russians to continue to nurture their language and culture (unlike the Mizrahim in the 1950s). The government subsidized Russian cultural institutions and Russian journalism. The immigration of hundreds of thousands of Russians encouraged Natan Sharansky to found a Russian political party, Yisrael Ba'aliyah. In 1999, Avigdor Lieberman set up Yisrael Beitenu as an expression of the successful absorption of the Russians and their ability to impose their cultural agenda. This created a multi-cultural dimension in their relations with veteran Israelis. Yisrael Ba'aliyah did poorly in the 2003 elections and dissolved following Sharansky's announcement that there was no longer a raison d'être for a Russian party.

In tandem, Lieberman and his party spearheaded a new program of political activism that relied on Russian support, while tilting towards a right wing stand on most issues. Before the elections for the seventeenth and eighteenth Knessets, Lieberman adopted a typical right wing Israeli platform and included his own additions regarding the future of the conflict and the civil status of Palestinians in Israel. From an organizational standpoint, Lieberman formed a political list based, not on Russians, but on Israelis such as former Likud right winger, Uzi Landau. From a political standpoint Yisrael Beitenu is a right wing political party through and through; however, it is a party that receives most of its support from the Russian stream. The party aims to draw votes from other sectors of Israeli society as well, as a right wing Israeli party that is not necessarily a Russian party. To sum up, the Russians have become an integral part of the Israeli political map. They have been successful in imposing their culture on Israeli society and even in having it financed by the state.

Israel finds itself in deep crisis because of political instability fueled by many factors. The fragile relations among the groups that make up Israeli society are a key factor in this instability. Israel will not be able to deal effectively with its intergroup tensions without granting clear institutional expression to these group affiliations and without changing from a regime based on liberal foundations to one based on consociational foundations anchored in the political structure and the law. Until Israel finds the political courage to make these fundamental changes, the country will continue to suffer political instability fueled by intergroup competition and unbalanced power relations.

7 Conclusion
The future of group politics in Israel

The political developments in Israel during the 1990s, due to the diverse political behavior of Israelis, indicate that the system was not as stable as it is depicted in the literature. The system was subject to strong oscillations from one side to the other, without ever stabilizing on a middle line.[1] This situation reflects the profound group divisions that cleave Israeli society, such that group identity and interest usually dictate patterns of political behavior and the course of the political system. In this realm, Israel is suffering from the failure of the "melting pot." In practice, the various groups in Israel have developed behavior patterns that are motivated by the power struggles between them and by mutual alienation.

The axes of the groups' struggle are the principal product of the discriminatory policy adopted by the members of the founding group of Israel, that is, the Ashkenazim. From the outset their intention was to establish an hegemonic ethnic state system based on conspicuous preference for their own interests, not a democratic regime that put the civic good first and foremost (Peleg, 2007; Rouhana, 1997; Smooha, 1990; 1997; Yiftachel 1996, 1999). In practice, the Ashkenazi-controlled ethnic system practiced a policy of discrimination against all other non-Ashkenazi groups (both indigenous and immigrants) and created a political and social system that legitimized ethnic group affiliations and even gave them precedence over the civic group affiliation. This paved the way for the group struggles that attest to the failure of the project of building an Israeli nation. Four such cleavages can be identified, that will continue to undermine the stability of the Israeli political system. Far-reaching reforms will be needed to deal with these conflicts and make it possible for the system to function in a stable fashion. These cleavages are: religious–secular, Mizrahi–Ashkenazi, Russian–Israeli/Jewish and Jewish/Israeli–Palestinians in Israel. The intensity of the contrast varies from one of these divides to another, reflecting the degree of opposition between the groups. The deepest schism is that between Jews and Palestinian in Israel, which is a national, cultural, political, religious, linguistic and class division (see Smooha 1989, 1992). The intensity of the other conflicts is less and may be reduced to various cultural, political and class divergences.[2]

Stability in a deeply divided society and the Israeli regime

Israel is an Ashkenazi "hegemonic ethnic system," in which the ethnic hegemony is preserved alongside with democratic procedures, including the implementation of a basic and solid procedure of democratic structure and conduct, such as elections, a parliamentary system, freedom of movement, and relatively open systems of media and communication. But despite the democratic representation, these regimes still facilitate an undemocratic expansion of the dominant ethno-nation. Such political systems are found in Sri-Lanka, Malaysia, Estonia, Latvia, Serbia, Canada since the 1980s, Macedonia until the Ohrid agreement in 2001 and Northern Ireland until the Good Friday (Belfast) agreement in 1998.

One aspect of "hegemonic ethnic states" is related to the instability of such a regime, political instability as strongly related to *regime illegitimacy* among minorities and marginal groups, which results in a combination of *social disorder* and breakdown of regime functions. This is often followed by the bypassing of the regime by disgruntled minorities, by increasing forms of political polarization and by intensifying waves of anti-governmental protest and violence (Peleg, 2007; McGarry and O'Leary, 1993).

However, the self-representation of many hegemonic ethnic states as democratic creates structural tensions, because it requires the state to go beyond lip service and empower minorities with some (though less than equal) formal political powers. The "cracks" and "crevices" between the open claims for democracy, and the denial of minority equality, harbor the tensions and conflicts typical of ethnic states (see Ghanem, Rouhana and Yiftachel, 1999; Mann, 1999; Yiftachel, 2006).

The susceptibility of such regimes to the surfacing of open ethnic conflict, and their chronic instability, are powerful engines of political change. Yet, this change may take varying, and at times contrasting, directions. We find a number of hegemonic ethnic systems which have responded to the pressures and contradictions of ethnic dominance with a series of democratization steps, such as Belgium, Spain, Greece, and most recently Canada, South Africa, Macedonia and Northern Ireland.

Contrary to the "hegemonic ethnic state" regime, the power sharing state regime is a specific type of arrangement of democratic *Civic State* model, which, structurally and essentially, prefers democracy and egalitarian components over ethnic-hegemonic ones in interactions with citizens, and should be understood as the extension of the liberal model, that is expressed by the implementation of consociational arrangements as an added value to the liberal citizenship (Lijphart, 1999; Lustick 1979; McGarry and O'Leary, 1993).

The consociational model eliminates the dominance of a particular group and the identification of the state with it. It grants full equality to all groups and makes the state part of the arrangements in the competition among groups; that is, identifying it with all groups on an equal basis. The arrangements include a genuine and sincere attempt to deal with ethnic divisions in order to guarantee equality among ethnic groups and their members. This is done on two main levels.

The first is the individual level. In democracies, competition among citizens as individuals is absolutely equal before the law. The second is the group level; as a supplement to the individual level, the elites of the various groups decide to add a group component to the liberal elements. The literature refers to such a system as "consociational democracy" (see Lijphart, 1977, 1984, 1999, 2002; Lustick, 1979).

The collective arrangements in the power-sharing system are manifested in four main domains:

1) A broad coalition of the different parties. Stability of the power-sharing system would be dependent upon a strong coalition between a broad spectrum of the elites of ethnic groups. Such a coalition would lead the country and be responsible for keeping the internal peace, and for running its internal and external affairs, while striving to reach consensus and compromise on problematic issues.
2) Right of veto for each of the main groups. Running the affairs of the power-sharing state regime correctly would demand the possibility of either group exercising a right of veto in extreme cases, even in the other group's internal affairs. Thus, the representatives of one group would have to take account of the other group's interests.
3) Fair representation for the main groups. The political and public common institutions of the power-sharing system would have to include fair and proportionate representation for each of the groups. Each group would have a "quota" reserved for its representatives. Certain offices such as President, Prime Minister and ministers would require the two groups to agree on proportional representation.
4) Internal autonomy for each group. The internal affairs of each group, such as education, culture, municipal government and so on, would be administered separately. Such autonomy might be territorial, personal or mixed, according to the arrangement reached between the groups' representatives. In dealing with overlapping issues, or with regions of mixed population, the representatives of the groups would have to cooperate in the correct management even of areas perceived to be separate.

The consociational arrangements include the tools that can satisfy the groups by realizing basic human needs, thereby improving group relations and achieving a peaceful settlement of national, ethnic and civil problems while developing civic values shared by all citizens, whatever their ethnic affiliation (see Lijphart 1969, 1977, 1984, 1999, 2002; Lustick, 1979).

The political instability has domestic significance within Israeli society with regard to internal solidarity, the goals of Zionism and the achievement of a constructive politics for the future. Thus, it is clear that the main project of Zionism – the creation of a Jewish-Israeli nation in the country – is facing huge obstacles. In fact, we are witnessing the emergence of groups that pursue their own interests while damaging those of other groups. This instability obviously has profound significance for Israel's relations with the Palestinian people. The essence of this significance lies in the impossibility of achieving the stability that would lead to far-reaching decisions concerning the future of the conflict and an arrangement acceptable to the Palestinians. Only an accord that is viewed by the major groups in Israeli society as not endangering the interests of the Israelis and the Jews, including groups such as the Russians, the settlers and the religious, will be welcomed by these groups. This means, consequently, that a peace settlement that coincides with Palestinian parameters for an agreement is impossible in the context of Israeli politics.

A relative stability prevails today because of the perceived common threat (real or spurious) posed by the Palestinian people and the Palestinian states. In the future, Israel will not be able to maintain the present format with regard to the relations among the groups. It will have to undergo a radical change to permit the various groups to: (a) have equal collective expression; (b) create personal autonomies based on consociational arrangements; and (c) enjoy liberal civic equality based on equal citizenship. This change will come at the expense of an order that discriminates against the non-dominant groups (Palestinians, ultra-orthodox, Mizrahim and Russians) and in favor of the founding group (the Ashkenazi). Today the Ashkenazim, or at least their representatives in the Knesset and the political, cultural, economic and social systems, concerned with preserving the relative advantages they enjoy, pose the major barrier to the process of democratization that is essential for Israeli society.

In light of what I have presented in this book and in light of the deepening conflict within the Israeli society, there is a need to substantially change the regime such that it: (a) seeks to create shared arrangements and power distribution; (b) organizes in a harmonious and less centralized way than it does now; and (c) rather than proposing to adopt a presidential political system in Israel, presses the government to be politically representative of the Knesset's ethnic, sectarian and geographical/regional structure. Having established that it is not satisfactory to adopt an electoral change or a change at the cabinet portfolios level, one cannot even append a real amendment to the constitution, as suggested by a few scholars and activists, in light of the deteriorated situation and instability resulting from the inequitable power distribution and the continued ethnic state system, where the Western-Ashkenazi group exercises hegemony over all walks of life in Israel. Any future arrangements must include a substantial change in the regime components, so that it seeks to rebuild a "consociocional democracy" based on arrangements of power-sharing and resources distribution in a just way between the different groups. This suggested system should be built on the basis of the political systems of Belgium and Switzerland while taking into consideration the local specialty of the country; this is at least one of the keys for future stability in Israel.

Notes

2 The Palestinian minority in Israel: resisting the "ethnocratic" system

1 This chapter is based on an analysis of surveys of Palestinian citizens of Israel conducted during the past decade. The bulk of the analysis is based on data from a survey conducted by the Institute for Peace Research at Givat Haviva in January–March 2001, under the joint direction of myself and Prof. Sammy Smooha of the Department of Sociology and Anthropology at the University of Haifa. The survey was based on a random sample taken from the voter registration lists. A total of 1202 respondents were interviewed anonymously, face-to-face, in their own homes. I would like to thank the Institute for Peace Research for its assistance, which made the fieldwork possible, and Professor Smooha for working with me and allowing me to publish some of the survey data in the present book.

   For comparison I have used data from two surveys conducted in 1994 and 1995: the second source of data is a survey I conducted with Professor Smooha in 1995, involving a representative sample of 1200 Israeli Palestinians (Muslims, Christians and Druze) selected at random from the voter registration lists and interviewed face-to-face in their homes. I would again like to thank Professor Smooha for allowing me to use some of these data.

   Some data is taken from a survey I conducted in 1994 while working on my doctoral dissertation in the Department of Political Science at the University of Haifa. I would like to take this opportunity to thank my advisers at the University of Haifa, Professor Gabriel Ben-Dor of the Department of Political Science, and Professor Majid Al-Haj of the Department of Sociology and Anthropology. This survey was a based on a representative sample of 768 respondents selected from the Palestinian population of Israel using the Kisch method.

2 The Jewish voting rate is actually higher than the figures cited here based on the data provided by the Israeli Central Bureau of Statistics. The rates are calculated as the number of voters out of all citizens including the hundreds of thousands of Jewish Israelis who live or stay overseas and who do not exercise their voting right.

3 See, for example, Sikkuy's annual report on the government's policy towards Arab citizens (Sikkuy, 1999).

4 The Likud candidate neglected the concerns of Palestinian citizens mostly from ideological considerations. The Labor candidate did not want to alienate Jewish voters with promises to the Arab citizens; besides, he understood that many Palestinian citizens considered him a better choice than the Likud candidate. See discussion of the "no-choice" motivated vote below.

5 In 1969 Mapai became the Labor party and ran on a joint list with Mapam, which had previously received a significant number of Arab votes.

6 In 1984, Mapam left the Labor party and joined Meretz, a left wing party.
7 In the Israeli electoral system, a party gains representation in the Knesset only if it gets 1.5 percent (or more) of the valid votes. Many coalitions among movements, some of them very different, were motivated by fear that if they ran separately they would not clear that threshold.
8 This is the result of the age structure of the Arab population, half of whom are younger than 18 and therefore not yet eligible to vote.

3 Mizrahi (Oriental) Jews and the Ashkenazi system: incorporation versus separation politics

1 Information here is taken from Shitrit, 2001, unless otherwise stated.
2 See the "Bow" website http://hakeshet.tripod.com – April 2003.

4 Jewish religious groups and the politics of identity in the "secular-Jewish" state

1 See the latest election slogan (2003) for the "Yahadut Hatorah": "So that we can live here."
2 In 1995, special courts were established for Judaization affairs under the Rabbinate's Religious Courts. In 2003, five of these were functioning.
3 Israeli Knesset website www.knesset.gov.il/docs/heb/neeman.htm
4 The Supreme Courts 1000\92 – Bavley against the Supreme Rabbinical Court – ruling "2"221.
5 See for example the Hapoel Hamizrahi executive committee's decision of June 21, 1971 against strikes and for "economic stability" in a report published by the Hapoel Hamizrahi Press in 1973.
6 Inapplicability of the Law for the Haredim orthodox girls constitutes, according to Don-Yihya (1997), a proof of the flexibility of Israeli democracy, that refrains from implementing laws that might result in breakaway for certain sectors.
7 During the 2003 election campaign Yahadut Hatorah representative Rabbi Ravitz presented himself in a TV electoral broadcast as a guardion of ecological values (and he did head the Knesset Committee for the quality of the environment).
8 The SHAS movement can also be included among the Mizrahi or Sephardi movements yet I will discuss SHAS here because of the control by Rabbis over the movement, though a major part of its supporters are not ultra-religious but rather traditional or even secular, voting for the party because of sectarian Mizrahi motives.
9 This chapter is mainly based on the 1999 book by Arie Dayan, *The Flowing Spring*, and Rahat's 1998 *SHAS: the spirit and the power*.
10 See the Knesset government website, www.knesset.gov.il
11 On the increase in the budgets transferred to SHAS institutions in the 1990s see Shahar Elan's *Haridym Ltd* (2000), tables on pages 255–59.

5 Russian immigrants: imposing multi-culturalism in the public sphere in Israel

1 Data from the Central Bureau of Statistics http://194.90.153.197/Shnaton54/st02_02.pdf
2 www.Knesset.Gov.il/docs/Heb/Neeman.htm
3 February 3, 2003, www.ynet.co.il.
4 The 1999 Elections Platform Collection, University of Haifa.
5 See for example the results of a survey that was published on January 6, 2009: www.politico.co.il/article.asp?rId = 641

6 From the party platform, the party's platform collection, the University of Haifa, 1999.

6 Group divisions, the external conflict and political instability in Israel since Oslo

1 Many of those who follow Israeli politics, especially Palestinians and Arabs, maintain that there is no difference between the right and left in Israel: they are all Zionists who adopt the same position with regard to the conflict and its solution. But from the perspective of most Israelis, the right and left represent positions that are substantially different, and of course their candidates for Prime Minister represent significantly different positions and platforms.
2 The Israel Democracy Institute claims that 77.4 percent of Arabs would support a constitution that recognizes the State of Israel as a Jewish and democratic state. Many have criticized the way the question was phrased: it links the identity of the state with equality for Arabs, without making clear the content of this identity from a constitutional and legal standpoint. The question should have been phrased as follows: "Do you support the identification of the state as a Jewish and democratic state in which Arabs enjoy equality?" The annual survey by the Mada al-Carmel Center in 2004 found that 62 percent of Arabs believe that Israel cannot be both a Jewish and a democratic country.
3 The rate of boycott for the eighteenth Knesset election in 2009 reached 46 percent.
4 This is despite the fact that Gesher stopped running as a separate list in 1996 and was, instead, guaranteed safe spots on the Knesset lists of the parties it ran with.
5 Moish Goldberg directed an impressive film on the first four months of the second Intifada, *A Million Bullets in October* (2007). The movie displays the eagerness of Israeli decision-makers and the Israeli army to escalate the conflict by deliberately squelching attempts to calm things down.
6 Sources: Draft budgets of the Ministry of Religious Affairs, 1983–2000; *Statistical Abstract of Israel 2005*. Note that in 2005 the number of those exempted from military service for religious reasons increased again, and the trend continued in 2006, as well. The "Tal Law" passed to create a new arrangement for Yeshiva students has not led to any appreciable change and has served chiefly as a lightning rod for criticism from both sides of the political barricades. Another effect was an increase in the number of ultra-orthodox students enrolled in "Collels" (institutions for married men) who joined the workforce. This was due to the cuts in the National Insurance allowances (such as the repeal of the Halpert law, officially known as the "Large Families Law").
7 2005 draft budget, www.pmo.gov.il.
8 www.nrg.co.il/online/1/ART1/805/361.html.
9 Take, for instance, the substance of remarks by SHAS's spiritual leader, Rabbi Ovadiya Yosef, who said, three days before the elections, that "whoever votes for Lieberman strengthens the devil." The party's political leader, MK Eli Yishai, went as far as to say "Heaven forfend that a son of Israel whose ancestors stood at Mount Sinai should vote for such a party. Their electoral platform is to open stores selling pork, to introduce civil marriage.... Woe to these people." See: www.nrg.co.il/online/1/ART1/850/757.html?hp=0&loc=1&tmp=3427.

7 Conclusion: the future of group politics in Israel

1 Some scholars and observers agree that there is no instability in the Israeli political system and argue that this instability is a result of the electoral system including the switch in 1996 to a system that separates the Knesset elections

from those for Prime Minister. I agree in part with this argument still. I believe that the explanation is more profound and lies in the group schisms that have intensified in the last decade and are manifested in the nature of voting, but which are broad and deep and will not be solved by technical measures such as the change of the election system.

2 Except for the non-Jewish Russians, who are nationally different from the Jews but do not currently accentuate this fact.

References

Aburaiya, Asam. 1989. "Developmental Leadership: the Case of the Islamic Movement in Um-Alfahim, Israel" (MA Thesis). Clark University, New England, USA.

Adalah (nongovernmental organization). 1998. *Legal Violations of Arab Rights in Israel*. Sehfa'amre: Adala.

Agasy, Yousel 1991. *Who is Israeli?* Rohovot: Chvoneem (in Hebrew).

Agnew, J. 1999. "Mapping Political Power Beyond State Boundaries: Territory, Identity and Movement in World Politics," *Millenium: Journal of International Studies* 28(3): 499–522

Al-Haj, Majid. 1988. "The Sociopolitical Structure of the Arabs in Israel: External vs. Internal Orientations," in John Hofman, ed., *The Arab-Jewish Relations in Israel: A Quest in Human Understanding*. Bristol, IN: Wyndham Hall Press, pp. 92–122.

— — 1995. *Education, Empowerment, and Control: The Case of the Arabs in Israel*. Albany, NY: SUNY Press.

— — 1996. "Political Organization by the Arab Population in Israel: The Development of a Center within Margins," in Baruch Knei-Paz and Moshe Lissak, eds., *Israel Toward the Year 2000*. Jerusalem: Magnes Press (in Hebrew), pp. 92–102.

— — 2003. "Education in the shadow of the conflict: Cultural hegemony vs. controlled multiculturalism," in Majid Al-Haj and Uri Ben-Eliezer, eds., *Sociology of Peace and War in Israel in a Changing Era*. Haifa: University of Haifa Press (in Hebrew).

— — 2004a. "The political culture of the 1990s immigrants from the former Soviet Union in Israel and their views toward the indigenous Arab minority: a case of ethnocratic multiculturalism," *Journal of Ethnic and Migration Studies* 30(4): 681–96.

— — 2004b. *Immigration and Ethnic Formation in a Deeply Divided Society: The Case of the 1990s Immigration from the Former Soviet Union in Israel*: Leiden: Brill.

Al-Haj, Majid and As'ad Ghanem, eds. 2004. *State & Society Journal* 4(1) (in Hebrew). Special volume about the Arab Minority in Israel. Dept. of Government & Political Philosophy, University of Haifa: Haifa.

Al-Haj, Majid and Elazar Leshem. 2000. *Immigration from the Former Soviet Union in Israel: Ten Years Later* (Research Report). Haifa: The Center for Multiculturalism and Educational Research.

Al-Haj, Majid and H. Rosenfeld. 1990. *The Arab Local Government in Israel*. Boulder, CO: Westview Press.

References

Almond, Gabriel and Sidney Verba. 1963. *The Civic Culture: Political Attitudes and Democracy in Five Nations*. Princeton, NJ: Princeton University Press.
Anderson, Benedict. 1991. *Imagined Communities: Reflections on the Origin and Spread of Nationalism*. London: Verso (second edition).
— — 1996. "Introduction," in G. Balakrishnan, ed., *Mapping the Nation*. New York: Verso, pp. 1–16.
Anderson, K. 2000. "Thinking 'Postnationality': Dialogue across Multicultural, Indigenous, and Settler Spaces," *Annals of the Association of American Geographers* 90(2): 381–91.
Arian, Asher. 1973. *The Elections in Israel*. Jerusalem: Jerusalem Academic Press.
— — ed. 1980. *The Election in Israel 1977*. Jerusalem: Jerusalem Academic Press.
— — 1990. *Politics and Government in Israel*. Tel Aviv: Zmora-Bitan (in Hebrew).
— — 1996. *The Second Republic*. Tel Aviv; Zmura Bitan (in Hebrew).
Arian, Asher and Michal Shamir, eds. 1999. *The Election in Israel 1999*. Jerusalem: The Israeli Institute for Democracy.
Arian, Asher *et al.*, 2004. *The Democracy Index*. Jerusalem: The Israel Democracy Institute.
— — 2005. *The Democracy Index*. Jerusalem: The Israel Democracy Institute.
Aronson, Geoffrey. 1996. *Settlements and the Israeli–Palestinian Negotiations*. Washington, DC: Institute of Palestine Studies.
Avineri, Shlomo. 1995. "The Hope Will Not Die," *Ha'aretz*, October 20 (in Hebrew).
Axtmann, Ronald. 1996. *Liberal democracy into the twenty-first century: globalization, integration, and the nation-state*. Manchester, UK: Manchester University Press.
Azoulay, Ariella and Adi Ophir. 2008. *The Regime which is not One: Occupation and Democracy Between the Sea and the River*. Tel Aviv: Resling.
Barber, B. 1995. *Jihad vs MacWorld*. New York: Ballantine.
Ben-Eliezer, Uri. 1993. "The Meaning of Political Participation in a Nonliberal Democracy: The Israeli Experience," *Comparative Politics* 25(4): 397–412.
Ben-Rafael, E., E. Olstein and E. Geist. 1998. *Perspectives of Identity and Language in the Absorption of Immigrants from the FSU*. Jerusalem: The Hebrew University.
Benski, T. 1993. "Testing Melting-Pot Theories in the Jewish Israeli Context," *Sociological Papers* 2(2): 1–46.
Ben-Zadok, E. 1993. "Oriental Jews in the Development Towns: Ethnicity, Economic Development, Budgets and Politics," in E. Ben-Zadok, ed., *Local Communities and the Israeli Polity*. New York: State University of New York Press, pp. 91–123.
Benziman, Uzi. 2006. *To Whom This Land*. Jerusalem: The Israel Democracy Institute.
Benziman, Uzi and Attalah Mansour. 1992. *Secondary Residences: The Arabs in Israel, their status and the policy towards them*. Jerusalem: Keter.
Berg, E. and S. Oras. 2000. "Writing Post-Soviet Estonia onto the World Map," *Political Geography* 19: 601–25.
Bermeo, Nancy. 1997. "Myths of Moderation: Confrontation and Conflict During Democratic Transitioins," *Comparative Politics* 29(3): 305–22.
Bernstein, Debie. 1979. " The Black Panthers:Conflict and Protest in the Israeli Society," *Magamot* 1: 65–80 (in Hebrew).

References

Brubaker, R. 1996. *Nationalism Reframed: Nationhood and the National Question in the New Europe.* London: Cambridge University Press.

Castells, M. 1997. *The Power of Identity: Economy, Society and Culture.* Oxford: Blackwell.

Central Bureau of Statistics. 2000. "Immigration to Israel 1998." Publication No. 1132 (June). Jerusalem: Central Bureau of Statistics (in Hebrew).

— — 2002. *Israeli Statistical Book 53.* Jerusalem: Central Bureau of Statistics.

Cohen, Asher and Bernard Susser. 2000. *Israel and the Politics of Jewish Identity*, London: Johns Hopkins University Press.

Cohen, E. 1972. "The Black Panthers and Israeli society," *Jewish Journal of Sociology* 14(1): 93–109.

Cohen, Raanan. 1985. "Process of Political Organization and Voting Patterns of the Palestinian minority" (MA Thesis). Faculty of Humanities, Tel Aviv University (in Hebrew).

Cohen, Yihezkel. 1993. *Military Service According to Halacha.* Jerusalem: The Movement for Torah and Work (in Hebrew).

Cohen, Y. and Y. Haberfeld. 1998. "Second-generation Jewish Immigrants in Israel: Have the Ethnic Gaps in Schooling and Earnings Declined?," *Ethnic and Racial Studies* 21(3): 507–28.

Collier, D. and S. Levitski. 1997. "Democracy with Adjectives: Conceptual Innovation in Comparative Research," *World Politics* 49(April): 430–51.

Connor, W. 1994. *Ethnonationalism: the Quest for Understanding.* Princeton, NJ: Princeton University Press.

Corney, Michael. 2001. *The Question of Jewish Identity.* Shregem: Nevo (in Hebrew).

Dayan, Arie. 1999. *The Flowing Spring: the story of the Shas movement.* Jerusalem: Keter.

de Tocquiville, E. 1961. *Democracy in America.* New York: Schocken Books.

Della-Pergola, Sergio. 2001. "Demography in Israel/Palestine: Trends, Prospects, Policy Implications." Lecture at the IUSSP XXIV General Population Conference, "Population Change and Political Transitions," Salvador de Bahia, August, S64.

Diskin, Avraham. 2001. *Jerusalem's Last Days: Guidelines for Examining the New Israeli Democracy.* Jerusalem: Floersheimer Institute.

Don-Yihya, Alizer. 1988. *Religious Institutions in the Political System.* Jerusalem: The Jerusalem Center for Public and State Affairs.

— — 1997. *The Politics of Regulation: Conflict Resolution on Religious Issues in Israel.* Jerusalem: Floersheimer Institute (in Hebrew).

Eisenstadt, S.N. 1968. *Israeli Society.* London: Weidenfeld & Nicolson.

— — 1985. *The Transformation of Israeli Society.* London: Weidenfeld & Nicolson.

Elan, Shahar. 1999. *The Postponing of the Military Service of the Religious Youth: A Policy Proposal.* Jerusalem: Floersheimer Institute.

— — 2000. *Haridym Ltd.* Jerusalem: Keter.

Esman, Milton, ed. 1977. *Ethnic Conflict in the Western World.* Ithaca, NY: Cornell University Press.

Falah, Ghazi. 1990. "Arabs Versus Jews in Galilee Competition for Regional Resources," *Geojournal* 21(4): 325–36.

Fars, Amin. 1996. *Poverty in Arab Society in Israel.* Beit Berl: Institute for Israeli Arab Studies (in Hebrew).

Fenster, T. and O. Yiftachel, eds. 1997. *Frontier Development and Indigenous Peoples.* Oxford: Pergamon.

Ferber, Pinhas. 1973. *Report to the 4th Mafdal Summit.* Tel Aviv: Hapoel Hamizrahi Press (in Hebrew).

Fien, Aharon. 1995. "Voting Trends of Recent Immigration from the Former Soviet Union," in Asher Arian and Michal Shamir, eds., *The Elections in Israel, 1992.* Albany, NY: SUNY Press, pp. 172–93.

Fincher, R. and J. Jacobs, eds. 1998. *Cities of Difference.* New York: Guilford Press.

Fond, Yusef. 1989. "Agudat Yisrael and Zionism – Ideology and Policy" (Doctoral Dissertation). Bar Ilan: Bar Ilan University (in Hebrew).

Foweraker, Joe and Todd Landman. 1997. *Citizenship rights and social movements.* Oxford: Oxford University Press.

Frankel, Rogovin E. 1996. "The 'Russian' Vote in The 1996 Israeli Elections," *East European Jewish Affairs* 26(1): 3–33.

Fredrickson, G. 1988. "Colonialism and Racism: United States and South Africa in Comparative Perspective," in G. Fredrickson, ed., *The Arrogance of Racism.* Middletown, CT: Wesleyan University Press, pp. 112–31.

Friedman, Menahem. 1988. "These are the Chronicles of the Status Quo: Religion and State in Israel," in V. Piluveky, ed., *Transition from Yeshuv To State, 1947–1949: Stability and Change.* Haifa: Hertzl Foundation for the Study of Zionism, pp. 22–28.

Gavison, Ruth. 1999. *Israel as a Jewish-Democratic State.* Jerusalem: Vanleer Institute.

Gavison, Ruth and Daphna Hacker, eds. 2002. *The Arab-Jewish Conflict in Israel.* Jerusalem: The Israel Democracy Institute.

Gitelman, Z. 1995. *Immigration and Identity.* New York: David and Susan Wilstein Jewish Policy Study.

Gitelman, Zvi and Ken Goldstein. 2001. "The Russian Revolution in Israeli Politics," in Asher Arian and Michal Shamer, eds., *The Election in Israel, 1999.* Jerusalem: The Israeli Institute for Democracy, pp. 203–32 (in Hebrew).

Ghanem, As'ad. 1990. "Ideological Trends on the Question of Jewish–Arab Coexistence Among Arabs in Israel. 1967–1989" (MA Thesis). Department of Political Science, University of Haifa (in Hebrew).

— — 1993. "The Perception by the Islamic Movement in Israel of the Regional Peace Process," in Ilan Pappe, ed., *Islamic Approaches to Peace in the Contemporary Arab World.* Giv'at Haviva: Institute for Peace Research, pp. 83–99 (in Hebrew).

— — 1995. "Municipal Leadership among the Arabs in Israel: Continuity and Change," *The New East* 37: 151–68 (in Hebrew).

— — 1996a. "The Palestinians in Israel Are Part of the Problem and Not of the Solution. Their Status in the Age of Peace," *State, Government, and International Relations* 41/42: 123–54 (in Hebrew).

— — 1996b. "Political Influence – Also to the Arabs in Israel," *Elections 1996 Papers 4*, Dean Center, Tel Aviv University.

— — 1996c. "Political Participation among Arabs in Israel" (Doctoral Dissertation). Department of Political Science, University of Haifa (in Hebrew).

— — 1997. "The Limits of Parliamentary Politics: The Arab Minority in Israel and the 1992 and 1996 Elections," *Israeli Affairs* 4(2): 72–93.

— — 1998 "State and Minority in Israel: The Case of the Ethnic State and the Predicament of its Minority," *Ethnic and Racial Studies* 21(3): 428–48.

—— 1999. "A Bi-national, Palestinian–Israeli State, at all the land of Palestine/Eretz Yisrael and the Status of the Arabs in Israel within this Frame," in Sara Ozacky-Lazar, As'ad Ghanem and Ilan Pappe, eds., *Theoretical Options for the Future of the Arabs in Israel*. Givaat Haviva: The Institute for Peace Research, pp. 271–303 (in Hebrew).

—— 2000. "The Palestinian Minority in Israel: the Challenge of the Jewish State and its Implications," *Third World Quarterly* 21(1): 87–104.

—— 2001a. *The Palestinian Arab Minority: A Political Study*. Albany, NY: SUNY Press.

—— 2001b. "The Palestinians in Israel: Political Orientation and Aspirations," *International Journal of Inter-Cultural Relations* 26: 135–52.

—— 2003. "Zionism, Post-Zionism, and Anti-Zionism in Israel: Jews and Arabs the Conflict over the Nature of the State," in Epraim Nemni, ed., *The Challenge of Post Zionism*. London: Zed Books, pp. 98–115.

—— 2004. "About the Situation of the Palestinian-Arab Minority in Israel," *State & Society Journal* 4(1) (in Hebrew). Special volume about the Arab minority in Israel. Dept. of Government & Political Philosophy, University of Haifa: Haifa.

—— 2005a. "The Bi-National Solution for the Israeli-Palestinian Crisis: Conceptual Background and Contemporary Debate," in Mahdi Abdul-Hadi, ed., *Palestinian–Israeli Impasse*. Jerusalem: PASSIA, pp.19–44.

—— 2005b. "Collective rights and Education: Lessons from Quebec in Canada," in Duane Champagne and Ismael Abu-Saad, eds., *Indigenous and Minority Education: International Perspective on Empowerment*. Beer-Sheva: Negev Center for Regional Development, pp. 136–60.

—— 2006. "Israel and the 'Danger of Demography'," in Jamil Hilal, ed., *Where Now for Palestine?* London: Zed books, pp. 98–116.

Ghanem, As'ad and Mohanad Mustafa. 2009. *Palestinians in Israel: Indigenous group politics in the Jewish state*. Ramallah: Madar (in Arabic).

Ghanem, As'ad and Sara Ozacky-Lazar. 1990. "The Green Line – Red Lines, the Arabs in Israel in View of the Intifada," *Skirot 2*, Giv'at Haviva: Institute for Peace Research (in Hebrew).

—— 1999. "The Arab Vote to the Fifteenth Knesset," *Sekirot* 24, Institute for Peace Research: Giv'at Haviva (in Hebrew).

—— 2001. "Israel as an Ethnic State and the Arab Vote in the 1999 Elections," in Asher Arian and Michal Shamir, eds., *The Elections in Israel, 1999*. Jerusalem: The Israeli Institute of Democracy (in Hebrew), pp. 72–93.

—— 2003. "The Status of the Palestinians in Israel in an Era of Peace: Part of the Problem but Not Part of the Solution," *Israel Affairs* 9(1–2): 263–89.

Ghanem, As'ad and Nadim Rouhana. 2001. "Citizenship and the Parliamentary Politics of Minorities in Ethnic States: the Palestinian Citizens of Israel," *Nationalism & Ethnic Politics* 7: 66–86.

Ghanem, As'ad, Nadim Rouhana and Oren Yiftachel. 1999. "Questioning 'Ethnic Democracy': A response to Sammy Smooha," *Israel Studies* 3(2): 253–66.

Greenberg, Haim. 1951. *Israeli Religion and the State of Israel*. New York: The Zionist Histadrut.

Grienstien, Ran. 1984. "The Israeli Heritage Movement (Tami): The Grow-up of the Religious Movement" (MA Thesis). Haifa: University of Haifa.

Grinberg, L.L. 1998. "From Periphery to the Core: Sources of Ethnic Political Leadership," in O. Yiftachel and A. Meir, eds., *Ethnic Frontiers and Peripheries:*

204 References

Landscapes of Development and Inequality in Israel. Boulder, CO: Westview Press, pp. 211–37.

— — 2007. *Imaginary Peace, War Talk*. Tel Aviv: Resling (in Hebrew).

Grylak, Moshe. 2007. "Perspective," *The Family: Jewish Home Monthly* 791: 8 (in Hebrew).

Gurr, Ted Robert. 1993. *Minorities at Risk: A Global View of Ethnopolitical Conflict*. Washington, DC: US Institute of Peace Press.

Gurr, Ted Robert, and Barbara Harff. 1994. *Ethnic Conflict in World Politics*. Boulder, CO: Westview Press.

Haidar, Aziz. 1991a. *The Arab Population in the Israeli Economy*. Tel Aviv: International Center for Middle East Peace (in Hebrew).

— — 1991b. *Needs and Welfare Services in the Arab Sector in Israel*. Tel Aviv: International Center for Middle East Peace (in Hebrew).

Harris, E. 2001. *Nationalism and Democratization: Politics of Slovakia and Slovenia*. Aldershot, UK: Ashgate.

Harvey, D. 1989. *The Condition of Postmodernity*. Oxford: Blackwell.

Hason, Shlomo. 2001. Scenarios for Israel: Relations Between Religion, Community and State. Jerusalem: Floersheimer Institute.

Hertsogh, Hana. 1986. *Political Ethnicity: Concepts vs. Reality*. Tel Aviv: Yad Tabinken and Hakibutz Hamiohad.

Hobsbawm, E. 1990. *Nations and Nationalism Since 1780*. Cambridge: Cambridge University Press.

Holmes, S. 1996. *Passion and Constraint: the Theory of Liberal Democracy*. Chicago, IL: University of Chicago Press.

Horowits, Neri. 2002. Jews, The City is Burning: Yahdut Hatora in the Elections: 1999–2001. Jerusalem: Floersheimer Institute.

Horowitz, Dan and Moshe Lisk, 1978. *From Yishuv To State*. Tel Aviv: Am-Ovid.

— — 1989. *Predicament in the Utopia*. Tel Aviv: Am-Ovid.

Horowitz, Donald. 1985. *Ethnic Groups in Conflict*. Berkeley: University of California Press.

— — 2002. *The deadly ethnic riot*. Berkeley: University of California Press.

Horowitz, Tamar. 1994. "The Influence of Soviet Political Culture on Immigrants Voters in Israel: The Elections of 1992," *Jews in Eastern Europe* 1(23): 5–22.

— — 1996. "Value-oriented Parameters in Migration Policies in the 1990s: The Israeli Experience," *International Migration* 34: 513–35.

— — 2003. "The Increasing Political Power of Immigrants from the Former Soviet Union in Israel: From Passive Citizenship to Active Citizenship," *International Migration* 41(1): 47–73.

Huntington, S. 1991. *The Third Wave: Democratization in the Late Twentieth Century*. Norman: University of Oklahoma Press.

Israeli, Yehuda. 1990. *The Age of the Kepa*. Jerusalem: Avivem (in Hebrew).

Jackson, P. and J. Penrose, eds. 1993. *Constructions of Race, Place and Nation*. London: UCL Press.

Jacobs, J. 1996. *Edge of Empire*. London: Routledge.

Jereis, Sabri. 1973. *The Arabs in Israel*. Beirut: The Institute for Palestinian Studies.

Kahwaji, Habib. 1972. *The Full Story of Al-Ard Movement*. Jerusalem: Arabi Publishing.

Kaufman, Ilana and Rachel Israeli. 1999. "Out of many, one: The vote of Arabs in Israel in the 1996 elections," in Asher Arian and Michal Shamir, eds., *The Elec-*

tions in Israel, 1996. Jerusalem: Israel Democracy Institute, pp. 107–48 (in Hebrew).
Katz, Z. 2000. "The Immigrants from the FSU and Political Life in Israel," *Jews from the Soviet Union in Transition* 4(19): 145–57 (in Hebrew).
Kemp, Adriana. 1998. "From Politics of Location to Politics of Significance: the Construction of Political Territory in Israel's First Years," *Journal of Area Studies* 12(1): 74–101.
— — 2000. "Territory and Consiosness in Israel," *Teoria Vbekurit* 16: 13–43.
Kemp, Adriana, David Newman, Uri Ram and Oren Yiftachel. 2004. *Israel in Conflict*. London: Sussex Academic Press.
Kenig, Ofer, Gideon Rahat and Reuven Hazan. 2005. "The Political Consequences of the Introduction and the Repeal of the Direct Elections for the Prime Minister," in Asher Arian and Michal Shamir, eds., *The Elections in Israel, 2003*. New York: Transaction Books, pp. 33–61.
Kildron, Nissem. 2000. *Pluralists Against Their Will. Multi-Pluralism in Israel*. Haifa: Haifa University Press.
Kimmerling, Baruch. 1998. "The New Israelis: Multiple cultures with no multiculturalism," *Al-Payim* 16: 264–308 (in Hebrew).
— — 1999. "Elections as a Battleground over Collective Identity," in Asher Arian and Michal Shamir, eds., *Elections in Israel, 1996*. Albany: New York State University Press, pp. 27–44.
— — 2001. *The End of the AHUSALIM Regime*. Jerusalem: Keter (in Hebrew).
Kook, R. 1998. "The Fact of Pluralism and Israeli National Identity," *Philosophy and Criticism* 24(6): 1–24.
Kretzmer, David. 1990. *The Legal Status of the Arabs in Israel*. Boulder, CO: Westview Press.
Kymlicka, Will. 1995a. *Multicultural Citizenship: a Liberal Theory of Minority Rights*. Oxford: Clarendon Press.
— — 1995b. *The Rights of Minority Cultures*. Oxford: Oxford University Press.
Kymlicka, Will and Wayne Norman. 1994. "Return of the citizenship: A survey of recent work on citizenship theory," *Ethics* 104: 352–81.
Landau, Yakov. 1971. *The Arab Minority in Israel: Political Aspects*. Tel Aviv: Maarachot.
— — 1993. *The Arab Minority in Israel: Political Aspects*. Tel Aviv: Am Oved.
Leshem, Elazar and Moshe Lesak. 2000. "The Formation of the Russian Community in Israel," *Jews from the Soviet Union in Transition* 4(19): 47–66 (in Hebrew).
Lijphart, Arend. 1969. "Consociational Democracy," *World Politics* 21(2) (January): 207–25.
— — 1977. *Democracy in Plural Societies*. New Haven, CT: Yale University Press.
— — 1984. *Democracies: Patterns of Majoritarian and Consensus Government in Twenty-One Countries*. New Haven, CT: Yale University Press.
— — 1999. *Patterns of Democracy: Governmental Forms and Performance in 36 Countries*. New Haven, CT: Yale University Press.
— — 2002. "The Wave of Power-Sharing Democracy," in Andrew Reynolds, ed., *The Architecture of Democracy*. Oxford: Oxford University Press, pp. 37–54.
Lingental, Nahom. 2002. "Religious Zionism, Between two Basic Intities," in Nahom Lingental and Shoki Friedman, eds., *Conflict Between Religion and the State*. Tel Aviv: Yideot Ahronot, pp. 125–56.

Linz, J. and A. Stepan. 1996. *Problems of Democratic Transition and Consolidation*. Baltimore, MD: Johns Hopkins University Press.

Lipset, Martin. 1959. "Some Social Requisites of Democracy: Economic Development and Democracy," *American Political Science Review* 53(1) (March): 69–105.

Lustick, Ian. 1979. "Stability in Deeply Divided Societies: Consociationalization vs Control," *World Politics* 31: 325–44.

—— 1980. *Arabs in the Jewish State: Israel's Control of a National Minority*. Austin: University of Texas Press.

—— 1987. "The Political Road to Binationalism. Arabs in Jewish Politics," in Ofira Selictar and Ian Peleg, eds., *The Emergence of a Binational Israel. The Second Republic in the Making*. London: Westview Press, pp. 97–123.

—— 1988. "Creeping Binationalism within the Green Line," *New Outlook* 31(7): 14–19.

—— 1993. *Unsettled States, Disputed Lands*. Ithaca, NY: Cornell University Press.

—— 1997. "Lijphart, Lakatos and Consociationalism," *World Politics* 69 (October): 88–117.

—— 1999. "Israel as a Non-Arab State: The Political Implications of Mass Immigration of Non-Jews," *Middle East Journal* 53(3): 417–33.

Mann, M. 1999. "The Dark Side of Democracy: The Modern Tradition of Ethnic and Political Cleansing," *New Left Review* 253 (June): 18–45.

—— 2000. "Democracy and Ethnic War," *Hagar: International Social Science Review* 1(2): 115–34.

Massey, D. 1994. *Space, Place and Gender*. Oxford: Blackwell.

Mawtner, Menahem, Avi Sagi and Ronen Shamir. 1998. *Multiculturalism at a Democratic and a Jewish State*. Tel Aviv: Ramot.

Maynes, C. 1993. "Containing Ethnic Conflict," *Foreign Policy*, 90 (Spring): 3–21.

McGarry, J. 1998. "Demographic Engineering: the State-Directed Movement of Ethnic Groups as a Technique of Conflict Regulation," *Ethnic and Racial Studies* 21(4): 613–38.

McGarry, John and Brendan O'Leary, eds. 1993. *The Politics of Ethnic Conflict*. New York: Routledge.

Meir, Tomas. 1989. *The Islamic Awakening in Israel*. Givat Haviv: The Institute for Arab Studies.

Ministry of Immigrant Absorption. 2002. *The Aliya Absorption – A Report*. Jerusalem: Ministry of Immigrant Absorption (in Hebrew).

Murphy, A. 1996. "The Sovereign State System as a Political-Territorial Ideal: Historical and Contemporary Considerations," in T. Biersteker and S. Weber, eds., *State Sovereignty as Social Construct*. Cambridge: Cambridge University Press, pp. 81–120.

Mustafa, Mohanad and As'ad Ghanem. 2007. " The Palestinians in Israel and the 2006 Knesset Elections: Political and Ideological Implications of the Election Boycott," *The Holy Land Studies* 6(1): 51–73.

Nakhleh, Khalil. 1977. "The goals of education for Arabs in Israel," *New Outlook* (April–May): 29–35.

—— 1979. *Palestinian Dilemma: Nationalist Conciousness and University Education in Israel*. Belmont, MA: The Association of Arab-American University Graduates.

—— 1982. "The Two Galilees," *Arab World Issues, Occasional Papers* 7 (September).

― ― 2008. *The Future of the Palestinian Minority in Israel*. Ramallah: Madar (in Arabic).
Neuberger, Benyamen. 1993. "The Arab Minority in Israeli Politics 1984–1992: From Marginality to Influence," *Asian and African Studies* 27(1&2) (March/July): 149–70.
Nie, N., S. Verba and J.O. Kim. 1974. "Participation and the Life Cycle," *Comparative Politics* 6: 319–40.
Nitzan, J. and S. Bichler. 2002. *The Global Political Economy of Israel*. London: Pluto Press.
Omi, M. and H. Winant. 1994. *Racial Formation in the United States: From the 1960s to the 1990s*. New York: Routledge.
Oren, Gidon. 1987. "From Religious Zionism to the Religion of Zionism" (Doctoral Dissertation). Jerusalem: The Hebrew University (in Hebrew).
Owna, Moshe. 1984. *Divergent Ways: The Religious Parties in Israel*. Alon-Shvot: Yad Sahpera (in Hebrew).
Ozacky-Lazar, Sarah. 1992. "The Elections for the Thirteenth Knesset among the Arabs in Israel." *Surveys of the Arabs in Israel* 9. Givat Haviva: The Institute for Peace Research (in Hebrew).
― ― 1996. "The Crystallization of Jewish–Arab Relations in Israel in the First Decade" (Doctoral Dissertation). Haifa: University of Haifa (in Hebrew).
Ozacky-Lazar, Sara and As'ad Ghanem. 1996. "Voting by the Arabs in Israel in the Elections for the Fourteenth Knesset," *a-Siyasa al-filastiniya (Palestinian Politics)* 11: 46–76 (in Arabic).
― ― 2003. *Or Commission Testimonies*. Tel Aviv: Keter (in Hebrew).
Ozacky-Lazar, Sara and Mustafa Kabha, eds. 2008. *Between vision and reality: The documents of the future visions for the Arabs in Israel 2006 – 2007*. Jerusalem: The Civic Reconciliation Forum (in Hebrew).
Ozacky-Lazar, Sara, As'ad Ghanem and Ilan Pappe, eds. 1999. *Theoretical Options for the Future of the Arabs in Israel*. Givaat Haviva: The Institute for Peace Research (in Hebrew).
Paasi, A. 1998. "Boundaries as a Social Process: Territoriality in the World of Flows," *Geopolitics* 3: 123–46.
― ― 1999. "The Social Construction of Territorial Identities," *Geography Research Forum* 18: 5–18.
Payes, Shany. 2005. *Palestinian NGOs in Israel: The Politics of Civil Society*. London: Tauris Academic Studies.
Pedahzur, Ami. 2000. *The Extreme Rightist Parties in Israel, From Growth to Decline?* Tel Aviv: Tel Aviv University.
Pedahzur, Ami and Daphna Canetti-Nisim. 2001. "Decline or Adaptation? The Changing Role of the Israeli Party as it is Reflected in the Parties Platforms," *Politika* 7: 15–31 (in Hebrew).
Peled, Yoav. 1998. " Towards a Redefinition of Jewish Nationalism in Israel? The Enigma of Shas," *Ethnic and Racial Studies* 21(4): 703–27.
― ― 2001. *Shas: The Challenge of Israelness*. Tel Aviv: Yideot Ahronot (in Hebrew).
Peleg, Ilan. 2007. *Democratization the Hegemonic State*. Cambridge: Cambridge University Press.
Piluvsky, V., ed. 1998. *Transition from Yeshuv to State, 1947–1949: Stability and Change*. Haifa: Hertzil Foundation for the Study of Zionism.

Rabushka, A. 1973. *Race and Politics in Urban Malaysia*. Palo Alto, CA: Hoover Institution Press, Stanford University.

Rahat, Menahem. 1998. *SHAS: the Spirit and the Power*. Kiryat Gat: Alpha.

Ram, Uri. 1995. *The Changing Agenda in Israeli Sociology: Theory, Ideology and Identity*. New York: State University of New York.

Ravitsky, Aviezer. 1993. *The Perceived End and the Jewish State*. Tel Aviv: Am Ovid.

—— 1998. *Religion, State and Israeli Philosophy*. Jerusalem: The Israeli Institute for Democracy (in Hebrew).

Reich, Bernard, Noah Dropkin and Mayrav Wurmser. 1993. "Soviet Jewish Immigration and the 1992 Israeli Knesset Elections," *Middle East Journal* 47(3): 464–78.

Rekhess, Eli. 1993. *The Arab Minority in Israel: Between Communism and Arab Nationalism*. Tel Aviv: Tel Aviv University Press.

Rouhana, Nadim. 1986. "Collective Identity and Arab Voting Patterns," in Asher Arian and Michal Shamir, eds., *The Elections in Israel, 1984*. Tel Aviv: Ramot Publishing.

—— 1990. "Palestinians in Israel: resurrecting the green line," *Journal of Palestine Studies* 19: 58–75.

—— 1997. *Identities in Conflict: Palestinian Citizens in an Ethnic Jewish State*. New Haven, CT: Yale University Press.

—— 1998. "Israel and its Arab Citizens: Predicaments in the Relationship Between Ethnic States and Ethnonational Minorities," *Third World Quarterly* 19(2): 277–96.

Rouhana, Nadim and As'ad Ghanem. 1993. "The Democratization of the Traditional Minority in an Ethnic Democracy: The Palestinians in Israel," in E. Kaufman, S. Abed and R. Rothstein, eds., *Democracy, Peace, and the Israeli-Palestinian Conflict*. Boulder, CO: Lynne Rienner Publishers, pp. 163–85.

—— 1998. "The crisis of minorities in ethnic states: the case of the Palestinian citizens in Israel," *International Journal of Middle East Studies* 30(3): 321–46 (equal contribution by the authors).

Rustow, Dankwart. 1970. "Transitions to Democracy," *Comparative Politics* 3: 337–63.

Sassen, S. 1998. *Globalization and its Discontents*. New York: Wiley and Sons.

Segev, Shmuel. 2008. *The Moroccan Connection*. Tel Aviv: Matar (in Hebrew).

Shabi, Aviva and Roni Shaked. 1994. *Hamas – From Believing in God to the Terror Track*. Jerusalem: Keter.

Shafir, G. 1995. *Immigrants and Nationalists: Ethnic Conflict and Accommodation in Catalonia, the Basque Country, Latvia and Estonia*. Albany, NY: SUNY Press.

—— 1996. "Zionism and Colonialism: a Comparative Approach," in M. Barnett, ed., *Israel in Comparative Perspective*. Albany, NY: SUNY Press, pp. 227–44).

Shafir, Gershon and Yoav Peled. 2002. *Being Israeli: The Dynamics of Multiple Citizenship*. Cambridge: Cambridge University Press.

Shamir, Michal and Asher Arian. 1999. "Collective Identity and Electoral Competition in Israel," *American Political Science Review* 93: 265–77.

Shamgar, Meir, ed. 2006. *Constitution with Consent*. Jerusalem: The Israel Democracy Institute.

Shapiro, Yonathan. 1976. *The Organization of Power*. Tel Aviv: Am Oved (in Hebrew).

— — 1977. *Democracy in Israel*. Ramat Gan: Massada (in Hebrew).
Shitrit, Shimon. 1999. "The Ohalim Movement," in Ophir Adi, ed., *Fifty to Fourty Eight*. Tel Aviv: Hakibutz Hamiuhad (in Hebrew), pp. 291–99.
— — 2001a. "The 21 Trap: Between Haridim and Mizrahim," in Yoav Peled, ed. *Shas: The Israeli Challenge*. Tel Aviv: Mishkal, pp. 21–51 (in Hebrew).
— — 2001b. "Oriental Politics in Israel" (Phd Dissertation). Jerusalem: The Hebrew University (in Hebrew).
Sibley, D. 1996. *Geographies of Exclusion*. London: Routledge.
Sikkuy (nongovernmental association). 1999. Annual report on the government's policy towards Arab citizens. Jerusalem: Sikkuy.
Smith, Anthony. 1991. *National Identity*. London: Penguin.
— — 1995. *Nations and Nationalism in a Global Era*. Cambridge: Polity.
Smooha, Sammy. 1978. *Israel: Pluralism & Conflict*. London: Routledge and Kegan Paul.
— — 1989. *Arabs and Jews in Israel*, vol. 1. Boulder, CO: Westview Press.
— — 1990. "Minority Status in an Ethnic Democracy: the Status of the Arab Minority in Israel," *Ethnic and Racial Studies* 13(3): 389–412.
— — 1992. *Arabs and Jews in Israel*, vol. 2. Boulder, CO: Westview Press.
— — 1993a. "Class, Ethnic, and National Schisms and Democracy in Israel," in Uri Ram, ed., *Israeli Society: Critical Aspects*. Tel Aviv: Berirot (in Hebrew), pp. 291–99.
— — 1993b. "Ethnic Relations in Israel," *Encyclopedia Hebraica*, A Supplementary Volume on The State of Israel: 435–56 (in Hebrew).
— — 1997. "Ethnic Democracy: Israel as an Archetype," *Israel Studies* 2(2): 198–241.
— — 2005. *Index of Arab–Jewish Relations in Israel 2004*. Haifa: University of Haifa Press.
Smooha, Sammy and As'ad Ghanem. 1996. "Ahmad Tibi's Roulette," *Haaretz*, January 21, 1996 (in Hebrew).
— — 2000. "Political Islam among the Arabs in Israel," in Theodor Hanf, ed., *Dealing with Difference: Religion, Ethnicity and Politics: Comparing Cases and Concepts*. Baden-Baden: Nomos Verlagsgesellschaft, pp. 143–73 (equal contribution by the authors).
Smooha, Sammy and Theodor Hanf. 1992. "The Diverse Modes of Conflict-Regulation in Deeply Divided Societes," *International Journal of Comparative Sociology* 33(1–2): 26–47.
Smooha, Sammy and D. Peretz. 1993. "Israel's 1992 elections: are they critical?" *The Middle East Journal* 47(3): 444–63.
Soysal, Y.N. 1994. *Limits of Citizenship: Migrants and Postnational Membership in Europe*. Chicago, IL: University of Chicago Press.
— — 2000. "Citizenship and Identity: Living in Diasporas in Post-War Europe," *Ethnic and Racial Studies* 23(1): 1–15.
Stasiulis, D. and N. Yuval-Davis, eds. 1995. *Unsettling Settler Societies: Articulations of Gender, Race, Ethnicity and Class*. London: Sage.
Sultany, Nimer. 2004. *Israel and the Palestinian Minority*. Haifa: Mada.
Swirski, S. 1989. *Israel: The Oriental Majority*. London: Zed Books.
Taylor, P. 1995. "Beyond Containers: Internationality, Interstateness, Interterritoriality," *Progress in Human Geography* 19(1): 1–15.
— — 1996. "The End of the Territorial State?" *Geography Research Forum* 16: 16–28.

Tellme, Efraim and Menahem Tellme. 1982. *Zionist Lexicon*. Tel Aviv: Maarev.
Tessler, Reki. 2003. *On the Name of God – Shas and the Religious Revolution*. Jerusalem: Keter.
Tilly, C. 1996. "The Emergence of Citizenship in France and Elsewhere," in C. Tilly, ed., *Citizenship, Identity and Social History*. London: Cambridge University Press, pp. 223–36.
Tschomsky, Dimitri. 2001. "Ethnicity and Citizenship in the Conception of the Israeli-Russians," *Tiuria Vibekurt* 19 (Autumn): 17–40 (in Hebrew).
Tzfadia, E. 2000. "Immigrant Dispersal in Settler Societies: Mizrahim and Russians in Israel under the Press of Hegemony," *Geography Research Forum* 20: 52–69.
Tzfadia, Erez and Oren Yiftachel. 2001. "Political Mobilisation in the Development Towns: the Mizrahi Struggle over Place," *Politika* (Israeli Journal of Political Science) 7: 79–96.
— — 2004. "Between Local and National: Mobilization in Israel's Peripheral Towns," *Cities* 21(1): 41–55.
Van den Berghe, Peirre. 1960. *Race and Racism*. New York: Wiley.
Vise, Shevah. 1997. "Analysis of Electoral Behavior of Immigrants from The Soviet Union," *Jews from the Soviet Union in Transition* 3(18): 233–45.
Warhaftig, Zerah. 1973. *Religion and State in Law*. Jerusalem: Ministry of Religion.
Yakobson, Alexander and Amnon Rubinstein. 2003. *Israel and the Family of Nations*. Tel Aviv: Schocken Publishing.
Yiftachel, Oren. 1992a. "The Ethnic Democracy Model and its Applicability to the Case of Israel," *Ethnic and Racial Studies* 15(1): 125–36.
— — 1992b *Planning a Mixed Region in Israel: The Political Geography of Arab–Jewish Relations in the Galilee*. Aldersho, UKt: Avebury.
— — 1996. "The Internal Frontier: The Territorial Control of Ethnic Minorities," *Regional Studies* 30(5): 493–508.
— — 1997. "Israeli Society and Jewish–Palestinian Reconciliation: 'Ethnocracy' and its Territorial Contradictions," *Middle East Journal* 51(4): 505–19.
— — 1998. "Democracy or Ethnocracy? Territory and Settler Politics in Israel/Palestine," *MERIP (Middle Eastern Research and Information)* 28(2): 8–14.
— — 1999. "'Ethnocracy': The Politics of Judaizing Israel/Palestine," *Constellations* 6(3): 364–90.
— — 2000. "Ethnocracy and its Discontents: Minorities, Protest and the Israeli Polity," *Critical Inquiry* 26(4) (Summer): 725–56.
— — 2006. *Ethnocracy: lands and the politics of identity Israel/Palestine*. Philadelphia: The University of Pennsylvania Press.
Yiftachel, Oren and As'ad Ghanem. 2004a. "Towards a Theory of Ethnocratic Regimes: learning from the Judaization of Israel/Palestine," in Eric Kaufmann, ed., *Rethinking Ethnicity*. London: Routledge, pp. 179–97.
— — 2004b. "Understanding 'ethnocratic' Regimes: the Politics of Seizing Contested Territories," *Political Geography* 23(6): 647–76.
Yiftachel, Oren and S. Kedar. 2000. "Landed Power: the Making of the Israeli Land Regime," *Teorya Uvikkoret* (Theory and Critique) 16: 67–100 (in Hebrew).
Yiftachel, Oren and A. Meir, eds. 1998. *Ethnic Frontiers and Peripheries: Landscapes of Inequality in Israel*. Boulder, CO: Westview Press.
Yishai, Yael. 1998. *Between Society and State: Civil Society in Israel*. Jerusalem: The Hebrew University (in Hebrew).

Youna, Yusi and Yehuda Shinhav. 2000. *What is Multiculturalism?* Tel Aviv: Babil (in Hebrew).
Youna, Y. and Y. Sporta. 2000. "Territorial and Living Policy: The limitation of the Citizenship Discourse," *Teoria Vabikoret* 16: 129–52.
Yuna, Cohen. 1980. *The Mafdal – Stand and Status*. Tel Aviv: Hamafdal (in Hebrew).
Yuval-Davis, N. 2000. "Multi-Layered Citizenship and the Boundaries of the Nation-State," *Hagar: International Social Science Review* 1(1): 112–27.
Zakaria, Fareed. 1997. "The Rise of Illiberal Democracy," *Foreign Affairs* 76(6): 22–43.
Zureik, Elia. 1979. *The Palestinians in Israel: A Study in Internal Colonialism*. London: Routledge and Kegan Paul.

Index

Abargil, Reuven 68
Abbas, Mahmoud 185
absorption package, Russian immigrants 137–9
absorption policy 60–1, 87–8
Abu-Hatzeira, Aharon 74, 75, 97, 113, 128–9
Aburaiya, Asam 39
accommodation politics, effects of multi-cultural policies 19–21
Agasy, Yousel 19, 60, 82
Agudat Yisrael 81, 85–7, 91, 94, 99–109, 112–17, 123, 125, 169; government involvement 102–5; opposition to Education Law and National Service Law for Girls 102
al-Aqsa Intifada 98, 174, 176
al-Ard 35–6
al-Fajr movement 36
Al-Haj, Majid 12, 24, 30, 45, 131, 132, 135, 141, 156, 160–1, 181
al-Midan 37
al-Nahda movement 36
al-Raya 36–7
Almond, Gabriel 52, 177
Alon Moreh settlement 71, 118–19
Alon, Beni 98
Aloni, Shulamit 109, 120–1
Anderson, K. 152
anti-war protests 186
apartheid states 7
Arab Movement for Change 42
Arab Palestinian Party 38
Arab Party 41
Arabic culture, attempts to eliminate 61–2
Arafat, Yassir 42, 180, 184–5
Arian, Asher 113, 114, 166, 169, 170, 177
Aronson, Geoffrey 153

Ashkenazi Jews: economic status 62; hegemony of 16–21
Ashkenazi–Mizrahi fissure 77–8; and political instability 170–1
Ashkenazi–secular group fissure 169–70
Asrat al-Jihad (Family of Jihad) 38
assimilation strategy, effects on Orientals and protest politics 18–19
autonomy: calls for 9, 31
Averini, Shlomo 56

Bar-Elan Street, Western Jerusalem 125
Barak, Ehud 56, 73, 98, 105, 110, 117, 121, 125, 148, 149, 157–8, 164–5, 168, 169, 171–2, 180, 184–5
Barakah, Mohammad 35
Basic Laws of the Knesset (1985) 25
Begin, Benny 150
Begin, Menahem 12, 64, 65–6, 73, 75, 96, 103, 126, 129
Begun, Yosef 148
Ben-Eliezer, Binyamin 125
Ben-Eliezer, Uri 49, 177
Ben-Elishar, Elyahu 67
Ben-Gurion, David 11, 43, 67, 85, 101, 102, 120, 121, 123
Ben-Rafael, E.E. 141
Ben-Zadok, E. 63, 68, 76
Benski, T. 64
Benziman, Uzi 24, 175
Bernstein, Debie 61, 69
bi-polar political systems 12–13
Bichler, S. 66, 74
Bin-Habib, Dolly 76
Bishara, Azmi 41, 167–8
Biton, Charlie 34, 68
Black Panther movement 34, 63, 68–71
British Mandate (1919–48) 37, 60, 94, 101

Index

Burg, Yosef 96, 128
burial rituals 139–40

Camp David (2000) 98, 148, 184–5
Canada: cultural diversity 11; demographic and geographic correspondence 4–5; open system 10
Canetti-Nisim, Daphna 131
Central Bureau of Statistics 20, 68, 133, 136–7, 158
change strategies, minority groups 3–10
Chetrit, Sami Shalom 180
Citizen and a State party 151
Citizenship Law (2003) 176
citizenship rights, Russian immigrants 139–41
citizenship: categories of 13–14; public opinion on 28–9
Civic culture (Almond/Verba) 52
civic state model 6–7, 191
civil-primordial explanations 166
clan allegiances, Palestinians 23
coalitions, Palestinian exclusion from 54–5, 168
Cohen, Amnon 156
Cohen, Asher 87, 89, 140
Cohen, E. 63, 70
Cohen, Raanan 43, 45
Cohen, Shalom 70
Cohen, Y. 62, 68, 85
Cold War 1–2, 3
collective-group status, perceptions 29
Comitern 32
Committee of Heads of Arab Local Councils 45
communications media 2, 110, 134–5, 143
Communist Party *see* Israel Communist Party (ICP)
conditional cultural diversity 12
conflict-oriented nationalism 179
consensus-based organizations, Palestinians 44–6
consociational democracies 6–7, 191–2
Construction Workers Union 72
cooperation strategy, effecting religious groups and demand politics 19
Corney, Michael 108
cultural diversity model 11–12
cultural identity: Jewish community in last decade 179–84; Russian immigrants 20, 141–3
cultural institutions, Russian immigrants 134–5

DA Party 150
Dahamsheh, Abdul Malek 41
Daran-Kaleb, Henrietta 76
Darawshe, Abdulwahab 40
Darweesh, Shiekh Abdullah Nimer 41
Dayan, Arie 107, 108, 109–10, 111, 117, 130
Dayan, Moshe 85
Declaration of Independence 101
declarative barriers to change 26
Degel Hatorah party 104, 107–8, 115
Della-Pergola, Sergio 132
demand politics, effects of cooperation strategy 19
Democratic Arab Party (DAP) 40–1, 43, 50, 54
Democratic bloc 151
Democratic Choice party 157
Democratic Front for Peace and Equality (DFPE) 32–5, 36, 41, 42, 49–50, 51
Democratic Movement for Change (Dash) 74, 128–9
demographic vulnerabilities 61
demographic weight 4–5
demonstrations: Mizrahi Jews 68–71; religious groups 117–19
Deri, Arye 104, 107–8, 109–10, 115, 169, 180
development towns: Oriental/Russian Jews in 19, 61, 62; support for Likud 64–6; voting trends in 63–4
Diaspora 80, 88, 89, 99–100
direct elections, Prime Minister 48, 50, 52–4, 167; repeal of 183
discrimination, Palestinians 24–6
Diskin, Avraham 67
diversified citizenship model 13
divide-and-conquer policy 5
divided states: minority claims and strategies 3–10; stability in 191–4
divorce 82–3, 91, 139–40
dominant populations 2
Don-Yihya, Alizer 90, 104, 129
Dropkin, Noah 162

Eastern Europeanism 182
Edri, Rafi 71
Education Law (1953) 84, 102
education: Ashkenazi/Mizrahim Jews 62; crisis in 120–1; and immigration 119–20; system of 83–4
educational institutions, Russian immigrants 143

Index

educational networks 109, 115, 120, 180
Egypt: peace agreement with 96–7; and Sinai Peninsular 114
Eisenstadt, S.N. 10
Elan, Shahar 85, 86, 88, 109, 110, 111
electoral boycotts 48–9
electoral system 52–4
electoral system change 182–3
electoral trends: 1949–2006 49–52; Arab Movement for Change 42; DAP 40–1; development towns 63–4; impact of religion 113–16; Islamic Movement 38–9; Israel Communist Party 33, 35; Labor Party 43–4; Mapai 43–4; National Union 150; NDA 41–2; Palestinians 46–52, 167–9; Russian immigrants 20, 152–60; Sons of the Village 36; Tami movement 74–5; Yemenite Union 66–7; Yisrael Ba'aliyah party 147–8; Yisrael Beitenu party 149
emancipation, Zionism as 81–2
employment: Mizrahi Jews 61–2, 63, 65, 68; Russian immigrants 20
Enlightenment 92
Equality Alliance 41
equality, Palestinian desire for 30–2
Eretz Yisrael 80–2
Eretz Yisrael Workers' Party *see* Mapai (Eretz Yisrael Workers' Party)
Estonia, as ethnic state 9, 16
ethnic democracy, Israel as 14–15
ethnic state model 7–8, 16, 20–1, 56–7
ethnic vote 50
ethnic-cultural societies, Russian immigrants 143
ethnic-nationalism 13
ethnocratic arrangements, effects on Palestinians/resistance politics 18
ethnocratic system, Israel as 15–16
ethnos/ethnicos 136
Europe, open system 10
exclusion, Palestinians 52–7
extra-Parliamentary political activity 177–8

Falah, Ghazi 10, 24
female military service 85, 91, 101, 102, 117, 123
Ferber, Pinhas 95
Fien, Aharon 152–3, 162
Fond, Yusef 100, 102–3, 112
For Justice and Brotherhood – Religious Mizrahim bloc 68
France: liberal democratic system 6; republicanism 13
Frankel, Rogovin 144
Frankenstein, Gila 98
Friedman, Menahem 86, 117, 130
Future vision of the Palestinians Arabs in Israel (Khatib) 178

Gabbai, Shosh 76
"Gahilit" forum 95
Gaon, Nissim 73–4
Gavison, Ruth 175
Gaza Strip: contact with Palestinians in Israel 38; discussions on future of 75–6; leadership in 23; Likud support for settlements in 65; occupation of 35–6, 45–6; Palestinian national movement in 168; Palestinian state in 27, 28–9, 30, 37, 166; return of 109; settlements in 65, 96, 118–19, 149, 152–3; use of military force in 150; war in 186; withdrawal from 95
Gaza-Jericho agreement (1993) 109
Geher faction 73
General Zionists 67
geographic concentration 4–5
Gerenovisky, Vladimir 151
Gesher party 171, 180, 181, 183
Gitelman, Zvi 145, 152, 153, 162, 170, 171, 172
Golan Heights 109–10
Golan Reinforcement Law 58
Goldstein, Baruch 119
Goldstein, Ken 145, 162, 170, 171, 172
Goren, Rabbi Shlomo 106
government involvement: Agudat Yisrael 102–5; Russian political parties 157–8; SHAS movement 106–11
Great Britain, liberal democratic system 6
Green line (1967 borders) 95
Greenberg, Haim 81–2
Grienstien, Ran 74, 76
Grinberg, L.L. 63, 64, 65, 179, 181
group identity, role in creation of political instability 167–72
group leadership 5
group level factors: demographic weight and geographic concentration 4–5; group leadership 5; indigenous vs immigrant status 4; internal solidarity 5
group politics, future of 190–4

group status perceptions 29
Grylak, Moshe 184
Gur, Avraham 150–1
Gurr, Ted Robert 3, 177
Gush Emunim movement 81, 96, 97, 118–19, 126–7

Haaretz 156
Haberfeld, Y. 62, 68
Hacker, Daphna 175
Hadash *see* Democratic Front for Peace and Equality (DFPE)
Haganah 93–4
Halacha 139–40
Hama'ayan movement 107, 109
Hamas 186
Hammer, Zevulun 96, 97–8, 128
Hamu, Eli 76
Hanf, Theodor 6
Hapoel Hamizrachi movement 93–5, 123; *see also* National Religious Party (NRP)
Haredim 81, 85–6, 100–1, 103, 113
Harff, Barbara 3
Hason, Shlomo 87
Hazan 183
Hazani, Michael 91
Hebrew University 36
Hebron agreement (1997) 98
hegemonic ethnic state, Israel as 9, 16–21, 191
Herrenvolk democracy 7
Hertsogh 62, 63, 65, 70
Herut movement 72
Higher Arab Follow-up Committee 45–6
Histadrut 63, 70, 72
history, Palestinian minority 22–3
holocaust 100–1
Horowits, Neri 86
Horowitz, Dan 10
Horowitz, Donald 3, 99, 100, 101, 105, 116
Horowitz, Tamar 137, 138–9, 143, 144, 147, 152, 153, 154, 155, 156, 162, 171
Housing Groups project 138
housing, Mizrahi Jews 68, 72, 77
Huntington, Samuel 6
Hussein, Ibrahim Nimr 45

Ibnaa al-Balad *see* Sons of the Village (Ibnaa al-Balad)
identity politics: cultural diversity model 11–12; diversified citizenship model 13; impact of post-Oslo era and second Intifada 172–84; instinct-civil model 12–13; Israel as an ethnic democracy 14–15; Israel as an ethnocratic system 15–16; and political stability 166–7; and Russian immigrants 153–4
ideological barriers to change 25
immigrant blocs, political parties 144–6
immigrant vs indigenous status 4
immigrants *see* Oriental immigrants; Russian immigrants
Immigrants' Heart for Israel party 151
immigration and education 119–20
Immigration for the sake of the Land of Israel 146
immigration policy 60
income gap, Ashkenazi/Mizrahim Jews 62
Independent North African Bloc 68
indigenous vs immigrant status 4, 8–9
instinct-civil model 12–13
institutions, exclusion from 25–6
integration: demands for 10; Palestinian demands for 31; Russian immigrants 133–6
intergroup relations, effects of peace process 184–7
intermarriage 139–40, 141
internal development, Palestinians 23
internal solidarity 5
international Jewish organizations 15
Intifadas 28, 45–6, 172–84
irredentist movements 9
Islamic colleges 38
Islamic Movement 37–41, 48, 50
"Israel 96" 76
Israel Communist Party (ICP) 32–5, 43, 47, 49, 51; Land Defense Committee 34
Israel Democracy Institute 174, 175–6
Israel Studies 15
Israeli Air Force 127–8
Israeli Defence Forces (IDF) 158–9; observance of Shabbat 82; *see also* military service
Israeli High Court 89, 117, 122
Israeli National Electricity Company 125
Israeli Social Struggle bloc 70
Israeli, Rachel 177
Israeli, Yehuda 95, 96, 97
Israeli–Russian fissure and political instability 171–2

Index

Itam, Efraim 98

Jabahat al-Ansar 37
Jbara, Husneya 44
Jerais, Sabri 33
Jewish Agency 87
Jewish code law 88–9
Jewish community, identity and politics in last decade 179–84
"Jewish majority" 58
Jewish National Fund 15
Jewish nationality 121
Jewish parties, Palestinians in 42–4
Jewishness of the state 174–6
Judaism 14–15
Judaization 88–9, 140

Kadima Party 51, 164, 165, 185–6
Kahwaji, Habib 33
Karin, Moshe 76
Kashrut, observance of 86–7
Katsav, Moshe 72
Katz, A. 153, 154, 156
Kaufman, Ilana 177
Kedar, S. 62
Kedma school network 180
Kemp, Adriana 62
Kenig, Ofer 183
Ketz shilton ha–Ohselim (Kimmerling) 180
Kewan, Muhammad 36–7
Khatib, Shawki 178
Kibbutz system 77
Kildron, Nissem 11
Kimmerling, Baruch 12, 20, 133, 134, 135, 152, 154, 165, 166, 180
Knesset Constitution, Law and Justice Committee 175–6
Knesset elections *see* electoral trends
Kook, Rabbi Abraham 81–2, 95
Kook, Rabbi Tsvi Yehuda 97
Kosher food 86
Kretzmer, David 18, 24

Labor and Rest Law (1951) 82, 94, 126; *see also* Shabbat
Labor education system 84
Labor Party 50, 51–3, 55, 56, 71, 104–5, 108, 165, 170–1; Mizrahi protests against 62–4; Russian immigrant blocs 145; Palestinian membership 43–4; *see also* Mapai
Landau, Yakov 36, 37, 40, 43
Lapid, Tommy 170, 172

Lapid, Yosef 126
Latvia, as ethnic state 16
Lautenberg Amendment (1989) 133
Law of Citizenship, as barrier to change 26
Law of Return 15; as barrier to change 26; crisis of 121–2; Palestinian opinion on 31; and right to citizenship 139–41; struggle for 87–8
Leader party 151–2
League for National Liberation 32
Lebanon war (1982) 45
legal barriers to change 25
legal dimension 82–3
lenient ethnic states 7–8
Lesak, Moshe 132
Leshem, Elazar 131, 132, 135, 156, 160–1
Levine, Isaac Meir 101, 123
Levine, Rabbi Yitzhak Meir 100
Levy, David 65, 71–3, 76, 171, 180
Levy, Moshe 75
liberal democratic system 6–7, 16
liberalism 13
Lieberman, Avigdor 146, 149, 150, 156, 157–8, 183
Lijphart, Arend 6, 7, 191, 192
Likud Party 47, 50, 63–4, 71, 72–3, 97, 107, 115, 170–1; Mizrahi support for 64–6; Palestinian membership 44; Russian immigrant blocs 145–6; in thirteenth Knesset elections 152–3
limited autonomy 9
Lingental, Nahom 80–1
Lisk, Moshe 10
Lithuania, as ethnic state 16
Lithuanian community 106
Lithuanian Haredim 113
Livneh, Isaac Meir 85
Livni, Tzipi 164, 185–6
local authority funding 45
local service provision, Islamic Movement 39
Lustick, Ian 5, 7, 47, 52, 56, 160, 191, 192

Ma'abarot 61, 63, 120
Ma'ayan Hachinuch Hatorani 84, 109, 115, 120
McGarry, John 191
Machiavelli 79
Mafdal *see* National Religious Party (NRP)
Magen, David 71

Index

Mahameed, Hashem 41
Makhul, Issam 35
Maki, see Israel Communist Party (ICP)
Malka, Udi 68
Mann, M. 191
Mansour, Attalah 24
Mapai (Eretz Yisrael Workers' Party) 47, 49, 51, 64, 67–8, 72, 84, 94–5, 167; Palestinian membership 43–4; see also Labor Party
Mapam (United Workers Party) 67, 94; Palestinian membership 42–3
marginalization, Palestinians 173–8
marriage 82–3, 91–2, 139–40
Martziano, Sa'adya 68
Masalha, Mawwaf 44
material privileges, Russian immigrants 137–9
Mawtner, Menachem 11, 12
Maynes, C. 6
Meir, Golda 69, 106
Meir, Tomas 38
membership: ICP 34–5; Islamic Movement 39–40
Meretz Party 50, 51, 170, 171; Palestinian membership 44
"Merging of the Exiles" 63
Merkaz Harav Institute 95
Mevaseret Tzion riots 77
Mikunis, Shmuel 32, 33
military service law 84–6, 101; crisis in 122–4
military service: females 85, 91, 101, 102, 117, 123; student exemption from 85–6, 101–2, 103, 122–4
Miller, Shoshana 122
Ministry of Education 102, 108–9, 120–1
Ministry of Immigrant Absorption 133, 138, 152
Ministry of Justice 177
Ministry of Religious Affairs 90–1, 184
Ministry of the Interior 96, 121–2, 139, 140–1, 155
minority claims and strategies: assimilation strategy 18–19; cooperation strategy 19; ethnocratic arrangements 18; group level factors 4–5; multi-cultural policies 19–21; state level factors 5–10
minority-state relationship, future of 57–9
Mizrahi Democratic Rainbow 76–7, 180
Mizrahi Jews: absorption policy 60–1; demographic vulnerabilities 61; experience of 61–2; immigration policy 60; leaders in large parties 72–3; non-parliamentary action and major demonstrations 68–70; parliamentary activities 72–6; political and social organizations 76–7; political approaches 63–77; political participation and organization 62–3; support for Likud 64–6; within large political elites 66–8
Mizrahi movement 93, 112; see also National Religious Party (NRP)
Mizrahi–Ashkenazi fissure and political instability 170–1
modernization processes, Palestinians 23
Mois, Hana 34
multi-cultural policies, effects on Russian immigrants and accommodation politics 19–21
multi-cultural system 11–12
Municipal Council 90–1
Muslim Brotherhood 37–8
Musrara neighborhood 68
Mustafa, Mohanad 48, 175, 176, 177, 178
Mwies, Hana 45

Naharie, Meshulam 121
Nakhleh, Khalil 10
Namir, Ora 142, 154
nation building 11–12
National Action Front 36
National Committee of Local Authorities 34
National Democratic Alliance (NDA) 35, 37, 41–2, 47–8, 50, 54
National Mizrahi and Mizrahi Bloc 67–8
National Progressive Movement (NPM) 36
National Religious Front bloc 95
National Religious Party (NRP) 67–8, 74, 84, 85, 90, 91, 93–9, 112–16, 125–6, 169; role in 1976 political crisis 126–9
National Service Law for Girls 102
national state, emergence of 79–80
National Union party 98, 150
National Unity Front 41, 47
Neeman, Yaakov 89, 140, 148
negative filtering 19
Netanyahu law 168
Netanyahu, Binyamin 55–6, 57, 73, 97, 105, 110, 164–5, 170, 171–2

Index

Neuberger, Benyamen 56
New Communist List 33
Nie, N. 177
Nitzan, J. 66, 74
non-governmental organizations (NGOs) 76–7
non-Jewish Russian immigrants 139–41
non-parliamentary action: Mizrahi Jews 68–71; religious groups 116–19
Novosti Nadlie 134
Nudelman, Michael 148, 159

O'Leary, Brendan 191
official education systems 84
Ohalim movement 71
Olmert, Ehud 126, 164, 185
One Israel bloc 73, 169
open systems 10
opposition status, Palestinian parties 54–5
Or Commission 176–7
Oren, Gidon 95, 118
Oriental immigrants: assimilation strategy 18–19; *see also* Mizrahi Jews
Oslo Accords 57, 97, 109, 121, 165–7, 170, 173, 179
Owna, Moshe 94, 96, 100, 101
Ozacky-Lazar, Sara 28, 36, 39, 40, 43, 44, 56, 167–8, 175
Ozen, Aharon 74

Palestine Communist Party (PCP) 32
Palestine Liberation Organization (PLO): in peace process 57; peace agreement with 172; recognition of 27, 37, 166; willingness to negotiate 165
Palestinian Authority 147, 148
Palestinian lists 51
Palestinian minority: collective-group status perceptions 29; conditions during last decade 173–8; consensus-based organizations 44–6; ethnographic arrangements affecting 18; future of 28–9; future of state–minority relationship 57–9; future vision of 178; history of 22–3; in Israeli political parties 42–4; needs and requirements 24–6; peace process revival 184–7; political achievements 52–7; political development 23–4; political mobilization and organization 32–46; political participation 46–52; recognition of the state 26–8; requirements of 30–2; voice of 26–32; voting patterns 49–52
Palestinian MKs 52–4
Palestinian nationalism 49, 174–5
Palestinian Party for Change 35
Palestinian Popular Front 35–6
Palestinian problem: need to solve 23–4; public opinion on 27, 30
Palestinian state, establishment of 27, 28–9, 30–2, 37, 40
Paolei Agadat Yisrael 100, 102, 103, 104, 114, 128
Pappe, Ilan 175
parliamentary activities: Mizrahi Jews 72–6; *see also* non-parliamentary action
parliamentary political participation trends, religious groups 112–16
Passover 86
Payes, Shany 178
peace process: Camp David talks 98, 148, 184–5; failure of 174; public opinion on 27; revival of 57, 184–7; role of Natan Sharansky 157; willingness to negotiate 165
Pedahzur, Ami 97, 98, 131
Peled, Matti 25
Peled, Yoav, 10, 13, 65, 130, 171
Peleg, Ilan 7, 10, 17, 190, 191
Peres, Shimon 47, 55–6, 57, 104, 108, 128, 164–5, 171–2
Perets, Yitzhak 122
Peretz, D. 56
Peretz, Rabbi 107
permanent opposition 54–5
policies as barriers to change 26
political achievements: Palestinian political parties 52–7; religious groups 119–29
political approaches, Mizrahi Jews 63–77
political crisis (1976) 126–9
political culture, Russian immigrants 137
political development, Palestinians 23–4
political instability: role of group identity 167–72; role of Israeli–Russian fissure 171–2; role of Mizrahi–Ashkenazi fissure 170–1; role of religious–secular fissure 169–70
political organization and mobilization: Mizrahi Jews 62–3, 76–7; Palestinians 32–46; religious groups 92–111; Russian immigrants 135–6, 143–60

political participation: Mizrahi Jews 62–3; Palestinians 46–52; religious groups 111–19; *see also* electoral trends
political parties: immigrant blocs 144–6; Mizrahi Jews in 66–8; Mizrahi leaders in 72–3
political perspectives, religious groups 112–13
political security 165–6
political stability, divided states 9, 166–7, 191–4
politics, Jewish community in last decade 179–84
Popular Front for the Liberation of Palestine 37
population dispersal strategy 18–19
Poraz, Avraham 141
Porush, Menachem 117
power-sharing, collective arrangements 192
Prime Minister, direct elections for 48, 50, 52–4, 167; repeal of 183
Prince (Machiavelli) 79
privileges, Russian immigrants 137–9
professional qualifications, Russian immigrants 20, 133, 137–8
Progressive List 36, 41
Progressive List for Peace (PLP) 50, 54
property, confiscation of 62
prophecy fulfilment, Zionism as 81
protest politics, assimilation strategy effecting 18–19
protest votes 48–9
public opinion polls, Palestinians 26–32

Rabbinical Courts, powers of 89–92, 115
Rabin, Yitzhak 45, 57, 58, 96, 97, 108–9, 115, 120–1, 123–4, 126–8, 145, 154, 164–5, 170
Rahat, Menahem 103, 104, 105, 108, 117, 183
Rakah *see* New Communist List
Ram, Uri 10
Raphael, Yitzhak 127, 128
Ravitsky, Aviezer 79, 118
Redco, Alexander 151
refugee problem, public opinion on 27–8
Reich, Bernard 162
Rekhess, Eli 32, 33, 34, 36, 178
religion: demands of 83; impact on voting trends 113–16; rift with the state 79–82

Religious Code Law (1953) 82–3, 91
religious councils, authority over 89–92
religious education system 84, 93, 120–1
Religious Front party 94
religious groups: effects of cooperation strategy 19; legal dimension 82–3; political organization 92–111; political participation 111–19; theological dimension 80–2
religious nature of the state 82–3
religious oppression 80
religious party agendas: education system 83–4; Jewish code law 88–9; Law of Return 87–8; military service law 84–6; Rabbinical Courts 89–92; Shabbat and Kashrut 86–7
Religious Services Law (1971) 90
religious–secular fissure and political instability 169–70
republicanism 13
resistance politics, ethnographic arrangements effecting 18
Rosenfeld, H. 24
Rouhana, Nadim 5, 7, 8, 15, 16, 18, 23, 24, 28, 44, 49, 52, 54, 56, 58, 59, 173, 174, 177, 190, 191
Rozon-Tsvi, Ariel 12
Russian immigrants: assimilation strategy 18–19; citizenship rights 139–41; demands of 136–43; effects of multi-cultural politics 19–21; integration or segregation 133–6; material privileges 137–9; political organization 143–60; political participation 152–60; political parties 146–52; political party blocs 144–6; preservation of cultural identity 141–3; voices of 181–2
Russian–Israeli fissure and political instability 171–2, 181–2

Sabra and Shatila massacre 97
Sagi, Avi 11, 12
Salah, Ra'ad 39
Sarid, Yossi 121
satellite lists 43
Schach, Rabbi Elazar 103–5, 106–8, 109, 114, 115, 117
Second Intifada, impact on identity politics 172–84
secondary return, right of 139–41
sectoral identity decline 183–4
secular Jews 113–14; friction points with ultra-orthodox Jews 117–18

secular state, rejection of 95–6
secular–religious fissure and political instability 169–70
Segev, Shmuel 182
segregation, Russian immigrants 133–6
separatist ethnic voting 66–8
separatist movements 9
Sephardim Jews *see* Mizrahi Jews
settlements, Occupied Territories 118–19, 127, 149, 152–3
Shabbat 83, 86–7, 94, 95, 99, 117–18, 125–6, 127–8
Shabi, Aviva 38
Shafir, Gershon 10, 13
Shahal, Moshe 142, 154
Shaked, Roni 38
Shaki, Avner 71
Shalit, Binyamin 122
Shalom-Chitrit, Sami 76
Shamgar, Meir 174, 176
Shamir, Michael 166, 169, 170
Shamir, Ronen, 11, 12
Shamir, Yitzhak 73, 104, 108–9, 115, 164–5
Sharansky without a mask (Nudelman) 159
Sharansky, Natan 141, 143–4, 146, 147, 148–9, 150, 153, 154, 157
Sharett, Moshe 182
Sharm el Sheikh Memoranda (1999) 98
Sharon, Ariel 44, 73, 85–6, 98, 103, 110, 115, 157, 165, 170–3, 180, 184–5
SHAS movement 50, 51, 56, 71, 75–6, 78, 83–4, 90–1, 97–8, 112–15, 117, 120–1, 140–1, 169–72, 179–81, 186–7; establishment of 106; government involvement 106–11; as guardians of Torah 105–11; secular Jews hatred for 155–6
She'a, Elly 76
Shemesh, Kochavi 68
Shenhab, Yehuda 76
Sheransky, Anatoli 134
Shinhav, Yehuda 12
Shinui party 98–9, 170, 172, 183–4
Shiran, Vicky 76
Shitrit, Bechor 67
Shitrit, Meir 72
Shitrit, Shimon 63, 66, 70, 71, 78, 91
Shobor school network 143
Shturm commission 118
sin, Zionism as 81
Sinai Peninsula 114
Smith, Anthony 6

Smooha, Sammy 6, 7, 10, 14, 15, 27, 28, 31, 54, 56, 59, 60, 65, 175, 190
social organizations, Mizrahi Jews 76–7
social welfare organizations, Russian immigrants 138–9
Socialist Workers' Party 32
Sons of the Village (Ibnaa al-Balad) 35–7, 41, 48
South Africa, apartheid 7, 70
Soviet Communist Party 32
Soviet Union: emigration from 132–4; relations with Israel 32, 142–3, 153
Sporta, Y. 62
Sri Lanka, as ethnic state 9
state funding allocations 26
state level factors 5–10
state recognition, Palestinians 26–8
state symbols 25
state: religious nature of 82–3; rift with religion 79–82
state–minority relationship, future of 57–9
status-quo 86–7; crisis over 125–6
Steinitz, Yuval 176
Stern, Esther 157
strikes 45–6, 57
structural barriers to change 25–6
student committees 36
students, exemption from military service 85–6, 101–2, 103, 122–4
Suissa, Yemin 71
Sultany, Nimer 176
Supreme Arab Monitoring Committee 186
Supreme Follow-up Committee 178
Susser, Bernard 87, 89, 140
Swirski, S. 62
Switzerland, cultural diversity 11

Tamam, Leon 74
Tami (Traditional Israel) movement 70–1, 73–5, 97, 114; decline of 75–6
Tarif, Saleh 44
taxation 39
Techiyah party 97, 98, 114
Tel Aviv Newspaper 155
Tel Aviv Social Institute 144
Tellme, Efraim and Menahem 100
Tentsir, Alex 151
territorial nationalism 6
Tessler, Reki 83, 111, 112
theoretical context: cultural diversity model 11–12; diversified citizenship model 13; instinct-civil model 12–13;

Israel as an "ethnic democracy" 14–15; Israel as an "ethnocratic system" 15–16
theological dimension: Zionism as emancipation 81–2; Zionism as fulfilment of prophecy 81; Zionism as a sin 81
"Tiberias" document 175
Tibi, Ahmad 35, 41–2
Tikvah party 151
Topaz, Dudu 74
Torah laws 82–3, 86–7, 91, 95, 100, 115, 117
Torah Religious Front bloc 102
Torah scholars 105
Torah Scholars Council 106
Torah studies 85
Torah, SHAS movement as guardians of 105–11
Toubi, Tawfiq 25, 33
traditional Jews 113–14
transit camps see Ma'abaro
Tsameret commission 118
Tschomsky, Dimitri 135–6
Turkey, as ethnic state 16
Tzefadia, E. 17, 19, 61, 62, 155

ultra-orthodox Jews 113–14; friction points with secular Jews 117–18
United Nations (UN): partition resolution (1947) 33; Security Council Resolution 242 37
United States: cultural diversity 11; influence of Diaspora 89; liberal democratic system 6; open system 10; settlements agreement 152–3
United Workers Party see Mapam (United Workers Party)
Unity and Aliya party 171
unity and immigration bloc 150–1

Van Leer Jerusalem Institute 175
Verba, Sidney 52, 177
Verma 134
Yeshivot 122–4
Veste 153
Vise, Shevah 134, 145, 154
Vistee 134
Vyshinsky, Andrey 182

Wadi Salib riots 65, 68

Warhaftig, Zerah 90, 91, 102, 121
Weizmann, Ezer 103
West Bank: contact with Palestinians in Israel 38; discussions on future of 75–6; leadership in 23; Likud support for settlements in 65; occupation of 35–6, 45–6; Palestinian national movement in 168; Palestinian state in 27, 28–9, 30, 37, 166; return of 109; settlements in 65, 96, 118–19, 127, 149, 152–3; use of military force in 150; withdrawal from 95
Whose land is it? A quest for Jewish–Arab compact in Israel (Benziman) 175
Wilensky, Esther 32
Wilner, Meir 32, 33
World Zionist Organization 15
Wurmser, Mayrav 162
Wye River agreement (1998) 98, 149

Yahadut Hatorah Hameuhedet see Agudat Yisrael
Yemenite Union 66–8
Yesviot system 86
Yiftachel, Oren 7, 8, 15, 16, 17, 18, 19, 24, 58, 61, 62, 155, 174, 190, 191
Yishai, Eli 110, 141, 185–6
Yishai, Yael 76
Yisrael Ba'aliyah party 51, 98, 141, 142, 146–9, 157–8, 160, 170, 171, 172, 181, 183; achievements of 55–6; voting trends 153–4, 155–6
Yisrael Beiteinu (Israel Our Home) party 140–3, 149, 157–8, 160, 170, 172, 183, 186–7; voting trends 156
Yosef, Rabbi Ovadiya 103–4, 106–8, 109, 110, 111, 113, 114, 115, 120, 156
Youna, Yusi 12, 62
Young Muslims 38–9
Yuna, Cohen 112

Zakat 39
Zionism: and anti-Zionism 54, 59; as emancipation 81–2; emergence of 92; in Europe 80; as fulfilment of prophecy 81 Palestinian perceptions of 31; as sin 81
Zionist Forum 134, 135, 143–4
Zionist movement 11–12, 93–4
Zureik, Elia 10

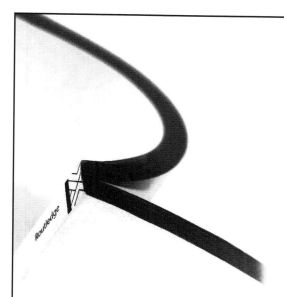

Routledge Paperbacks Direct

Bringing you the cream of our hardback publishing at paperback prices

This exciting new initiative makes the best of our hardback publishing available in paperback format for authors and individual customers.

Routledge Paperbacks Direct is an ever-evolving programme with new titles being added regularly.

To take a look at the titles available, visit our website.

www.routledgepaperbacksdirect.com

ROUTLEDGE Revivals

Are there some elusive titles you've been searching for but thought you'd never be able to find?

Well this may be the end of your quest. We now offer a fantastic opportunity to discover past brilliance and purchase previously out of print and unavailable titles by some of the greatest academic scholars of the last 120 years.

Routledge Revivals is an exciting new programme whereby key titles from the distinguished and extensive backlists of the many acclaimed imprints associated with Routledge are re-issued.

The programme draws upon the backlists of Kegan Paul, Trench & Trubner, Routledge & Kegan Paul, Methuen, Allen & Unwin and Routledge itself.

Routledge Revivals spans the whole of the Humanities and Social Sciences, and includes works by scholars such as Emile Durkheim, Max Weber, Simone Weil and Martin Buber.

FOR MORE INFORMATION

Please email us at **reference@routledge.com** or visit:
www.routledge.com/books/series/Routledge_Revivals

www.routledge.com

ROUTLEDGE INTERNATIONAL HANDBOOKS

Routledge International Handbooks is an outstanding, award-winning series that provides cutting-edge overviews of classic research, current research and future trends in Social Science, Humanities and STM.

Each *Handbook*:

- is introduced and contextualised by leading figures in the field
- features specially commissioned original essays
- draws upon an international team of expert contributors
- provides a comprehensive overview of a sub-discipline.

Routledge International Handbooks aim to address new developments in the sphere, while at the same time providing an authoritative guide to theory and method, the key sub-disciplines and the primary debates of today.

If you would like more information on our on-going *Handbooks* publishing programme, please contact us.

Tel: +44 (0)20 701 76566
Email: reference@routledge.com

www.routledge.com/reference

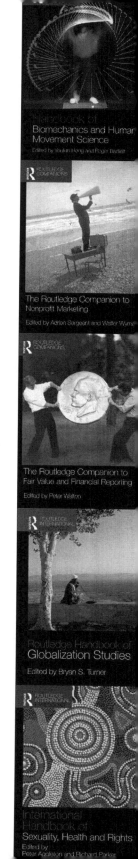

eBooks – at www.eBookstore.tandf.co.uk

A library at your fingertips!

eBooks are electronic versions of printed books. You can store them on your PC/laptop or browse them online.

They have advantages for anyone needing rapid access to a wide variety of published, copyright information.

eBooks can help your research by enabling you to bookmark chapters, annotate text and use instant searches to find specific words or phrases. Several eBook files would fit on even a small laptop or PDA.

NEW: Save money by eSubscribing: cheap, online access to any eBook for as long as you need it.

Annual subscription packages

We now offer special low-cost bulk subscriptions to packages of eBooks in certain subject areas. These are available to libraries or to individuals.

For more information please contact webmaster.ebooks@tandf.co.uk

We're continually developing the eBook concept, so keep up to date by visiting the website.

www.eBookstore.tandf.co.uk